ᵍ Modelling the Middl

Modelling the Middle Ages

The History and Theory of England's Economic Development

JOHN HATCHER

AND

MARK BAILEY

OXFORD
UNIVERSITY PRESS

OXFORD
UNIVERSITY PRESS

Great Clarendon Street, Oxford OX2 6DP

Oxford University Press is a department of the University of Oxford.
It furthers the University's objective of excellence in research, scholarship,
and education by publishing worldwide in

Oxford New York

Athens Auckland Bangkok Bogotá Buenos Aires Cape Town
Chennai Dar es Salaam Delhi Florence Hong Kong Istanbul Karachi
Kolkata Kuala Lumpur Madrid Melbourne Mexico City Mumbai
Nairobi Paris São Paulo Shanghai Singapore Taipei Tokyo Toronto Warsaw

and associated companies in Berlin Ibadan

Oxford is a registered trade mark of Oxford University Press
in the UK and certain other countries

Published in the United States
by Oxford University Press Inc., New York

British Library Cataloguing in Publication Data

Data available

Library of Congress Cataloging-in-Publication Data
Hatcher, John.
Modelling the Middle Ages : economic development in theory and practice / John
Hatcher, Mark Bailey.
p. cm.
Includes bibliographical references and index.
1. Great Britain—Economic conditions. 2. Great Britain—History—Medieval period,
1066–1485. 3. Europe—Economic conditions—To 1492. 4. Europe—History—476–1492.
I. Bailey, Mark. II. Title.
HC254 .H37 2001
330.94′01—dc21
00–066922

ISBN 0–19–924411–1
ISBN 0–19–924412–X (pbk.)

1 3 5 7 9 10 8 6 4 2

Typeset by Graphicraft Limited, Hong Kong
Printed in Great Britain
on acid-free paper by
Biddles Ltd,
Guildford and King's Lynn

To Janice and Julie

❦ Foreword ❧

Behind the writing of this book lie a variety of motives. Perhaps the first to emerge was an awareness of the pressing need of undergraduate students studying the medieval economy for an introduction to the theory and practice behind the grand models of development which dominate the subject. But this was combined with our long-standing dissatisfaction with some of the intellectual and empirical content of these models, with the extent of their influence over the shaping of medieval and later periods of history, and with the manner in which they are being applied by non-medievalists and non-historians with little knowledge of the sources and character of the Middle Ages. Explanations of how and why history has taken the course that it over the last couple of millennia has too often come down to a championing of the supremacy of either the ubiquity of class conflict, the impulse to trade, or the desire to reproduce. The urge to ruck, the urge to truck, or the urge to . . . copulate; there must be more to the process of history than this! We were also disconcerted by the prevalence in some parts of our discipline of a culture of categorization which has resulted in repeated attempts to pack historians off to one or another of these schools of thought. For example, we have been deemed to be members of the Postan, or even the Malthusian, school of history, despite the fact that we have each written a number of pieces which ought to have led to our prompt expulsion. After all, a leading argument in Hatcher's *Plague, Population and the English Economy,*

1350–1530, published in 1977, is that population manifestly did not behave in a Malthusian manner in this era, and the central message of 'Serfdom and Villeinage in England' is that demographic and economic forces provide a totally inadequate explanation of the history of freedom and unfreedom; moreover, Bailey's very first publications —*A Marginal Economy?* and 'The Concept of the Margin'—are sustained refutations of the key role which Postan assigned to marginal regions in his basically Ricardian model of pre- and post-Black Death economic development.

Since the book is driven by such a variety of motives, it is hardly surprising that it has proved far more demanding to write than either of us initially expected. At one level it is intended to provide a basic guide to the concepts expounded in the eighteenth and nineteenth centuries by Adam Smith, Thomas Malthus, David Ricardo, Karl Marx, and Johan von Thünen which, in the hands of twentieth-century historians and social scientists, have been moulded into three grand and conflicting explanatory models which trumpet either the claims of 'commercialization', or 'population and resources', or 'class power and property relations' to be the prime mover of history. In three central chapters each of these models is constructed on its own terms from the basic theory through to the corpus of evidence which has been assembled in its support. Yet the processes of dismantling these elaborate edifices and examining their constituent parts, of probing their internal strengths and weaknesses, of testing their theories against our knowledge of the history, and of assessing the validity of their claims to supremacy, are far more than exercises in simplification. Inevitably we found ourselves reconstructing the economic history of the medieval era, and straying into the philosophy and methods of history and the nature of causality, and at the same time hoping that we had something of value to say to specialist medievalists as well as to non-medievalists.

We are acutely aware that in attempting to hit so many targets and to confront so large a number of broad issues within so few pages, many important areas have not been adequately covered and others entirely missed or misrepresented. In self-defence we would like to spell out what this book is not, as well as what it is. It is not a book which aspires to join the ranks of eminent works contributing to the philosophy and practice of history. It is emphatically not intended to press the merits of one of the traditional models against those of the others, nor does it put forward a new or revised model. At heart it is a refutation of the claims of all such models accurately to represent and explain the historical themes and periods which they address. Further, while an examination of Neo-Malthusian, Smithian, and Marxist approaches provides the core of the book, we have deliberately not dwelt on the full range of variants which exist under these umbrellas, or on the subtle variations of interpretation within each model and the controversies which surround them. In our reconstructions of the key elements and assessments of the strengths and weaknesses of the three grand supermodels, we have drawn as faithfully as possible from the published work of their leading exponents, and have tried to provide balanced critical commentaries rooted in precise citations from their published work. But, in the interests of clarity and brevity, we have not attempted to track the evolution over time of the perspectives and interpretations of each of these historians, and we are aware that we have not necessarily represented all the nuances of their latest or definitive positions. Often, in the course of their careers, historians shift positions and change minds in the light of further reflection, debate, and greater knowledge, but to have included a long series of intellectual biographies would have resulted in a very different, much longer, and, we believe, far more confusing book.

In the course of writing this book we have accumulated many debts. Richard Britnell and Duncan Bythell offered valuable advice during the early days of the undertaking, and also provided many helpful comments on a preliminary version of the text. Our chapter on Marxist models was improved by the perceptive criticisms of Steve

Rigby, and Jim Golby effectively combined the pleasures of the Syrah grape with an invaluable initiation into the implications of Chaos Theory for the social sciences. It goes without saying, of course, especially in a book of this kind, that the responsibility for the views expressed in the succeeding pages lies solely with the authors.

J. H. and M. B.

❧ *Contents* ❧

❧ *Figures* ❧

❧ *Table* ❧

❧ *Abbreviations* ❧

AHEW, ii	H. E. Hallam (ed.), *Agrarian History of England and Wales*, ii. *1040–1350* (Cambridge, 1988)
AHEW, iii	E. Miller (ed.), *Agrarian History of England and Wales*, iii. *1348–1500* (Cambridge, 1991)
CEHE, i	M. M. Postan (ed.), *The Cambridge Economic History of Europe*, i. *Agrarian Life in the Middle Ages*, 2nd edn. (Cambridge, 1966)
CEHE, ii	M. M. Postan and E. Miller (eds.), *The Cambridge Economic History of Europe*, ii. *Trade and Industry in the Middle Ages* (Cambridge, 1987)
EcHR	*Economic History Review*
P & P	*Past and Present*

I

Methods and Models

The economic history of the Middle Ages has proved an exceptionally fertile field for the cultivation of models. As any newcomer to the subject will soon come to appreciate, much of what historians write is imbued with an awareness of theory and abstract concepts, and interpretations of the period resonate with the influence of a number of grand but conflicting models of the processes of long-term change and development.

Studies devoted to the expansion of population and settlement in the twelfth and thirteenth centuries abound with references to the economic theories of Thomas Malthus and David Ricardo, who flourished at the turn of the eighteenth and nineteenth centuries; the principles of free trade enunciated by their contemporary, Adam Smith, permeate much of the work done on towns, trade, and commercial development; and the ideas of Karl Marx loom equally large whenever relations between landlords and tenants are investigated. Historians seeking to describe how early fourteenth-century London was supplied with food and fuel have applied the

2 / *Methods and Models*

abstract speculations of a nineteenth-century Prussian farmer—Johann von Thünen;[1] and when the nature of family and landholding among medieval English villagers is examined, reference is frequently made to the concepts proposed by a nineteenth-century Russian social scientist, Chayanov, and sometimes also to those of the Bolshevik thinker and revolutionary, V. I. Lenin.[2]

Preoccupation with theory shows no sign of abating. Studies published in the last few years include a book devoted to the use of 'closure theory' to illuminate English society in the later Middle Ages,[3] another which seeks to reveal the workings of the English manorial system by the application of general equilibrium theory and Pareto mapping,[4] another which seeks to analyse growth and stagnation in the European (especially the English) medieval economy using a 'rigorous' model which comprises a complex series of mathematical equations,[5] and yet another which aims to achieve a similar goal by the application of economic 'growth theory'.[6] Moreover, the aftershocks of the 'Brenner Debate' of the late 1970s, which was devoted to the contrasting and conflicting methods of analysing the processes and causality of change in the European economy in the

[1] B. M. S. Campbell, J. A. Galloway, D. Keene, and M. Murphy, *A Medieval Capital and its Grain Supply: Agricultural Production and Consumption in the London Region, c.1300*, Historical Geography Research Series, 30 (1993); J. A. Galloway, D. Keene, and M. Murphy, 'Fuelling the City: Production and Distribution of Firewood and Fuel in London's Region, 1290–1400', *EcHR*, 2nd ser., 49 (1996).

[2] R. H. Hilton, 'The Peasantry as a Class', in R. H. Hilton (ed.), *The English Peasantry in the Later Middle Ages* (Oxford, 1975), 6–7; R. M. Smith, 'Some Issues concerning Families and their Property in Rural England, 1250–1800', in R. M. Smith (ed.), *Land, Kinship and Life-Cycle* (Cambridge, 1984), 6–8, 11–12; P. Gattrell, 'Historians and Peasant Studies of Medieval English Society in a Russian Context', *P&P* 96 (1982).

[3] S. H. Rigby, *English Society in the Later Middle Ages: Class, Status and Gender* (1995).

[4] R. M. Townsend, *The Medieval Village Economy: A Study of the Pareto Mapping in General Equilibrium Models* (Princeton, 1993).

[5] K. G. Persson, *Pre-industrial Economic Growth: Social Organisation and Technical Progress in Europe* (Oxford, 1988). Discussed below, pp. 156–9, 161–2.

[6] G. D. Snooks, *Economics Without Time: A Science Blind to the Forces of Historical Change* (1993), part II; *idem*, 'The Dynamic Role of the Market in the Anglo-Norman Economy and Beyond, 1086–1300', in R. H. Britnell and B. M. S. Campbell (eds.), *A Commercialising Economy: England 1086–c.1300* (Manchester, 1995). Discussed below, pp. 159–61.

medieval and early modern centuries, continue to reverberate through much of the literature.[7]

There are many reasons why the medieval period has proved so attractive to the builders of historical models, and theorizing so attractive to medieval historians. The Middle Ages lasted for half a millennium and more, and during this long and distinctive era transformations occurred in many central areas of economic and social life. The numbers of people living in England probably trebled in the two hundred years or so after the making of Domesday Book in 1086, and then fell precipitously. Up to the early fourteenth century settlement expanded on a grand scale and land was farmed more intensively; the manor, demesne farming, and serfdom flourished; towns, trade, and markets multiplied, and industrial activity both broadened and increased. By stark contrast, in the fourteenth and fifteenth centuries the population was cut by more than a half, both rural and urban settlement suffered massive contraction, levels of trade and economic activity slumped, there was a wholesale abandonment by landlords of farming in favour of renting and, while serfdom went into terminal decline, living standards soared.

Merely to describe these colossal changes in detail is a formidable challenge, and the provision of adequate explanations for them is an undertaking which historians are still struggling to fulfil. Why did the distinctive features of what is often termed the 'feudal era' evolve and dissolve when they did? Were the relations between landlords and tenants essentially conflictive in nature? Was the medieval economy underdeveloped, and if so why? When and why did economic growth take place, and what stimulated growth and

---

[7] The original contributions to the debate, which first appeared in *Past & Present* between 1975 and 1982, are republished in T. H. Aston and C. H. E. Philpin (eds.), *The Brenner Debate: Agrarian Class Structure and Economic Development in Pre-industrial Europe* (Cambridge, 1985). Examples of subsequent work which explicitly address the issues raised by Brenner in the debate include: J. Hatcher, 'English Serfdom and Villeinage: Towards a Reassessment', *P&P* 90 (1981); R. W. Hoyle, 'Tenure and the Land Market in Early Modern England: or a Late Contribution to the Brenner Debate', *EcHR*, 2nd ser., 43 (1990); M. Mate, 'The East Sussex Land Market and Agrarian Class Structure in the Late Middle Ages', *P&P* 139 (1993).

what restrained it? How did money and the market come to assume greater significance over barter, payments in kind, and personal service, and with what implications for patterns of production and consumption? And even if we resolve these medieval puzzles, there is the task of fitting the Middle Ages into yet broader schemes of change over still longer periods. Any attempt to do so inevitably raises questions of ever greater scope and complexity—such as when and why did the transition from a feudal to a capitalist economy occur, and why was England the first country to industrialize?—and the search for answers necessarily involves breadths of scholarship and sweeps of speculation on an even greater scale.

The sheer size and complexity of the major processes of economic and social change mean that historians cannot hope to describe, analyse, and explain them by the gathering and narrating of factual information alone. Facts need to be weighed and interpreted. Surviving sources are often patchy in coverage, and their contents are not fully known or understood. Theory and speculation are therefore indispensable ingredients of any grand survey, and in their attempts to impose some degree of coherence and clarity on their work historians often draw upon abstract concepts and models whose primary objective is to provide a manageable working framework.

Naturally, the scale and character of the models and theories which are applied to history vary enormously in content and structure, from those designed to focus on a single place or sector of the economy at a particular time, to overarching hypotheses which regard the Middle Ages as merely one step in the development of Western, or even world, civilization. Some are venerable, while others are novel. Some have been created or adapted by economists and theorists rather than historians, while others are propounded by historians who lack a specialist knowledge of the Middle Ages. Some are imbued more with a poetic than an analytic method,[8] while

---

[8] Sir John Hicks (*A Theory of Economic History* (Oxford, 1969), 2) described the 'grand designs' of Arnold Toynbee (*A Study of History*, 3 vols. (1934)) and Oswald Spengler (*Decline of the West* (first published in German in 1918)) as 'historical patterns which have more aesthetic than scientific appeal'.

others, though they may lack aesthetic appeal, are firmly rooted in the methodology of the social sciences.[9]

The resort to theory by historians is not always made explicit, or even done consciously, partly no doubt because the conclusions towards which a lot of theory leads are those which the systematic historian would intuitively have expected. But other historians take pride in spelling out the theoretical underpinnings of their arguments. Nor are theories and models used only to illuminate and explain the past. In fact the reverse is sometimes practised, and the past used as a testing ground for theories and models. There are historians as well as social scientists who begin with a theory or judgement, and then study a piece of history in order to see whether the facts validate or contradict it. Thus, they work in the reverse direction to most historians, who would begin with the facts and see if there is a theory which can assist in their elaboration and interpretation.

Historical Methods

History is a vast subject, the historical profession is a broad church, and many sects dispute within it. There is no single correct method of writing history. Historians have a variety of aims and carry them out in various ways, and they also perform the same tasks in different ways.[10] Within each branch of the subject there are some who deny the usefulness of theory, or even see it as positively harmful, and others who delight in the embracing of each new scientific or pseudo-scientific fashion. Those who are resistant to the use of theory commonly maintain that historical events are

---

[9] For example, D. C. North's model based on institutions and institutional arrangements (discussed below, pp. 192–7), and R. Brenner's variant of the Marxist model (discussed below, pp. 73–6).

[10] For a lively account of the historian's craft, see R. J. Evans, *In Defence of History* (1997).

unique, that the forces which mould them are multifarious, and that the variety of experience in the past is too vast to be squeezed into any model or adequately accounted for by any abstraction. In contention, those who are addicted to the use of theory maintain that historians who deny its value and overstress the uniqueness of events are blind to the similarities which exist between occurrences and recurrences over time, and are therefore doomed to remain mere chroniclers producing interesting but largely unconnected anecdotes which contribute little to answering the big questions of history.

In practice, scarcely anything that historians seek to accomplish can be achieved in a strictly factual and objective manner. The bare facts rarely take us far. The first task of a historian is usually held to be description—the reconstruction of what happened in the past. But even this basic job calls for the selection of the events to be described and a decision about the amount of attention to be given to each of them. Having selected the events or subject area to be studied, it is not usually possible or desirable to write an account which relates everything that happened, even within a strictly defined time frame. Furthermore, the mass of information thrown up by research is commonly disparate and often conflicting. Evidence has to be weighed, not all of it will be equally convincing or significant, some will be unreliable or trivial, and the probability is that not all of it will point in the same direction. Even the most particular of topics blessed with excellent records, especially in remote periods such as the Middle Ages, are likely to have gaps in the coverage of the sources which have to be bridged by surmise of one sort or another.

So although a historian may profess to be guided by the facts alone and decry any form of subjectivity or speculation, in practice almost all historical accounts must involve the selection of those facts deemed to be the most accurate and important, and some assessment of their relative significance. In this manner, even those who profess themselves to be resistant to the charms of quantification frequently resort to judgements which ought to be based on the weighing of information or some form of counting. The most political of biographies will therefore tend to rest upon the selection and ranking of facts in order of significance, and will contain verdicts on the relative merits of different courses of action, on the competence of ministers and advisers, kings and queens and so on, which are in essence, or should be, exercises in comparison which involve measurement.

Few historians, of course, are content to limit themselves to the description of individual events and, in addition to describing whole series of events across broad periods, they routinely seek to explain how and why things happened as they did, and what their relative significance was. The broader the topic under study, and the more the historian seeks to explain rather than merely to describe, the more he or she is driven beyond the limited security offered by plain facts. Given the complexity of history, and the mass of miscellaneous and often contradictory indications which surviving evidence yields up to the researcher, it would seem indispensable that historians should adopt a systematic approach to their material, should sort and grade it, ask pertinent questions of it and, if appropriate, place it within a conceptual framework. When performing such tasks some historians will overtly add theory to the hard evidence at their disposal, while others will go further and adopt the framework of a model.

Economic Theory and Economic History

Studying the past requires historians to acquaint themselves with the resources and methods of a range of disciplines from the sciences to the arts, according to the subjects which they choose to bring under their scrutiny. The use of concepts, models, and theory is especially appropriate for the study of economic history, which shares a common subject matter with economics.[11] Economic history does not deal primarily with the discovery and presentation of unvarnished facts. It is essentially a problem-centred discipline which seeks to provide general answers as well as descriptions of particular instances, and aims to establish not just what happened, but how it happened and why. To achieve this, facts must be interpreted and ranked in order of significance, and potential relationships between sets of facts must be examined. Progress towards accomplishing such tasks is frequently assisted by the use of appropriate economic theory. Theory based upon general patterns of behaviour may well help the historian to separate the typical piece of evidence from the untypical, the general from the particular, and to discern patterns in the evidence and fill gaps with plausible assumptions. Economics teaches us that although it is impossible to predict the behaviour of individuals, it is possible to draw useful conclusions about how large groups might behave in given situations. Thus, whereas any particular consumer may act according to his or her own idiosyncratic motives, demand theory and consumer theory can be helpful when looking at the total body of consumers and the whole market for a commodity, and for analysing how they will react to changes in price, quality, substitute commodities, and so on.

Economics is a major discipline whose practitioners far outnumber those historians who write about economic subjects in the past, and it has a substantial and very rapidly growing body of theory at its command. It would therefore be remiss of any economic historian to neglect to consider that branch of theory which is relevant to the topic which he or she is studying. But this does not mean that the application of theory to historical problems is necessarily either straightforward or helpful. The dilemma for the economic historian

---

[11] For the nature of economic history and its relationship with economics, see J. Hicks, *A Theory of Economic History* (Oxford, 1969); M. M. Postan, *Fact and Relevance: Essays on Historical Method* (Cambridge, 1971); D. C. Coleman, *History and the Economic Past: The Rise and Decline of Economic History* (Oxford, 1987); W. N. Parker (ed.), *Economic History and the Modern Economist* (Oxford, 1986); C. M. Cipolla, *Between Two Cultures: An Introduction to Economic History* (Oxford, 1991).

is frequently not whether to use theory, but which theory to use and how to use it. Should theory be added routinely to the facts that are available, and a range of different concepts borrowed according to whichever seems applicable to a particular historical event or problem? Or should the facts be incorporated within a single theory or common set of concepts, which collectively comprise a coherent and generalized explanatory model? If the former, the resultant work is liable to lack consistency and coherence, if the latter, there is a danger that the facts will be made to fit the model rather than the model being fashioned to fit the facts.

On occasion, the use of theory may erect barriers to understanding, rather than assisting in their dismantling. It is an intuitively plausible proposition to most medieval economic historians that in the course of the twelfth and thirteenth centuries the proliferation of markets, improvements in the efficiency with which they operated, and the broadening of the range of goods available on them, made it easier and more attractive for farmers to engage in buying and selling and encouraged those with spare resources to produce more for the market, and that in turn these developments encouraged increases in productivity as well as a further growth in towns, trade, and industry. Equally unexceptionable is the proposition that the actual outcome at any particular time and in any particular location or situation, depended upon a wide range of additional factors: negative and positive, accidental and determined, political, social, and legal as well as economic. However, the new economic literature which might lend theoretical support to these commonsensical propositions is not only fragmented into a number of different branches (including path dependency, endogenous growth, general equilibrium search, 'new' trade theory, and coordination failure), much of it is highly mathematical in nature and therefore rendered virtually inaccessible to specialist historians.[12] Ideally one should have an

---

[12] For an insight into the methods which are now being adopted, see P. Krugman, *Geography and Trade* (Leuven and London, 1991).

equally good grasp of the theory and the history, but in practice this can very rarely be the case.

While history which has no theory is often lacking a valuable dimension, the application of theory to history without a sufficient awareness of its limitations can be positively misleading. This is more often the fault of the historian than of the theory. There is some bad theory, but most of it is good; however, by no means all of the good theory is appropriate to the uses to which it is put. As has been said many times, the past is a foreign country, and some things were done very differently there. Consequently economic theory fashioned to fit contemporary economies cannot necessarily be transported backwards in time and applied to distant periods without modification. In order to function in as scientific a manner as possible economic theory has to be founded upon sets of assumptions, primarily about human behaviour in any given set of circumstances, and this behaviour must be held consistent and rational within the terms of agreed economic laws. But, while these sets of assumptions about the behaviour of the generality of people may be valid when applied to the present day or to relatively recent times, they may well be inappropriate to more distant times. For example, it is an essential underpinning of neoclassical economics that individuals and business organizations will seek to maximize income and profit, but in the Middle Ages labourers displayed a strong desire for leisure when wages were high and their basic subsistence needs had been met, while for the great landlords the maximization of income often took second place, because they were warriors, churchmen, politicians, and dispensers of hospitality and patronage as well as owners of assets. Moreover, much economic theory is predicated upon the operation of free markets, but in the Middle Ages the working of the land, labour, and capital markets was severely distorted by a variety of non-economic forces, including custom, villeinage, and religious teaching.

Modelling the Middle Ages

This short book is not about historical method in general, but rather the differing approaches which have been adopted for the study of the medieval economy. Even less than that, far from attempting to cover all the theories, concepts, and models which abound in the historiography of the Middle Ages, it will concentrate upon the three leading schools of thought which have long predominated, and which are commonly conveniently grouped together under the shorthand titles of 'commercialization', 'Marxist', and 'demographic'. The next three chapters are devoted to each of these in turn, and all are shown to comprise a powerful mixture of evidence and theory that has been augmented and refined over many decades. No less should be expected, for the writing of the history of all periods and parts of the world has often been framed with reference to one or other model derived from these schools of thought, and they still exert great influence over the literature of the medieval West. Yet, despite occasional efforts to incorporate elements from all three approaches into new explanations, the same events and processes continue to be explained in exclusive and starkly conflicting terms because each of these grand supermodels has at its heart either population, commerce, or class relations.

The manner in which the assumptions which drive these models can impinge on the writing of history, in both a helpful and a harmful manner, may be illustrated in a simple fashion by noting how small pieces of evidence which in themselves are of little moment, may be imbued with greater significance. For instance, in the records of the thirteenth century one may find notices of the taming of an acre or two of moorland for the growing of corn, of the decision of a manorial official to accept money from an unfree tenant rather than require him to perform the customary service of a day of unpaid labour, or of the fining of a tenant for the inadequate performance of a labour service. The first stage in assessing the significance of such scraps will be to determine how frequently they occur and whether they are indicative of general patterns. If they are shown to be untypical, they will naturally have little or no role to play in any explanation; but if they are deemed to be part of a general phenomenon, the next tasks of the historian will be to explain why they are taking place and to discover what the longer term effects of such events may have been. If many small patches of moorland were being brought under the plough, it might be concluded that there was a general drift towards the cultivation of poorer soils; frequent payments in cash rather than in labour may be taken as evidence of an increasing use of money; and large numbers of incompetent villein labourers may been seen as symptomatic of a growing resentment at having to perform servile duties.

One might go further, and seek to use accumulations of such instances to highlight leading currents of economic and social change, and perhaps even to provide an explanation as to why history took one course rather than another. Thus, the conversion of a patch of moorland to arable might, in terms of a demographic model based upon Malthusian and Ricardian theory, be seen as a small step on a relentless journey towards the margins of subsistence by a society in which population was increasing faster than the resources to support it; the payment of money rather than the performance of a labour service might be seen in Smithian terms in a model stressing commercialization, as indicative of the inexorable rise of a money economy at the expense of a feudal economy; and the reluctant villein labourer might be viewed, in Marxist terms, as emblematic of the inexorable struggle between the irreconcilable interests of tenants and landlords which would eventually bring about the collapse of the feudal system.

In this manner, order can be imposed upon the chaos of vast numbers of pieces of information, and answers formulated to some of the most crucial questions. Yet there is an obvious cost. When a historian proceeds from the particular to the general, his or her work remorselessly moves further from its factual base and inevitably becomes ever more speculative. The sorting of the typical from the untypical can involve far more than mere counting, and the sorting of the significant from the insignificant inevitably relies heavily upon the judgement of the person doing the sorting. Simple counting is normally not sufficient to produce definitive answers, because the survival of evidence is haphazard and the patterns it reveals frequently differ from place to place and from time to time. In the years before the Black Death, at the same time as arable fields were being carved out of the bracken on the exposed infertile slopes of Bodmin moor and Dartmoor, a large-scale retreat from cultivation was occurring in the uplands of Derbyshire and Staffordshire.[13] How, then, is the general trend to be established?

Moreover, the processes of sorting evidence and of identifying the general trend from a mass of particulars is an exercise in simplification as well as in quantification and speculation. If order is to be produced out of chaos, the modeller can only do so by abstracting common themes from the vast mass of seemingly unique and unrepeatable events of history. And this can only be done by divining general characteristics in ostensibly unique events. However, historians are only human, and since the mass of evidence available to them will almost certainly contain a wide range of instances capable of lending support to almost any hypothesis, they are often cruelly exposed to the temptation of finding the evidence to fit the hypothesis rather than vice versa. Even facts are rarely permitted to be neutral. Sometimes pieces of evidence may be imbued with a significance considerably greater than they would otherwise warrant because they presage general changes that the historian with hindsight knows will subsequently come about. At other times some occurrences are deemed to be of more consequence than others because they are held to show the workings of core elements

---

[13] *The Agrarian History of England and Wales*, ii, *1042–1350*, ed. H. E. Hallam (Cambridge, 1988), 233–4 , 243–4.

rather than peripheral matters, though naturally what constitutes the core and what the periphery is usually open to debate.

In addition to variations in the quality of the judgement exercised by historians, the conflicting positions they adopt often reflect a difference of approach or even philosophy, and it is in the nature of medieval history that the great majority of controversies over the interpretation of evidence cannot result in a demonstrably clear outcome, in which one position can be proved to be wrong and the other right. A good example is provided by the debate about whether or not the demesne farms of landlords were contracting in the mid-twelfth century, which has rumbled on over many decades. The main protagonists—M. M. Postan and R. V. Lennard—differed not only on the general issues of what was happening at the time, but over the very particular ones of what could be read from surviving documents.[14] To put it crudely, Lennard maintained that each documentary source—in this instance the estate surveys of the individual manors of the abbey of Glastonbury which record the number of plough teams, the acreage of the demesne, and the level of rents—ought to be interpreted largely by reference to what the document itself actually says, while for Postan any sensible interpretation should take context into account and be formulated in the light of what can be seen to be happening elsewhere. Postan expressed the issue in terms of the relationship between 'general trend and local and temporary contingencies', and went on to pronounce that '[l]ocal causes are very frequently no more than local effects of general factors'. In other words, for Postan if two alternative conclusions might be drawn from a particular document, the one which is more likely to be true is the one which is in accord with

[14] M. M. Postan, 'Glastonbury Estates in the Twelfth Century', *EcHR* 5 (1953); R. Lennard, 'The Demesnes of Glastonbury Abbey in the Eleventh and Twelfth Centuries', *EcHR* 8 (1956); M. M. Postan, 'Glastonbury Estates in the Twelfth Century: A Reply', *EcHR* 9 (1956); R. Lennard, 'Glastonbury Estates: A Rejoinder', *EcHR* 28 (1975); M. M. Postan, 'The Glastonbury Estates: A Restatement', *EcHR* 38 (1975). A further exchange on these and related themes between A. R. Bridbury and M. M. Postan was published three years later ('The Farming Out of Manors', *EcHR* 31 (1978), 503–20, 521–5).

the generality of evidence in the country or region at large. The problem is, however, how accurately can the general trend be discerned and accounted for?

The models that are formulated to encompass broad topics and long periods of history often appear extremely complex, and as they attempt to subsume more and more of the enormous range of historical experience which is continually being unearthed, they have to become ever more elaborate. But complexity and elaboration is often superficial, since it stems primarily from the multiplicity of abstractions that need to be adopted, and from the arcane language in which they are frequently expressed. By contrast with their theoretical superstructures, the factual bases of most models are ruthless exercises in simplification, which depend upon stereotypes and broad categories to represent what would otherwise prove an overwhelming range and diversity of innumerable pieces of evidence. Thus, for models purporting to demonstrate the intensity of the pressures of rising population on scarce resources in the thirteenth century, the remorselessness of struggles between landlords and villeins, or the inexorable rise of the money economy, instances of cultivated moorland reverting to pasture, or of tenants willingly paying part of their rent in kind by working reasonably competently for their lord, must be deemed to be of less significance than contrary instances. It is the ploughing up of thin soils, the preference for rents in cash, and the existence of recalcitrant villeins which are seen to reflect the dynamic elements in the economy, and to signal the direction in which it is travelling.

Naturally, the majority of those who construct models do not wittingly proceed in defiance or ignorance of the distortions which their methods can inflict on the individual facts of history. They are in search of a greater truth, which they believe can be reached only by concentrating on the wood rather than the trees within it. Yet, the prime test of the validity of any model must be the extent to which it is built upon historical reality, and that reality is constantly shifting as more and more evidence accumulates. The historians and social scientists who drive the models also have a tendency to pursue ever more ambitious goals, and when they do so the maintenance of internal coherence and consistency becomes an ever more challenging intellectual task, and they apply further doses of abstraction in an attempt to control the rapidly multiplying confusion of factual evidence.

Moreover, selecting those pieces of evidence which are the most representative or significant at any given time, however difficult it might prove to be, is only the first stage in proving the reliability of a model. For most of the grand historical models, and in particular the three models which form the core of this book, are explanatory models which seek to give the reasons behind such vast historical processes as the rise and decline of serfdom and feudalism, the rise of the money economy and capitalism, the rise and contraction of economic activity, and the growth of urbanization and industrialization. Since such changes spanned very many centuries and penetrated almost all sectors of economic, social, and political life, the list of events which might form a part of the description, timing, and distribution of such changes is almost infinite, while the list which can be compiled of factors which may have driven or impeded such processes is also very large. Few economic processes are determined by economic factors alone. Economic activity may be deeply affected by war, by the law, by weather, and by the incidence of disease, as well as by the relative scarcity of land and labour or the size of the money supply. More than this, of course, the listing of potential influences and causal factors is but a first step in providing an explanation of crucial historical processes. If causality is to be determined, all relevant factors have to be assigned weight and those of lesser significance distinguished from those of greater, and, most important and most difficult of all, it is necessary to to rank the positive and negative influences in order of strength.

Not surprisingly therefore there is a pronounced tendency for the models which are the most ambitious in terms of the scale and complexity of the events and processes which they are seeking to describe and explain, to have at their core a relatively simple set of assumptions, as well as a limited number of variables and a strictly regulated body of evidence. In fact, the simplification of complex historical reality often proceeds much further. Those who devise and redesign models soon find that it is impossible to incorporate more than a severely restricted number of events and causal factors without creating a major increase in complexity and a severe loss of coherence. Moreover, not only do models incorporate merely a small proportion of the range of possible elements, few of the elements that are privileged by selection are ever allowed to move freely. The greater the variability and independence which the elements of the model are allowed to enjoy, the greater the difficulty the modeller encounters in attempting to analyse their relative importance and the manner in which they may impact on one another. It is necessary, therefore, to hold constant the majority of the select band of elements which are incorporated into the models, in order that attention may be focused more effectively upon those which are deemed to be the most important, and thus allowed to move. It is obviously easier to predict the consequences of rising population on the welfare of the peasantry if such crucial elements as the behaviour of landlords, the weather, the levels of technology and taxation, are held to be constant, rather than allowed to vary as they did in practice.

In fact many models go further still and account for economic and social change by raising a single factor, or a combination of closely related factors, to the status of 'prime mover', thereby reducing all other potential forces to secondary or ancillary roles. The championing of a 'prime mover' in history is usually achieved by allowing all other variables a steady rather than a dynamic influence or by making their behaviour dependent upon the chosen prime cause. Thus, in a model devoted to emphasizing the supremacy of demographic forces, the behaviour of landlords and peasants may be taken to be relatively fixed, or, if it is allowed to change, it is assumed to have done so as a consequence of the rise or fall of population. Likewise, in models devoted to emphasizing the supremacy of class relations, the rise and fall of population cannot be permitted to exercise a powerful influence, but instead must be relegated to secondary importance or even made a function of the independently changing behaviour of landlords and tenants.

It is normally deemed essential that change is generated within the model itself, by the interaction of the elements which have been chosen to be included within it. These chosen elements are sometimes termed 'endogenous'. In a demographically-based model such endogenous elements would embrace population, land, landlords and tenants, and the relations and reactions between them would include the fact that landlords charged rents which tenants had to pay to occupy the land, that land is the means by which landlords and tenants derived most of their income, that the majority of tenants produced their own subsistence, and so on. 'Exogenous' factors, by contrast, are not generally included within models, and even if they are they cannot be allowed to exert significant influence over the operation of the model. This is because exogenous factors are by definition independent of other factors and follow their own paths, and consequently have a tendency to undermine the coherence and internal consistency of models based on logical principles and predictable outcomes.

Climate and disease are two phenomena which are commonly considered to be exogenous, and all three leading medieval supermodels therefore downplay their significance. The standard Malthusian population and resources model sees the inexorable rise of population eventually leading to an economic watershed precipitated by falling living standards, agricultural crises, and sharply increased levels of mortality. But a deterioration in the climate can also cause living standards to fall, agricultural output to decline and death rates to rise, since bad weather reduces the yields of grain and animal products, which leaves the peasants with less to eat and forces food prices upwards. Europe does indeed appear to have experienced a long-term climatic deterioration which commenced around the turn of the thirteenth and fourteenth centuries, and extended periods of extremely high rainfall in the late 1310s were especially disastrous for agriculture.

Obviously, catastrophic weather cannot easily be incorporated within a Malthusian model, for climate fluctuates according to forces which operate independently of the level of population or the productivity of the land. Thus, if the causes of the long-term depression of living standards are to rest primarily with the excessive growth of population, which is the leading endogenous factor in the Malthusian model, then it is necessary for its proponents to limit severely the power granted to climatic fluctuations. Accordingly, the contribution of climatic deterioration to the creation of the crisis may be said to have lain merely in the exacerbation or acceleration of a pre-existing trend, which had been created by the inexorable rise of population over the preceding centuries, and which by itself was bound to lead to crisis. Climatic change might be admitted as an influential, and even as an independent, cause of economic change in certain restricted regions, such as low-lying coasts prone to flooding, and for certain periods of time, such as 1315 to 1322, but overall the prime causal agent was the long-term imbalance between the level of the population and the resources available to support it. It was this worsening imbalance which made a profound and extended crisis of subsistence inevitable. In other words, the most that this model might concede is that impact of the exogenous force will be conditioned by existing endogenous forces and be secondary to them.

Epidemic disease poses similar or even greater problems for the builders of internally consistent models. In Malthusian modelling, mortality is primarily dependent on movements in living standards: it rises when welfare declines and falls when it improves. In this manner the persistently high death rates of the later thirteenth and early fourteenth centuries may be viewed as a consequence of the chronic poverty which afflicted much of the population, and this underlying vulnerability also ensured that mortality frequently soared to crisis levels when harvests failed. But the phenomenal death rates which resulted from the massive outbreaks of epidemic disease which began with the Black Death of 1347–50 are not easily subsumed within the workings of a model which depends primarily on the rational and predictable effects of changes in the balance between population and resources, or for that matter the state of class relations or the degree of commercialization.

At first sight, and for some historians at second and third sight as well, the waxing and waning of a disease like bubonic plague would seem to be due primarily to changes in the virulence of its causative agent—a bacterium called a bacillus—and in the behaviour of the insects which carried it and the mammals which carried the insects, rather than to changes within human society and economy. If this is admitted, the only course for the modeller is to downgrade the impact which the disease and its consequent mortality had on economy and society, and to allow plague to have some effect on the timing and speed of change but little or none on its scale and direction.

This chapter has sought to sketch how and why historians and social scientists have constructed and adopted grand supermodels in their quest to describe and explain economic and social development. Although relatively few historians have chosen to imprison their writings wholly within the walls of strict theoretical models, very many more, consciously and unconsciously, use the concepts which underpin them to assist in the tasks of sorting and interpreting evidence and formulating explanations of particular and short-term events and processes as well as general and long-term.

It is in these and in many other ways that the conflicting tenets of the three leading models, derived in turn from the theories and concepts of Malthus, Marx, and Smith, continue to reverberate through our historiography and mould the ways in which we regard the medieval centuries. In the next three chapters we conduct a detailed review of the theoretical underpinnings and evidentiary bases of each of these models, and assess their overall strengths and weaknesses.

2

Population and Resources

The Theory

Agriculture dominated the economy of medieval England, and the great bulk of the country's resources were devoted to providing the basic subsistence needs of its inhabitants. There were many towns, of course, some of them of an appreciable size; trade was commonplace, both within England and with nations overseas; and small-scale industrial production was widespread. But at the very least 80 per cent of the population lived in the countryside and were directly engaged in farming the land. Moreover, agricultural production relied on the muscle-power of the men and women who worked the soil and tended the livestock, assisted only by draught animals and basic equipment. Farming technology changed but slowly, and most farms were small and utilized little capital. Hence the relationship between the numbers of people and the amount of land available to support them was of overwhelming significance to the economy, and the balance of this relationship was subject to dramatic change over time.

It is upon fundamentals such as these that the model variously named as the 'population and resources', 'demographic', or 'neo-Malthusian' model is founded.[1] It puts forward robust explanations of the operation of the medieval economy and society, and of long-term trends in economic growth and the distribution of incomes, which have at their core a set of simple economic relationships between land and labour. The most fundamental proposition involves the relative scarcity of these two prime factors of production. Because a scarce factor will tend to be expensive relative to one which is in abundant supply, it follows that land will be expensive when it is scarce relative to labour, and so too will the products of the land: foodstuffs and raw materials like leather, wool, and wood. The counterpart of the scarcity of land is, of course, the abundance of labour, and labour will be cheap when it is abundant. In an agrarian economy with a large peasant sector the direct results of land scarcity are that there will be too little land and too little employment to satisfy the demand for them, so people will pay high rents for the holdings they occupy and the purchasing power of their wages will be low when they are hired. If the relationship between land and labour is reversed, and land becomes plentiful and labour scarce, then the price of land and its products will fall relative to labour.

There is clear potential for applying such basic supply and demand analysis to conditions prevailing not just in the European Middle Ages, but in pre-industrial eras throughout the world.[2] In the centuries before large-scale urbanization and industrialization, there is abundant evidence to show that over the longer term there

[1] For an introductory overview, see D. B. Grigg, *Population Growth and Agrarian Change: An Historical Perspective* (1980); for more advanced reading, see the essays in M. S. Teitelbaum and J. M. Winter (eds.), *Population and Resources in Western Intellectual Traditions* (Cambridge, 1989).

[2] For the application of Malthusian analysis to the writing of Chinese history, see K. Chao, *Man and Land in Chinese History: An Economic Analysis* (Stanford, Conn., 1986); K. Deng, 'A Critical Survey of Recent Research in Chinese Economic History', *EcHR*, 2nd ser., 52 (1999), 13–14.

was a strong correlation between rising population, on the one hand, and increasing land values and agricultural prices, and falling real wages, and, on the other, between declining population, falling prices and land values, and rising real wages. By this analysis the Middle Ages falls into two sharply contrasting periods: with the broad experience of much of the era up to the early fourteenth century conforming to the former set of circumstances, and the latter characteristics persisting throughout much of the late fourteenth and fifteenth centuries.

Further powerful economic laws and concepts can also be brought to bear to explain and amplify the experience of these centuries. First, and most important, is the law of diminishing returns, which states that if additional units of one factor of production (labour, land, or capital) are employed while the others are held constant, the output generated by each additional unit will eventually fall. As applied to a fixed area of land, with labour the variable and capital the constant, the law has obvious relevance to the workings of an agricultural economy. If increasing numbers of workers are employed to farm a given piece of land, initially both the average productivity of the workers and the total amount of output from the land will tend to rise. For example, two men may be more than twice as productive as one on an area of, say, one hundred acres, and three men more than 50 per cent more productive than two, and so on. But eventually, as more workers are employed on the hundred acres, the average amount produced by each worker will reach a peak and then fall progressively, although the total amount yielded by that land may continue to rise. Therefore, for each area of land, to which a certain amount of capital is applied, there is an optimum number of workers. Below this number average returns will increase as each unit of labour is added, and above it they will diminish, since each additional worker will produce less than the average amount produced by those who are already employed.

Major advances in the analysis of the workings of agricultural economies and of the relationship between the land and people within them were achieved by David Ricardo (1772–1823) and Thomas Malthus (1766–1834), and their work has exercised a profound influence over all succeeding generations of historians and economists.[3] Ricardo had a particular interest in constructing theoretical models to predict the likely consequences of a rising demand for agricultural produce caused by an increasing population, and in doing so he refined and extended the concept of diminishing returns. Starting from the premiss that people would settle first on the most fertile lands, Ricardo argued that an increasing supply of people and demand for foodstuffs would result both in the application of more labour to the lands which were already being cultivated, and in the colonization of lands which had previously lain idle. As population continued to rise, diminishing returns would inevitably become apparent on the older-settled lands as more and more people were forced to live on them, while continuous extensions of the margin of cultivation would eventually result in the farming of second-, third-, and even fourth-rate soils. Population pressure would also be likely to produce excessively exploitative patterns of cultivation which would result in declining yields per acre, especially on the poorer soils. Thus, such an economy would eventually suffer from falling output per acre as well as from falling output per person.

From the law of diminishing returns flows the classical theory of economic rent. Economic rent is an abstract concept and quite distinct from the amount of rent which is actually paid to a landlord, but it is a means of demonstrating the intuitive belief that rents will rise when the demand for land increases. The economic rent on any piece of land is held to be equal to the difference between the cost of producing a given output on that land and the cost of

---

[3] Ricardo's main contributions to this field are contained in *The Principles of Political Economy*, first published in 1817, and those of Malthus are contained in *An Essay on the Principle of Population*, first published in 1798. For discussions of the nature and significance of their work, see e.g. D. P. O'Brien, *The Classical Economists* (Oxford, 1975); M. Blaug, *Ricardian Economics: An Historical Study* (New Haven, 1958); J. Dupaquier, A. Fauve-Chamoux, and E. Grebenik (eds.), *Malthus, Past and Present* (1983); W. Peterson, *Malthus* (1979).

producing the same output on land which is just on the borderline of being worth farming. Ricardo postulated that because land is always there and its supply is effectively fixed, in times of great abundance even lands of the best quality might in theory command no rent at all. But two things happen as the demand for land increases. First, the community is driven to employ land that was previously thought not good enough to farm. This drives up the rent of the best land, because fertile land is able to produce its output at less cost than the newly cultivated poorer land (the economic rent being the cost advantage which the best land enjoys). Likewise, it is the rising rental of the best land which makes the poorer land worth farming. Second, the best land is used more intensively, which increases the product of that land and thereby also pushes up the potential money rent, as the landowner is able to capture this productivity rise in the form of higher exactions. Further increases in the demand for land will, in similar fashion, lead to the spread of farming to progressively poorer and poorer lands, and successive attempts will be made to farm lands more intensively, thereby forcing rents ever higher.

Malthus tackled the relationship between population and resources from a different perspective. He held that the human race has an innate drive to reproduce, and that consequently population will always have a tendency to grow. But whereas in ideal conditions population has the capacity to expand at a geometric rate, the food supply in the longer term is capable of expanding only in arithmetical progression. Malthus thus produced an overtly pessimistic model which predicts that crises will loom periodically as rising numbers eventually move too far ahead of subsistence. Initially Malthus stressed that whenever population was too high relative to the productive resources of the nation, 'positive checks' in the form of famines and disease would force up death rates and lead to reductions in the numbers of people. But later he also proposed a less cataclysmic alternative in which, instead of moving inexorably towards crisis as living standards fell, society would avoid the worst consequences by adopting a range of 'preventive' or 'prudential'

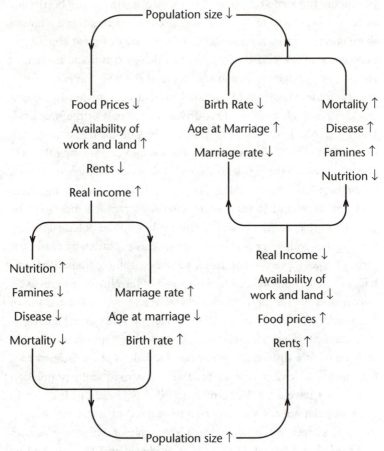

FIG. 1. The two versions of the basic Malthusian model

measures, such as delayed marriage, family limitation, and celibacy, which would have the effect of lowering the birth rate and thereby stifling any further growth of numbers. The elegant simplicity of the two versions of the Malthusian model are expressed in Figure 1.

From these basic hypotheses demographers and historians have written in terms of recurrent two-phase 'Malthusian cycles'. In the high-pressure version of the model, phase one sees a progressive build-up of population until competition for land, food, and employment drives family incomes down to a level which threatens subsistence crises. It is at this point that checks in the form of rising death rate, and probably also falling birth rate, will begin to occur, the latter due to the effects of malnutrition on conception and infant mortality, while the scarcity of land and employment also restrains the ability of couples to marry and establish families. The culmination of phase one necessarily results in the onset of phase two, namely a decline in population. As population declines so land becomes progressively cheaper and more plentiful, and living standards and employment opportunities will eventually improve to such an extent that the checks cease to operate. When this occurs population decline would be halted and numbers would begin to grow again, and thus the downswing in the cycle would be converted into an upswing.

Here we have a model of a self-contained ecosystem, with built-in mechanisms for self-correction. This 'motion biseculaire' is driven by the motive power of population, with its inherent tendency to grow unless checked. Expressed in engineering terms the two phases of the cycle are reciprocating and, like the rise and fall of a piston in an engine, 'the phase of increasing population and falling incomes is automatically succeeded and counterbalanced by the phase of falling population and rising incomes'.[4]

There are therefore two main elements in the position of those who espouse a Malthusian or neo-Malthusian position: one is that the rise and fall of population was the pre-eminent force in determining economic fundamentals and economic change in the pre-industrial era, the other is that population rose and fell in a predictable manner. In the words of Emmanuel Le Roy Ladurie, an avowed neo-Malthusian, England until the late seventeenth century and France until the eighteenth century were trapped in an

---

4 M. M. Postan and J. Hatcher, 'Population and Class Relations in Feudal Society', in T. H. Aston and C. H. E. Philpin (eds.), *The Brenner Debate: Agrarian Class Structure and Economic Development in Pre-industrial Europe* (Cambridge, 1985), 69.

'infernal cycle of agrarian-type Malthusian misfortunes'.[5] Ladurie terms his approach neo-Malthusian because, unlike Malthus who placed overwhelming emphasis on food supply and on those diseases which flowed directly from its insufficiency, he allows semi-autonomous 'biological' or epidemic factors to play a part in regulating population. However, although waves of epidemic disease may arise from the operation of independent biological factors, according to Ladurie their ultimate impact will be largely determined by prevailing economic and social conditions, which in turn are determined primarily by demographic factors.[6]

An uncompromising Malthusian stance would regard both the agrarian crises of 1315–22 and the Black Death of 1348–50 as positive checks which were the direct and inevitable consequence of overpopulation in Western Europe. In support it might also be argued that the transmission of plague was facilitated by the high densities of population and the proliferation of commercial networks which had built up in previous centuries, and that its impact upon communities was exacerbated by overcrowding, poverty, and malnutrition. Furthermore, by pointing to evidence that population had already begun to decline before the arrival of plague, it can be argued that the role played by epidemic disease in shaping the course of economic and social change was strictly limited and that the Black Death acted merely as an accelerator of trends which were already decisively underway.

It is possible to go much further, in theory at least, and elevate demographic forces and their consequential effects to the status of constant and predictive determinants of all major aspects of economic and social life. The rise and fall of population thereby becomes not merely the primary causal factor determining living standards, the distribution of wealth, the structure of the economy and its pattern of development, but social structures, institutions,

5 E. Le Roy Ladurie, 'A Reply to Robert Brenner', in Aston and Philpin (eds.), *Brenner Debate*, 104–5.
6 Ibid., 102–3.

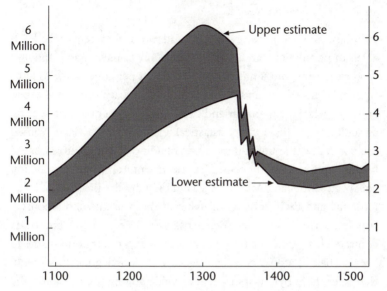

FIG. 2. Long-term flows in English population

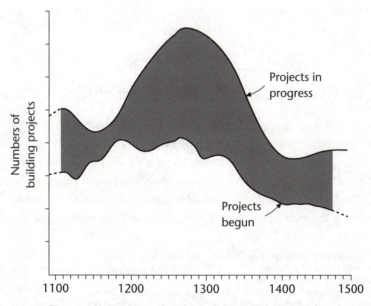

FIG. 3. Chronology of major building works on medieval
English cathedrals and abbeys

attitudes, and, perhaps, even legal and political systems too. High levels of population can be claimed not only to have made land and food expensive, but landlords powerful and peasants weak; to have strengthened serfdom and demesne farming; to have stimulated urban and commercial expansion and, through the generation of soaring agricultural profits for ecclesiastical institutions, to have primed the boom in cathedral and monastic building which occurred in the twelfth and thirteenth centuries. Furthermore, when population collapsed in the later Middle Ages not only did the incomes of landlords fall and the standards of living of the peasants and labourers rise, but serfdom declined, demesnes were leased, towns and trade contracted, and the building of cathedrals and monasteries came to a virtual halt.[7] Barons and knights faced with declining incomes sought to bolster them by the spoils of war, while among the peasantry the relative scarcity of people and easy availability of land led to the weakening and contraction of kin networks as access to holdings no longer depended upon inheritance and the maintenance of family ties.[8]

The Evidence of Population Pressure

How well does a neat Malthusian model, amplified and extended by the more elaborate theories of Ricardo, fit the facts of the Middle Ages? Certainly, the changes which took place in the level of population were spectacular. Most historians now accept that the population of England at least doubled and probably almost trebled between the end of the eleventh century and the opening of the

[7] See the remarkably close correlation between estimated English population movements and fluctuations in building projects in English cathedrals and abbeys between 1100 and 1500, exhibited in Figs. 2 and 3.

[8] For example, M. M. Postan, 'The Social Consequences of the Hundred Years War', in *idem, Medieval Agriculture and General Problems of the Medieval Economy* (Cambridge, 1973), esp. 60–1; Z. Razi, 'The Myth of the Immutable English Family', *P&P* 40 (1993), 22–44.

fourteenth, perhaps reaching 6 million at its peak.[9] Thereafter, first the famines of 1315–17 and then the recurrent plagues of later years resulted in massive losses, to be succeeded by a prolonged era of decline and stagnation. At the lowest point in the later fifteenth century there may well have been scarcely more than 2 million people in the country, perhaps no more than there had been four hundred years before, and there are few signs of sustained recovery before the first quarter of the sixteenth century.[10]

The foremost pioneer in the application of economic and demographic theory to the study of the English Middle Ages was M. M. Postan. When Postan began writing in the 1930s, the subject lacked a coherent general framework within which to fit the swelling tide of facts that was flowing from research on the records of particular estates, localities, trades, and towns. With bold strokes he sought to paint such a framework and to outline the sharply contrasting characteristics of the earlier and later medieval centuries. In his work on rural England, Postan elucidated the ebbs and flows of agricultural prosperity, and attempted to establish the nature of the interrelationship between population, settlement, and land use. His interest in relating economic fluctuations to demographic changes in turn led him to consider aspects of economic underdevelopment and the nature of growth in pre-industrial economies, and also the impact of changes in population and settlement on the incomes of landlords, peasants, and labourers. In the interpretation of the empirical evidence available to him, and the drawing from it of general principles, Postan made extensive use of the work of Malthus and, more particularly, of Ricardo. In so doing he argued

[9] R. M. Smith, 'Demographic Developments in Rural England, 1300–48: A Survey', in B. M. S. Campbell (ed.), *Before the Black Death: Studies in the 'Crisis' of the Early Fourteenth Century* (Manchester, 1991), 49; E. Miller and J. Hatcher, *Medieval England: Towns, Commerce and Crafts, 1086–1348* (1995), 393.

[10] L. R. Poos, 'The Rural Population of Essex in the Later Middle Ages', *EcHR*, 2nd ser., 38 (1985), 530; J. Hatcher, 'Mortality in the Fifteenth Century: Some New Evidence', *EcHR*, 2nd ser., 39 (1986); R. H. Britnell, *The Commercialisation of English Society, 1000–1500*, 2nd edn. (Manchester, 1996), 155–6; M. Bailey, 'Demographic Decline in Late Medieval England: Some Thoughts on Recent Research', *EcHR*, 2nd ser., 49 (1996).

that overall there was a reassuringly close fit between theory and practice.[11]

For Postan and his followers the key to understanding the dynamic forces behind economic fluctuations lay in establishing the changing balance between land and labour. This did not depend on computing accurate figures of total population, though occasionally such figures may be available for a particular manor: the best example being a rare long-run series of the number of resident adult males on the Somerset manor of Taunton, which showed an astonishing rise of 228 per cent between 1212 and 1312.[12] But even if reliable evidence of demographic trends were to exist for wide areas of England, according to Postan 'very little meaning could be read into total figures of population, no matter how accurate . . . much more significant than global numbers of population is its dynamics, i.e. the speed and direction of its movements and its changing relation to other economic factors'.[13] When this maxim is applied to the 'long thirteenth century', the crucial issue is not the aggregate level of the English population at its peak, but the degree to which population growth was matched by the extension of land colonization and the intensification of land use, and, even more importantly, the extent to which symptoms of an imbalance between land and labour became apparent.

Thus population statistics are of less importance than indicators of economic change and well-being, such as land values, holding size, and real wages. If such indicators point strongly towards an

[11] Most of Postan's leading essays on the Middle Ages have been republished in M. M. Postan, *Essays on Medieval Agriculture and General Problems of the Medieval Economy* (Cambridge, 1973) and *Essays on Medieval Trade and Finance* (Cambridge, 1973), and these together with his 'Medieval Agrarian Society in its Prime', in *The Cambridge Economic History of Europe*, i. *Agrarian Life in the Middle Ages*, ed. M. M. Postan, 2nd edn. (Cambridge, 1966), 548–659 (hereafter cited as *CEHE*, i), provide the best introduction to his work.

[12] J. Z. Titow, 'Some Evidence of the Thirteenth-Century Population Increase', *EcHR*, 2nd ser., 14 (1961).

[13] M. M. Postan, *The Medieval Economy and Society: An Economic History of Britain 1100–1500* (1972), 31.

extreme degree of overpopulation at the turn of the thirteenth and fourteenth centuries, then it follows that the population downturn of the fourteenth century would be best explained by the triggering of endogenous demographic checks. In the words of Postan, 'It will not be too fanciful . . . to see in the falling production of the later centuries a natural punishment of earlier over-expansion.'[14] The case for a demographic downturn along Malthusian lines around *c.*1300 has been argued so many times that it has become something of an orthodoxy. In essence, the evidence is fitted to the theoretical underpinnings outlined above by considering it within four broad categories: the performance of agriculture at the extensive, and intensive, margins of cultivation; peasant welfare; and towns, trade, and markets.

The Extensive Margin of Cultivation

The distribution of settlement, population, and plough teams recorded in the Domesday survey indicates that England was an old-settled country by the late eleventh century, especially in the south and east. Here Anglo-Saxon colonization had concentrated on the most fertile soils, and in particular the strong loams and better clays. In densely settled parts of the country the scope for further large-scale colonization was generally restricted to those areas of poorer soil or difficult access which had hitherto been avoided: in particular, virgin areas of marshland, woodland, downland, and heathland. The regions with the greatest opportunities for large-scale expansion lay in the north and west of England.

The twelfth and thirteenth centuries witnessed a rising tide of new settlement and land colonization throughout the nation, the pace and extent depending upon the local availability of wasteland. In anciently-settled regions cultivators grubbed out small assarts from

---

[14] *Medieval Agriculture and General Problems*, 14 (the paper from which the quotation is drawn was first presented in 1950).

the pastures, woods, and scrubland around the edges of their villages. Opportunist peasants who did not inherit land migrated from these overcrowded areas onto the heavier and less manageable clays, and onto thin and acidic heathlands. The northern silt fens of East Anglia, and the marshlands of Kent and Holderness, underwent progressive reclamation. Woodlands in the Weald and the forest of Arden were cleared, and Postan reported that the thin downlands and heathlands of the Chilterns and Breckland were brought into use. In the more remote harsh and inaccessible reaches of northern and western England the process was even more spectacular: on Dartmoor, the Pennines, and the Lake District, a multitude of new settlements were founded bearing place names which reveal their late origins. It was as if England had been rotated anti-clockwise on its diagonal axis, resulting in a flow of settlers into the sparsely populated wastes of the north and west.[15]

The process and extent of new colonization in England are well recorded and largely uncontentious. However, the significance of such colonization to the 'population–resources' model centres on the inherent infertility of the newly-won soils. While some intakes were of good quality, most were, 'to use a humdrum adjective, poor', so that population growth compelled farmers 'to overflow into lands worse than those ranking as second rate'. Without significant improvements in farming techniques, this 'land was worth ploughing only for a short while, after which the stored up fertility of the soil would be mined and the land would lie exhausted'.[16] Implicit in the work of Postan and Titow is the belief that falling yields soon became apparent on the newly colonized lands of the thirteenth century, a belief based on anecdotal evidence of 'barren' and 'debilitated' arable land in such regions.[17]

[15] Postan, 'Agrarian Society in its Prime', 548–52; Postan, *The Medieval Economy and Society*, 15–26.
[16] Ibid. 18,19, 24.
[17] Postan, 'Agrarian Society in its Prime', 556–8; Postan, *Medieval Economy and Society*, 23–6; J. Z. Titow, *English Rural Society, 1200–1350* (1969), 93–5.

In accordance with Ricardo's theories in which the best land would be used first, assarts were usually destined to be marginal in fertility as well as in location, and the later the assart the more marginal it was likely to be. But Postan also noted the perplexing tendency for land newly assarted from the waste to fetch higher rents than that which had been in cultivation for some time, and he suggested that the explanation for this apparent inversion of values lay in the inability of the older land to maintain its fertility, which made it worth less than intrinsically poorer land whose fertility was as yet unexhausted.[18] If the extension of the margin of cultivation onto barren soils in inhospitable regions proved the existence of overpopulation, the subsequent failure of those soils greatly exacerbated it.

Such ominous strains would be first in evidence not on good soils and well-located settlements in the heartlands of England, but on poor soils and in marginal regions. For, as Postan maintained, the latter were a litmus test of the changing fortunes of the economy because their very marginality made them particularly sensitive to the stirrings of a downturn. Any fall in the level of population, or—strictly speaking—in the price of grain consequent upon a fall in population, would quickly result in the abandonment of some of these meagre and unrewarding lands. A clear and widespread contraction in grain production did indeed occur after the catastrophic crop failures and livestock epidemics of the years from 1315 to 1322, and this downturn was most marked in marginal regions and on marginal soils.[19]

The retreat at the extensive margin of cultivation is a central theme of the population–resources model, for as the price of grain fell relative to the cost of labour so the acreage under crops continued to contract. The tide of medieval settlement and arable cultivation swelled to its highest point in the late thirteenth century,

---

[18] 'Agrarian Society in its Prime', 557–8.
[19] E. Miller and J. Hatcher, *Medieval England: Rural Society and Economic Change, 1086–1348* (1978), 61–3.

and ebbed to its lowest by the mid-fifteenth century. In the later Middle Ages, vast tracts of arable land were turned over to pasture or abandoned to the advancing wastes, and in village after village houses lay dilapidated and tenants were hard to find. On the poorest soils, and in the least favoured regions, the contraction was most dramatic. 'Villages on the furthest frontiers of cultivation . . . contracted, some of them to the brink of demise.' The fifteenth century is depicted as the most sustained agricultural depression in documented English history, and in a graphic and evocative image John Saltmarsh viewed the remains of crumbling churches in the Norfolk Breckland, and assumed they had been 'built by the latest pioneer settlers of the high Middle Ages, never enlarged and early abandoned'.[20]

During the era in which Postan was formulating his hypotheses many other scholars were producing evidence which could be used to support them, and in more recent decades the factual foundations of the broad contours of his chronology and interpretation have continued to be significantly reinforced. The conspectus of a relentless expansion of English settlement which inexorably resulted in the cultivation of ever poorer soils until, eventually, this centuries-long process was halted and then reversed in the decades before the arrival of the Black Death, resonates through the regional chapters of the second volume of the *Agrarian History of England and Wales*, published in 1988.[21] In this massive collaborative work we learn, for example, that 'increasing land hunger' from the mid-thirteenth century finally led to the colonization of tracts of the High Weald of Sussex and Kent, 'a wild, inmost region of broken hills and unkindly, cold wet soils'; that around the same time innumerable farmsteads proliferated in the most inhospitable locations in Devon and Cornwall, high up on Bodmin Moor and Dartmoor, and

---

[20] J. Saltmarsh, 'Plague and Economic Decline in England in the Later Middle Ages', *Cambridge Historical Journal*, 7 (1941), 24.

[21] *Agrarian History of England and Wales*, ii. *1040–1350*, ed. H. E. Hallam (Cambridge, 1988) (hereafter cited as *AHEW*).

on the heathlands of Goonhilly and Carnmenellis, where families grew crops as well as kept animals; while in Yorkshire 'additions to the arable fields in the townships lower down the Calder valley (Yorks.) were no longer being made in the early fourteenth century [but] . . . higher up the valley, at Holmfirth, Sowerby and Hipperholme no less than 777 $^1/2$ acres of assart are recorded in the court rolls between 1307 and 1316'. In the west midlands, '[a]lready by the thirteenth century and even earlier, land now classified as grade IV, "only suitable for low output enterprises" because of its "severe limitations" for agricultural use, was being cultivated', and by the later thirteenth century 'the poor quality of land left for clearance' was resulting in a severe slowdown of the pace of assarting in the region, even in the Derbyshire Peak Forest and the Chilterns; while in the east midlands '[S]o strong and traditional . . . was the thrust of demand for arable that the fourth zone of negligible arable potential was penetrated for a time from the late thirteenth century'. Over much of central, southern, and eastern England the scope for substantial further expansion was curtailed at a much earlier date, and inevitably such late new assarts as were able to be carved out were mainly on poorer soils and in unfavourable locations. In crowded eastern England 'by the early fourteenth century reclamation had . . . long since advanced far into highly marginal lands', like the 2,400 acres of 'moorish land and marshes' at Elm (Cambs.), of which only a tenth could be cultivated each year, and sizeable areas of the spectacular intakes from the sea in Lincolnshire, Norfolk, and Cambridgeshire had been won only at considerable expense and great risk of subsequent loss.[22]

Postan maintained that the high tide of medieval population swept ever larger numbers of people onto 'lands on which [no] society would draw except in times of real land hunger'.[23] Since the

---

[22] Ibid.: P. F. Brandon, 184, J. Hatcher, 242–4, E. Miller, 253–4; C. Dyer, 231–2; J. A. Raftis, 200–1; H. E. Hallam, 173, 174.
[23] Postan, 'Agrarian Society in its Prime', 551–2.

supply of even the poorest land was eventually bound to run out, by c.1300 the centuries-long process of reclamation had virtually ground to a halt to be followed by agricultural crises and rural retrenchment. Since Postan wrote, much additional evidence has been gathered which may be used to lend support to his gloomy hypotheses, and although regional differences in scale and chronology have emerged, with assarting continuing up to 1349 in some of the less densely settled regions like the south-west and the Kent and Sussex Weald,[24] for most parts of the country the peaking of colonization has been confirmed around 1300 and signs of retreat after 1320 have multiplied.[25] From the perspective of population–resources modelling, therefore, the firm conclusion may be drawn that the limits to the supply of new cultivable land had been reached, and that this was accompanied by falling yields at the extensive margin of cultivation, which together helped to precipitate a crisis of subsistence and promote a series of decisive economic changes whose ramifications were to reverberate through the fifteenth century as well as the fourteenth.

The Intensive Margin of Cultivation

Just as the pressure of a rising population encouraged the colonization of new lands, so it also encouraged farmers to intensify agricultural production on existing farmlands. But technology lagged, and although the potential for some increases in output is implicit in

---

[24] *AHEW*, ii. 184–5, 242–5.

[25] The structure of the second volume of *The Agrarian History of England and Wales* does not facilitate coverage of the early fourteenth-century crisis and the subsequent retreat of cultivation before the Black Death, but some of the contributors to the regional chapters in the next volume do refer to these matters: *The Agrarian History of England and Wales*, iii. *1348–1500*, ed. E. Miller (Cambridge, 1991), 34–5, 106–8. See also A. H. R. Baker, 'Evidence in the *Nonarum Inquisitiones* of Contracting Arable Lands in England during the Early Fourteenth Century', *EcHR*, 2nd ser., 19 (1966); Miller and Hatcher, *Rural Society and Economic Change*, 53–63; J. A. Raftis, *Assart Data and Land Values: Two Studies in the East Midlands, 1200–1350* (Toronto, 1974), esp. 19–22, 49; Campbell (ed.), *Before the Black Death*, esp. 184–208.

Ricardo's model, he believed that the law of diminishing returns would ultimately ensure that output would not keep pace with the growth in population. Accordingly, the medieval evidence is interpreted to show that despite attempts made by farmers to raise yields per acre, the onset of diminishing returns in agriculture would be rapid and ultimately overwhelming. For Postan, 'the most distinguishing attribute of medieval [agrarian] technology was its immobility compared to the technology of modern times.'[26] Indeed, it can be argued that the progressive colonization of poorer land in the twelfth and thirteenth centuries does not merely demonstrate the failure of output to match population increase, it is highly suggestive of the existence of diminishing returns on the old-settled land.

Postan was not insensitive to the attempts of medieval farmers to increase output per acre, but he judged most of their efforts to be centred on improvements in land management and increased labour inputs rather than new capital-intensive inventions, especially among the hard-pressed peasantry who had few resources except their own labour. The digging in of marl, lime, sand, or seaweed could improve the workability and fertility of soils, but only a small portion of the arable benefited. For, as Postan pointed out, these practices were not normally cost-effective. Certainly, for demesne farmers the cost could be very high, despite the cheapness of labour: the abbot of Bury St Edmunds paid no less than 40*d.* an acre to marl about 10 per cent of his demesne at Tivetshall (Norfolk) in 1250.[27] At these prices marling an acre could cost as much as buying an acre. The amounts that could profitably be invested to upgrade buildings and the narrow range of carts and farm implements used at the time were also strictly limited, and

---

[26] Postan, *Medieval Economy and Society*, 41. For further discussions by Postan of the nature and significance of investment and technological improvements, see ibid. 41–52; M. M. Postan, 'Investment in Medieval Agriculture', *Journal of Economic History*, 27 (1967); *idem*, 'Why Was Medieval Science so Backward', in Postan, *Medieval Agriculture and General Problems*. See also Titow, *English Rural Society*, 37–42.

[27] *AHEW*, ii. 285.

further encouraged landlords to invest in 'width' rather than in 'depth', that is in buying more land rather than trying to improve the land which they already owned. The growing of leguminous crops could also lead to improved yields of grain by helping to replenish nitrates. The acreage devoted to beans, vetches, and peas undoubtedly expanded, and in some parts of the country, including Norfolk and Holderness, it reached substantial proportions, but overall such crops were marginal and primarily grown for animal fodder rather than as aids to successful corn cultivation. A recent estimate suggests that nationally they accounted for just 6 per cent of the demesne sown acreage in the period 1250–99.[28] Prevailing attitudes encouraged a traditional approach to agriculture, and the system of communal farming was not conducive to technical innovation. Even if new ideas emerged, their diffusion was restricted by the generally static and subsistence nature of the peasant economy, and the inherent characteristics of the manorial regime meant that landlords did not invest in the farms of their tenants.

Attempts by medieval farmers to raise output by reorganizing the layout of open field systems and the rotations of crops grown on them also receive considerable attention. Knowledge of the nature and variety of local field systems has expanded since the population–resources model was first outlined, yet Postan was always aware that local differences in topography had resulted in the adoption of field systems of varying intensity, such as the use of the famous infield–outfield system on less fertile soils. He also discerned that the rising demand for grain encouraged many villages to reorganize their fields so as to reduce the area of arable land left fallow each year, and that as a consequence two-field systems, which left half the land fallow each year, progressively gave way to three-field

---

[28] B. M. S. Campbell and M. Overton, 'A New Perspective on Medieval and Early Modern Agriculture: Six Centuries of Norfolk Farming, *c.*1250–*c.*1850', *P&P* 141 (1993), 59 n. 49.

rotations. Yet it was argued that this straightforward and seemingly rational process was by no means free of adverse consequences, because some of the land which had previously benefited from lying fallow every other year began to suffer from declining yields when it was cultivated two years in three. Moreover, when coupled with the piecemeal ploughing up of village wastes and grasslands, the balance of land use was tilted even further towards arable at the expense of pasture. The growing scarcity of grassland in the farming systems practised by medieval villages is demonstrated by the high price placed on meadowland, which in predominantly grain-producing districts rose even more rapidly than that of arable land.[29]

Thirteenth-century agriculture is thus depicted as moving remorselessly towards a 'grain monoculture', a shift which is viewed as one of the most significant economic events of the High Middle Ages. Whatever changes might occur in land management, labour inputs, or even capital investment, land productivity was ultimately dependent on the supply of fertilizer, that is animal manure. A rise in the area under crops each year therefore required a concomitant rise in the amount of manure. However, it was not possible to increase livestock numbers progressively when the amount of land devoted to pasture was falling. It therefore follows that the numbers of livestock became ever more inadequate as the thirteenth century wore on, and dwindling supplies of manure undermined the fertility of the cultivated area.

Postan backed up his 'working hypothesis' by producing evidence of the numbers of animals owned by the peasantry from a short series of exceptionally informative tax returns of a scattering of villages in south Wiltshire, Suffolk, and Huntingdonshire, and additional supporting evidence was later derived from parts of

[29] Postan, 'Agrarian Society in its Prime', 554.

Bedfordshire and the West Riding of Yorkshire.[30] Taking account of the fact that these records list the livestock of the peasantry who were wealthy enough to be taxed, the picture they reveal may be regarded as indicative of a progressive and ultimately harmful over-specialization on arable farming. Surprisingly few pigs were kept. Even in the ideal 'sheep country' of south Wiltshire and Black-bourne, average peasant flocks were small, but perhaps it is of even more significance that nearly one-third of taxpayers in Suffolk, two-fifths of those in Huntingdonshire and Wiltshire, over half of those in Ripon, and more than two-thirds of those in Bedfordshire, had no sheep at all. Finally, draught animals were everywhere deficient in numbers, even in the favoured arable regions of Hun-tingdonshire and Bedfordshire. Many villagers were so chronically short of plough beasts that they must have been compelled to plough with their cows to the detriment of their milk yield, or to spend money on hiring draught animals from their richer neighbours.

It is held, therefore, that although the attempts to intensify agri-cultural production did sometimes result in some increases in out-put per acre, these fell far short of what was required to keep pace with the growing demands of a rising population; that enhancements of output per acre were commonly achieved only at the expense of decreasing marginal returns to labour, as more and more time was applied to existing lands to less and less effect, or of decreasing returns to capital, as applications of marl or expensive drainage operations failed to prove cost-effective; and that yet other measures, such as the conversion from a two-field to a three-field system, sometimes resulted in falling yields per acre. Moreover, the 'worst case' interpretation of the period draws further powerful support from the proliferation of references in thirteenth- and early fourteenth-century manorial accounts to impoverished lands, and from Titow's monumental calculations of grain yields on the incomparably docu-

[30] M. M. Postan, 'Village Livestock in the Thirteenth Century', *EcHR*, 2nd ser., 15 (1962); *idem*, 'Agrarian Society in its Prime', 554–6. For additional evidence and discus-sion, see Miller and Hatcher, *Rural Society and Economic Change*, 152–5.

mented manors of the bishopric of Winchester, which Postan hailed as demonstrating that a significant decline in output occurred at the turn of the thirteenth and fourteenth centuries.[31]

Taken together, all this evidence was used to demonstrate that not only did England's expanding resource base fail to keep pace with the growth in population, but that its capacity actually diminished when the demands placed on it were at their heaviest. In Postan's words, 'after a time the marginal character of the marginal lands was bound to assert itself, and the honeymoon of high yields was succeeded by long years of reckoning'.[32] He believed in the metabolism of organic field systems, in their potential for decay and their need for renewal, and held that the exhaustion of England's soils was not easily or swiftly rectifiable. During the course of the thirteenth century arable lands deteriorated under unsustainable pressure, and they required a century or more to recuperate, as the low yields of the later fourteenth and fifteenth centuries demonstrated. Thus, the excessive pressures generated by the long upswing in population were instrumental in bringing about a protracted subsequent downswing.[33]

Peasant Welfare

Such profoundly negative developments in the agricultural base of the country were bound to have adverse consequences for the well-being of the mass of the population. Since the holding of land provided the main source of subsistence and income for the vast majority living in thirteenth-century England, it follows that the living standards of the peasantry will primarily be determined by

[31] J. Z. Titow, *Winchester Yields: A Study in Medieval Agricultural Productivity* (Cambridge, 1972); Postan, *Medieval Economy and Society*, 62–3. A statistical analysis of the Winchester grain yield data by M. Desai has demonstrated that they do not exhibit a declining trend ('The Agrarian Crisis in Medieval England: A Malthusian Tragedy or a Failure of Entitlements', *Bulletin of Economic Research* (1991)).

[32] 'Economic Foundations of Medieval Society', in Postan, *Medieval Agriculture and General Problems*, 14.

[33] Postan, *Medieval Economy and Society*, 66–72.

the output of that landholding. Hence Postan placed much emphasis on the evidence of the smallness of the average landholding and,
most importantly, of its further diminution in the course of the
thirteenth century. Once again it was the growth of population which
denied land to an increasing proportion of people and created
intense pressure to subdivide holdings, a process facilitated in
some parts by partible inheritance (the division of lands among all
male heirs) and by an active market for land among the peasantry.
Fewer acres meant lower incomes for the masses, a more precarious existence, and rising impoverishment.

It is generally accepted that the produce of at least 10 acres of
decent land was required to provide for the basic needs of an average family and meet its obligations to its landlord; and some would
put the requirement nearer 20 acres.[34] Yet Postan produced statistics
from a range of estates in the mid- and late thirteenth century which
revealed that almost half of all tenants held less than a quarter
virgate (*c.*8 acres), and these he added to the broadly similar findings
which Kosminsky had produced from the landholdings of thousands
of freemen and villeins in a swathe of six counties across central
England recorded in the Hundred Rolls of 1279.[35]

Subsequent analyses of manorial surveys throughout the country have added greatly to the range and scale of our information
on landholding patterns, and transformed Postan's assertions of a
proliferating lesser peasantry hungry for land into a proven fact. The
county-based data given in Table 1 can be readily supplemented

---

[34] See the discussions in R. H. Hilton, *A Medieval Society: The West Midlands at the End of the Thirteenth Century* (1966), 114–15; Titow, *English Rural Society*, 79–93; C. Dyer, *Standards of Living in the Later Middle Ages: Social Change in England, c.1200–1520* (Cambridge, 1989), 110–40. The most recent assessment is pessimistic: H. Kitsikopolous concludes a reconstruction of the budgets of middling tenants with 18 acres of arable and 2 acres of common meadow, by claiming that approximately half of the English peasantry must have 'struggled to keep itself alive between harvests' ('Standards of Living and Capital Formation in Pre-plague England: A Peasant Budget Model', *EcHR*, new ser., 53 (2000), 237–61).

[35] 'Agrarian Society in its Prime', 617–22; E. A. Kosminsky, *Studies in the Agrarian History of England in the Thirteenth Century* (Oxford, 1956), esp. tables on 216 and 223.

TABLE 1. The size of tenant landholdings in England, c.1260–1340 (by percentage)

County	0–5 acres	0–10 acres
Suffolk	41%	72%
Sussex	50%	63%
Northumberland	30%	35%
Yorkshire	42%	52%
Lancashire	32%	59%

Sources: *AHEW* i. 606, 624, 631, 687. Bury St Edmunds manors in 1285 (7,337 tenancies); manors of the bishop of Chichester, c.1250 and the archbishop of Canterbury, 1285 (2,168 tenancies); Inquisitions Post Mortem and manorial surveys: Northumberland, 1244–1352 (910 tenancies); Yorkshire, 1259–1320 (746 tenancies); Lancashire, 1311–46 (503 tenancies).

by those derived from the records of estates with lands in a number of counties. On the manors of Westminster Abbey in the early fourteenth century, situated mainly in Hertfordshire, Middlesex, and Surrey, 52 per cent of tenants held 10 acres or less, while on the manors of the bishop of Worcester in 1299, situated in Worcestershire, Warwickshire, and Gloucestershire, 44 per cent of tenants held less than 14 acres.[36] Whereas average holdings may well have been somewhat larger in the north and west of England, the quality of their soil was generally lower and the climate harsher, and morcellation could reach Lilliputian proportions on the best lands of the favoured south-east: on five fenland manors of Spalding

[36] B. Harvey, *Westminster Abbey and its Estates in the Middle Ages* (Oxford, 1977), 436–7; C. Dyer, *Lords and Peasants in a Changing Society: The Estates of the Bishop of Worcester, 680–1540* (Cambridge, 1980), 88.

priory in 1259/60 more than 72 per cent of tenants held under 10 acres, while a number of Norfolk manors had a median holding size of less than a single acre.[37]

What is more, even these doleful statistics fail to reveal the true extent of potential poverty. For they are derived from manorial surveys which almost invariably record only those people who held land directly from the lord. Evidence of those lesser people who held land as subtenants of other tenants would reduce the average size of landholdings still further and, of course, there are many other indications that substantial and rising numbers of landless persons were residing in villages as either squatters or servants.

The thirteenth century was an age of increasing land values when the rents paid by most peasants grew, despite the prevalence of freeholders and customary tenants whose rents were fixed by law or constrained by custom. The rising value of land found its clearest expression in those parts of the market where demand and supply were able to operate with least hindrance. Consequently, the rents charged for leaseholds and tenancies-at-will often ran extremely high, and were calculated in shillings per acre rather than pence. This was not just in the crowded south and east of England, for even allowing for the possibility of large customary acres, land leased at 2s. 6d. and 3s. an 'acre' at Bamburgh (Northumb.) and 2s. 9d. per 'acre' at Tanshelf (Yorks.) was remarkably expensive. And if the annual rent of 6d. per acre on the bishop of Coventry and Lichfield's waste at Longdon (Staffs.) seems low, he charged in addition entry fines which rose to an astronomical 10s. an acre.[38]

Although normally far lower than free market rents, the payments demanded of customary tenants in cash and in kind also tended upwards as holdings were split and as generation succeeded generation. Entry fines, which were paid when a new tenant inherited or entered a holding, were more flexible than customary rents, and on many estates 'they mounted at an ever greater speed until by

[37] *AHEW*, ii. 966–7.
[38] Miller and Hatcher, *Rural Society and Economic Change*, 45–6; *AHEW*, ii. 228–9.

the turn of the thirteenth and fourteenth centuries they reached exceptional heights'.[39] The longest series comes from the Winchester manor of Fonthill (Wilts.), where fines rose from an average of 1s.–1s. 8d. a virgate in 1214 to 8s.–46s. 8d. in the late thirteenth and early fourteenth centuries, but in the fertile vale of Taunton and at Sedgemoor in Somerset, some truly extraordinary fines of £40, £60, and even £80 were levied for entry into a virgate of perhaps 40 acres.[40] Although entry fines were considerably lower than this in most of the rest of England—on the estates of Peterborough Abbey, for example, the highest payment was closer to £5 per virgate—the overall trend in fines, as well as in rents, was decisively upwards during the course of the thirteenth century.[41] In addition to rents and entry fines paid in cash, many customary tenants were liable to perform labour services and pay a variety of seigneurial charges. According to Postan, the claims of landlords, the Church (through tithes and death duties), and the state (through taxation) could result in the forfeiture of at least half of the gross product of a holding.[42] The combination of large charges and small landholdings commonly made impoverishment inevitable.

Welfare was also determined by the prices of grain and wage labour, because peasants as well as landless labourers routinely needed both to purchase food and to find employment in order to survive, and they too moved in adverse directions during the thirteenth century. Overall the price of most basic commodities, and in particular grain, rose faster than money wage rates in the thirteenth century, thereby driving real wages down, until they plunged to unsustainable depths in the succession of famine years from 1315. According to the most recent compilations of data by D. Farmer, the real wages of agricultural labourers fell by a third between 1208/20 and

[39] Postan, 'Agrarian Society in its Prime', 553.

[40] Titow, *English Rural Society*, 75–8.

[41] E. King, *Peterborough Abbey, 1086–1310: A Study in the Land Market* (Cambridge, 1973), 166.

[42] Postan, 'Agrarian Society in its Prime', 603–4. This frequently quoted figure is discussed in S. H. Rigby, *English Society in the Later Middle Ages: Class, Status and Gender* (1995), 31–3, and found to be an overestimate.

1290/1300.[43] Such movements, it is argued, offer a crude index of the worsening balance between population and resources, because the trend of grain prices reflects the growing insufficiency of the supply of corn in the economy, while the trend of wages reflects the growing surplus of labour.

Thus, there is compelling evidence of a severe long-term decline in peasant welfare, and the data on real wages, land rents, and holding size point to a nadir at the turn of the thirteenth and fourteenth centuries. In accordance with the projections of population and resources modelling, this doleful state of affairs is the direct consequence of mounting overpopulation, and this ushered in a period when positive Malthusian-style checks operated on the population to force it down.

The theory that population growth inevitably erodes living standards, and that sustained improvements in the welfare of the masses are likely to be achieved only under conditions of demographic decline, also derives substantial support from the experience of the later Middle Ages when population and agricultural prices fell and wages rose. By the middle of the fifteenth century the purchasing power of a day's labour seems to have more than doubled. Gains in earnings accrued as the surplus of labour which blighted the later thirteenth century was transformed into shortage, and employment opportunities abounded for women as well as men. Rents inevitably followed agricultural prices downwards. The contraction in the area under cultivation was underway by the 1330s and 1340s, and by the close of the fourteenth century rents had contracted sharply throughout England, and most continued to fall still further thereafter. Even by the dawn of the sixteenth century there were only sporadic signs of a sustained recovery.[44] All of which was greatly

[43] *AHEW*, ii. 778.

[44] For Postan's views of the later Middle Ages, see, *inter alia*, 'The Fifteenth Century', *EcHR*, 9 (1939) and 'Some Economic Evidence of a Declining Population in the Later Middle Ages', *EcHR*, 2nd ser., 2 (1950), both reprinted in *Medieval Agriculture and General Problems*; *Medieval Economy and Society*, 35–9, 105–9, 139–42. For up-to-date and detailed presentations and analyses of the evidence, see *AHEW*, iii, *passim*.

to the benefit of the fifteenth-century peasantry, the majority of whom held comfortably more land than their predecessors and on markedly more favourable terms.

Towns, Trade, and Markets

If the growing population of the thirteenth century could not be adequately absorbed in the home village, and if land colonization was slowing to a virtual halt, then the employment opportunities offered by crafts, towns, and trade represented the only outlets for surpluses of rural manpower. Commercial activity in medieval England was undertaken at three levels. First, all smallholders had to engage in some exchange of basic goods and services in order to subsist, and all landholders needed to sell some of their produce in order to secure the cash with which to pay their rents. Second, specialized production of raw or manufactured goods took place in various localities throughout England and entered inter-regional trade, and, third, some commodities, notably wool, woollen cloth, and minerals, were exported. Thus, Postan accepted that 'some opportunities for trade were therefore to be found in all places and, above all, at all times'.[45]

Clearly, then, the variety of occupational and wage-labouring opportunities available in the countryside offered some compensation for the remorseless tendency towards smaller landholdings in the thirteenth century. Whereas agricultural labouring for lords and other villagers probably provided the bulk of rural employment, various craft, industrial, and retailing activities furnished further opportunities to supplement the income which could be derived from the landholding. Welcome additions to the family pot might also come from fishing, snaring birds, and catching wild animals. Peasants frequently had dual occupations, working as carpenters,

[45] Postan, *Medieval Economy and Society*, 183.

thatchers, and so on when their services were needed. If they were skilled they might fashion items for the local market, and one of the most common ways in which smallholders might gain a few extra pennies was by brewing and selling ale. Rural textile production was widespread and created considerable part-time and some full-time employment in the home, but large-scale industrial employment, such as the mining, refining, and working of metals, was more localized because it depended upon the proximity of raw materials.

Although the range of potential by-employments could be surprisingly broad, the real issue is whether the income they provided to smallholding and landless families was sufficient to compensate them for their lack of acres and, in the thirteenth and early fourteenth centuries, the escalating price of their food. Unfortunately, no explicit evidence about peasant household budgets exists from the Middle Ages, and therefore we cannot know the contribution which by-employments made to household income. Notwithstanding this lack of certainty, the proponents of population–resources models downplay the cumulative importance of commerce and urbanization in medieval economic development, and consequently are pessimistic about their implications for peasant welfare.

Since such an assumption cannot be based upon adequate hard evidence, it has to be supported by a number of a priori arguments and a range of circumstantial evidence. For example, if one accepts that medieval agriculture was largely geared to subsistence, then it follows that the proportion of people who were fully engaged in trade and industry must have been relatively small. Support for this argument can be derived from what we know of towns. We cannot be certain of the numbers of people living in towns, but since many historians are comfortable with the estimate that the proportion did not exceed 15 per cent of the population *c.*1300, the ability of towns to provide compensation for the deficiencies of the countryside would seem to have been severely restricted. Town streets were not paved with gold and many who migrated there simply exchanged one form of poverty for another. In the words of A. R.

Bridbury, 'thirteenth-century towns were not so much populated as swollen and choked with people, all hoping for the living that the countryside could no longer give them, and all but a few hoping in vain.'[46] Similarly, it is stressed that rural by-employments could do no more than enable smallholders to subsist—though barely—in good years. 'The supplementary income from wages would not wholly compensate for the acres they lacked'; such employment was too 'incomplete and discontinuous', too poorly paid in real terms, and too prone to dry up in bad years to have significantly alleviated rural poverty in the late thirteenth century.[47]

The urban and commercial sectors did not operate in opposition to the agricultural sector, but were part of the same interlocked economy, and were likewise moulded by the rise and fall of population. The collapse of population and the decline in agricultural prosperity in the later Middle Ages induced a severe contraction in the volume of goods which were traded and in the size and fortunes of most towns. The majority of village markets ceased to function in the fifteenth century, and town after town sought relief from taxation and annual payments by complaining to the Crown about depopulation and impoverishment. The growing value of labour, and the redistribution of incomes in favour of the masses, did stimulate some sectoral expansion, based principally on a growing demand for basic consumer goods which had previously been unaffordable. Demand for woollen textiles was especially buoyant both at home and overseas, particularly for cloth of modest quality, and production flourished in a number of rural areas as the countryside enjoyed the advantage over towns of having a less regulated environment and a supply of labour which was both cheaper and more flexible. However, falling agricultural prices made manufactured goods

---

[46] A. R. Bridbury, *Economic Growth: England in the Later Middle Ages* (1962), 55. The plentiful flow of migrants into Norwich in the early fourteenth century 'simply increased the number of urban poor' (E. Rutledge, 'Immigration and Population Growth in Early Fourteenth-Century Norwich', *Urban History Year Book* (1988), 28).

[47] Postan, 'Agrarian Society in its Prime', 624; Postan, *Medieval Economy and Society*, 132–4.

relatively more expensive and many of these industries ceased to expand after the close of the fourteenth century, and some clearly declined markedly thereafter. Even in the case of the market leader, woollen textiles, domestic demand could not compensate for the loss of overseas markets in the mid-fifteenth century.[48] Overall, there-fore, although the volume of trade and non-agricultural production in the late fourteenth and fifteenth centuries may not have fallen as much as population, in an overwhelmingly agrarian economy, with a pronounced emphasis on arable farming, it was inevitable that no major sector would escape recession. 'That the total national income and wealth was declining is shown by almost every statist-ical index available to historians.'[49]

The Strengths and Weaknesses of the Case

The population and resources model thus shows what happened to the medieval economy and society and also why it happened. The compelling manner in which Postan expounded his arguments, their intellectual roots in the theories of two of the greatest classical economists, and their impressive empirical foundations, produced a model of immense power and influence. Yet more force was added to the demographic factor by the contemporaneous work of William Abel,[50] and a long succession of historians, led by Emmanuel Le Roy Ladurie and Sir John Habbakuk, have helped

---

[48] Postan, 'Agrarian Society in its Prime', 568.

[49] Postan, 'The Fifteenth Century', 42. For recent examinations of the fifteenth-century economy, see R. H. Britnell, 'The Economic Context', in A. J. Pollard (ed.), *The Wars of the Roses* (1995); J. Hatcher, 'The Great Slump of the Mid-fifteenth Century', in R. H. Britnell and J. Hatcher (eds.), *Progress and Problems in Medieval England: Essays in Honour of Edward Miller* (Cambridge, 1996), 237–72; P. Nightingale, 'England and the European Depression of the Mid-fifteenth Century', *Journal of European Economic History*, 26 (1997).

[50] W. Abel, *Die Wüstungen des ausgehenden Mittelalters*, 2nd edn. (Stuttgart, 1955); W. Abel, *Agricultural Fluctuations in Europe from the Thirteenth to the Twentieth Centuries* (1980 edn., first published in 1935).

to ensure the continued prominence of the model in explaining economic development in modern as well as medieval times.[51] In the resounding words of Habbakuk:

Rising population, rising prices, rising agricultural profits, low real incomes for the mass of the population, unfavourable terms of trade for industry—with variations depending on changes in social institutions, this might stand for a description of the thirteenth century, the sixteenth century and the early seventeenth, and the period 1750–1815. Falling or stationary population with depressed agricultural profits but higher mass incomes might be said to be characteristic of the intervening periods.[52]

With such powerful and widely-based support, it is small wonder that those who believe in alternative theories of historical development should complain that the Malthusian model, rooted in demographic determinism, has assumed the status of orthodoxy which, 'served by the reputation of the historians who defend it, is crushing our historiography with its tentacles'.[53]

Because of the immense influence which it has exerted over the historical literature, and the manner in which it has been repeatedly used to explain vast sweeps of history, the population–resources model has inevitably attracted sustained criticism as well as support. The model is frequently portrayed by professional historians as well as undergraduates as a simplistic and crude elucidation of Malthusian determinism. However, Postan, its major architect, claimed a relatively modest role for what he called his 'working hypotheses', and refuted the 'slipshod . . . imputations of Malthusian creed'.[54] In his seminal paper of 1950 Postan declared that the primary subject of his

[51] E. Le Roy Ladurie, *Les Paysans de Languedoc*, 2 vols. (Paris, 1966); *idem*, 'En Haute-Normandie: Malthus ou Marx?', *Annales ESC* 31 (1978); and various essays in *idem*, *Territoire de l'historien*, 2 vols. (Paris, 1973–8); H. J. Habbakuk, *Population Growth and Economic Development since 1750* (Leicester, 1972); *idem*, 'The Economic History of Modern Britain', in D. V. Glass and D. E. C. Eversley (eds.), *Population in History* (1965).

[52] 'Economic History of Modern Britain', 148.

[53] G. Bois, 'Against the Neo-Malthusian Orthodoxy', in Aston and Philpin (eds.), *Brenner Debate*, 107.

[54] Postan and Hatcher, 'Population and Class Relations in Feudal Society', 70.

studies was 'the economic base of medieval society . . . population and land settlement, techniques of production and the general trends of economic activity: in short all those economic facts which can be discussed without concentrating on the workings of legal and social institutions and upon relations of class to class'.[55] Then again, in his last contribution before his death, Postan maintained that he, and other historians of similar persuasion, had never sought to 'present demographic factors as an omnipresent and omnipotent force behind every economic and social activity or every feature of economic and social organisation', or to 'account for the abiding features of the medieval economy and society, its structure, institutions or attitudes, by demographic factors alone'. Instead, he claimed that the stated aim 'was far more limited, namely, to relate periodic movements or economic fluctuations—repeat fluctuations—to concomitant demographic changes—repeat changes—over time'.[56]

Coming as they do from its most distinguished proponent, these are very significant limitations on the range and applicability of the demographic model. The theories which underpin it are undoubtedly at their most robust when focusing on the nature and power of the economic forces set in motion by the rise and fall of population. In terms of the actual history of the Middle Ages, the model would seem at its strongest when applied to the experience of the 'long thirteenth century', and the onset of the extremely adverse conditions experienced by the European economy on the eve of the Black Death. In a pioneering study based on the estates of the bishop of Winchester in the thirteenth and early fourteenth centuries, Postan and Titow analysed the links between death rates and the yield and price of grain. Not surprisingly they found that when prices rose mortality increased, which is what might be expected in any underdeveloped agrarian society, but much more significantly

---

[55] Presented in 1950 to the Ninth International Congress of Historical Sciences in Paris, reprinted as 'The Economic Foundations of Medieval Society', in Postan, *Medieval Agriculture and General Problems*, 3–27 (quotation on p. 3).
[56] Postan and Hatcher, 'Population and Class Relations', 64–5.

they also discovered that as the thirteenth century wore on similar increases in prices resulted in ever greater levels of mortality as the poorest peasants increasingly starved to death or succumbed to ailments related to malnutrition.[57] From some perspectives, therefore, the appalling famines and almost universal distress of 1315–22, during which more than 10 per cent of the population died, would seem to constitute an exemplary case of a Malthusian crisis. Moreover, the extent and strength of the downturn during and after these catastrophes, when according to Postan 'the population figures came tumbling down',[58] could suggest that the arrival of plague merely led to an acceleration of a pre-existing and endogenously induced crisis of subsistence.

Yet the case for a neo-Malthusian interpretation of this era is not as strong as it might appear to be.[59] Even if it is accepted that early fourteenth-century England was suffering from a significant degree of overpopulation—and it can scarcely be doubted that the long rise in population resulted in 'a journey to the margin' for substantial parts of the economy, and in greater economic instability and uncertainty for a growing proportion of the people—this state of affairs need not by itself have led to the severe and long-enduring crises which were actually experienced throughout most of Europe. First, it is possible that the exceptional and extraordinary combination of harvest failures and animal murrains between 1315 and

---

[57] M. M. Postan and J. Z. Titow, 'Heriots and Prices on Winchester Manors', in Postan, *Medieval Agriculture and General Problems*, 150–85. This work has been subjected to much criticism and amendment, and it has been noted that heriots, which were originally taken by Postan to have almost always indicated a death, were often levied when a holding was sold. Nonetheless, the Malthusian correlation between rising prices and increased distress, leading to forced sales of land as well as increased deaths, still appears to hold.

[58] Postan, *Medieval Agriculture and General Problems*, 14.

[59] For critiques of Postan's views and the case for a Malthusian crisis, see e.g. H. E. Hallam, 'The Postan Thesis' and 'The Malthusian Problem', *Rural England, 1066–1348* (1981 edn.), 10–16, 245–64; B. Harvey, 'Introduction: The "Crisis" of the Early Fourteenth Century', in B. M. S. Campbell (ed.), *Before the Black Death: Studies in the 'Crisis' of the Early Fourteenth Century* (Manchester, 1991), 1–24; Rigby, *English Society in the Later Middle Ages*, 87–95; Desai, 'Agrarian Crisis in Medieval England'; and, of course, the various contributions in the *Brenner Debate*.

1322 would have killed a large number of people irrespective of prevailing levels of peasant welfare, if they were a product of freak conditions rather than of a systemic crisis of subsistence. Second, the emphasis in Postan's writings on overpopulation and 'punishing death rates' is redolent of the more pessimistic conjectures of Malthus, and of a 'high pressure' demographic regime in which crisis mortality eventually overwhelms a high birth rate. Yet Malthus himself came to accept that there could be another, less cataclysmic, outcome to the pressure of population on resources. Societies could avert a crisis of mortality if they took measures to reduce the birth rate, instead of proceeding remorselessly towards the precipice. These steps he termed prudential restraints or preventative checks, as opposed to the positive checks which 'shorten the natural duration of human life'. They included the delay or avoidance of marriage, which were occasioned by low wages and the scarcity of employment opportunities as well as by conscious decisions, and the limitation of births within marriage, though Malthus himself was opposed to contraception.[60]

In other words, it is possible that, without the intervention of the disastrous weather and livestock epidemics of 1315–22, and the arrival of plague in 1348–9, declining living standards would have led to the adoption of prudential checks on the number of births, which would have ended the growth of population, and possibly forced numbers downwards for a time until a sufficient improvement in living conditions came about. Thereafter, to follow Malthus's own speculations, the level of population would have proceeded to experience a series of oscillations, first downwards and then upwards,[61] rather than plunging catastrophically for a century and more. On the other hand, why should the search for the cause of

---

[60] In later editions of his *Essay on the Principle of Population*, Malthus laid progressively greater emphasis on moral restraint, alongside vice and misery, as a check to population growth (T. R. Malthus, *An Essay on the Principle of Population*, ed. D. Winch (Cambridge, 1992), pp. xiii–xiv, 21–9).

[61] Ibid. 25–7.

population change in the early fourteenth century, or any other era for that matter, be conducted in terms of a choice between prudential or positive checks? Surely it is far more likely that the behaviour of population was influenced by both. Moreover, to move even further outside the conventional neo-Malthusian framework, the extreme difficulty of constructing a plausible hypothesis which avoids giving significant weight to the exogenous factors of freak weather conditions and bubonic plague must be confronted.

Despite the closeness of the fit between the concepts developed by Malthus and Ricardo and Postan's belief that the long period of expansion sowed the seeds of an inevitable catastrophe which began in the early fourteenth century, Postan made no sustained attempt to explain the later Middle Ages in Malthusian and Ricardian terms. The experience of the later Middle Ages, when population fell by more than a half—and possibly by as much as two-thirds—and failed to sustain a recovery before the early decades of the sixteenth century, bears little or no resemblance to the second cycle of a Malthusian model, or even to the dynamic of a more loosely structured 'population and resources' approach.[62] The inability of population to rise during a prolonged era of very high wages and abundant cheap land, clearly poses a major problem for any hypothesis which regards living standards as the prime determinant of the level and trend of population. Malthus listed among his positive checks on population growth 'the whole train of common diseases and epidemics, wars, pestilence, plague and famine',[63] but the arrival and then persistence of plague would seem to have had far less to do with the preceding era of expansion, or of its culmination in overpopulation, than with the independent behaviour of micro-organisms, fleas, and the rodents which carried them.

---

[62] This argument is stressed in J. Hatcher, *Plague, Population and the English Economy, 1348–1530* (1977) and M. Bailey, 'Demographic Decline in Late Medieval England: Some Thoughts on Recent Research', *EcHR*, 2nd ser., 49 (1996), 1–19.

[63] Malthus, *Essay on the Principle of Population*, ed. Winch, 23.

Postan briefly speculated that the excessive demands placed on arable lands during the thirteenth century may have resulted in long-term damage to the soil, and that this reduced productivity and diminished the capacity of the resource base to the extent that it held back demographic recovery for much of the fifteenth century. But it is much more convincing to see the reduced agricultural yields of the later Middle Ages as a consequence of low population levels rather than their cause. The low yields of the later Middle Ages were primarily the result of a reduction in the intensity of farming during a period of agricultural recession and high labour costs. If low yields had been responsible for holding back population, then it would have been high prices rather than low prices which dominated the closing decades of the fourteenth century and virtually the whole of the fifteenth. An insufficiency of resources cannot be the reason why the late medieval population did not recover.

Another weakness of the population–resources model is the widening gap which has emerged between its general descriptions of events and the welter of local evidence uncovered in recent years. The model was constructed at a time when few local studies had been undertaken, and initially the typicality of the evidence it employed and the universality of its application was not seriously questioned. However, the explosion of research into the medieval economy during the past two decades has established that some of the more pessimistic predictions of the model are inappropriate for certain regions and places. For example, land productivity did not suffer a widespread secular decline in the late thirteenth century, and some farms achieved good yields per acre while simultaneously eliminating fallows.[64] Similarly, some regions of poor soil which were identified by Postan as exemplifying decline at the external margin of cultivation, actually developed diverse economies capable of

---

[64] See below, pp. 145–6.

absorbing population growth, in which arable farming constituted a serviceable adjunct to other activities.[65]

As our knowledge of other sectors of the medieval economy has grown in the past few decades, so too has the scope for challenging the overwhelming dominance accorded in this model to agriculture and the level of population. In particular, it is argued that the stimulus given to productivity and employment by the expansion of towns, trade, and industry has been seriously underestimated, and that if such commercial developments were to be granted due weight they would invalidate any simple or linear relationship between rising population and available resources. The central premiss of the population and resources model that there were only slight and tardy increases in productivity in the High Middle Ages has also been forcefully challenged. The theories of Malthus and Ricardo to all intents and purposes exclude the possibility of sustained substantial improvements in productivity, and instead argue that any gains in productivity will eventually be swamped by increasing numbers.[66] Yet, as the experience of England during the later eighteenth and nineteenth centuries demonstrates, it is possible for progress in agricultural technology and the development of the non-agrarian sectors of the economy to provide increases in the supply of food, employment, and wealth on a scale sufficient to accommodate sharply rising population. Some would see great strides being taken in this direction before 1300, and these themes are described and assessed in Chapter 4.

Demographically-driven models have also long been subject to criticism because the stress which they lay on the workings of market forces leads them to understate the impact of fluctuations

[65] M. Bailey, 'The Concept of the Margin in the Medieval English Economy', *EcHR*, 2nd ser., 42 (1989), 1–17.

[66] Although Ricardo accepted that increasing marginal returns were possible in some sectors of agriculture, trade, and manufacture, he was criticized by other classical economists for underestimating the capacity of innovation to delay or even reverse the onset of diminishing returns.

in the amount of money in the economy.[67] As we have seen, in models based on the rise and fall of population it is shifts in the balance between the numbers of people and the resources available to support them which are held responsible for movements in the prices of food, land, and labour; but prices may also be inflated or deflated by changes in the amount of money in circulation. Money did matter, and there would appear to be little doubt, for example, that the fluctuations which can be observed in the output of English mints in the second and third quarter of the fourteenth century played a significant part in the sharp deflation of food prices in the decades just prior to the Black Death and their rapid inflation in the decades just after, and the case has been repeatedly made for a contraction in the money supply triggering the recession of the mid-fifteenth century. Furthermore, the long-term, large-scale expansion of the coinage, and the broad stability of its silver content, certainly assisted the economic development of England in the twelfth and thirteenth centuries.

Some monetarist historians have gone further and argued that much of the evidence used to bolster demographic models is suspect, since the major price cycles of the Middle Ages were primarily driven not by the rise and fall of population but by fluctuations in the supply of money, which in turn were driven primarily by the output of European silver mines. Postan was seeking to supplant such interpretations when he formulated his models, and he frequently engaged directly with monetary hypotheses and those who propagated them.[68] Postan readily conceded that because

in the twelfth and thirteenth centuries, i.e. the period when prices were rising, European supplies of silver from the mines of Hungary, the Hartz

---

[67] See below pp. 138–9, 186–92 for a further discussion of the role of money in economic development.

[68] For Postan's views on money in the medieval economy, see e.g. 'Economic Foundations of Medieval Society', 7–13; 'The Trade of Medieval Europe: The North', in *CEHE*, ii. 210–17; *Medieval Economy and Society*, 235–45. See also W. C. Robinson, 'Money, Population and Economic Change in Late Medieval Europe', *EcHR*, 2nd ser., 12 (1959), 63–76 and M. M. Postan, 'Note', ibid. 77–82.

mountains, Tyrol and elsewhere, grew very fast; and that the fourteenth and the first half of the fifteenth century, when prices were falling, coincided with a rapid decline of output in the older fields of silver mining. The conclusion that prices fell or rose through changes in the supply of newly mined bullion is therefore very difficult to resist.

But he then proceeded to raise a whole series of reasons why this conclusion should be resisted, many of which remain powerful today.[69]

None more so than the fact that, in any given era, the prices of major commodities moved at different rates and sometimes in different directions, whereas fluctuations in the money supply should have resulted in broad uniformity rather than diversity. Postan stressed that in the thirteenth century 'steep and continuous changes in food prices unaccompanied by similar changes in other prices make it more or less certain that the relative costs of agricultural production were rising, and this . . . indicates a growing pressure of population against land'.[70] It is possible to go further, and demonstrate that what happened to prices, especially relative prices, in the longer term strongly points to the operation of powerful 'real' forces bringing about changes in demand and supply. Although there is a very rough correlation between rising food prices and rising money supply in the later twelfth and thirteenth centuries, and falling food prices and falling money supply in the later fourteenth and fifteenth centuries, this correlation does not hold for prices in general, and what is more wages—the price of labour—behaved in a directly contrary manner. The levels of prices for the whole range of goods expected to be consumed by labouring and peasant households were actually marginally *lower* on average at the turn of the thirteenth and fourteenth centuries, when the money supply was at its highest, than they were in the second half of the fifteenth century, but even more striking is the fact that the money wages paid to unskilled and semi-skilled labourers were two to three

---

[69] 'Economic Foundations of Medieval Society', 8.
[70] 'Trade of Medieval Europe', 210.

times higher.[71] There was clearly far more to the operation of the medieval economy than the amount of money within it.

The fiercest and most sustained assaults on the Malthusian/ Ricardian interpretation of economic and social development in the Middle Ages have come from those who support alternative and conflicting grand explanatory supermodels. Viewed from the perspective of model-builders the study of medieval economic and social history can seem to resemble the clash of the Titans, but it is important to stress the existence of a number of distinctions which can become blurred in the historiography. In particular, the propounding, construction, and elaboration of theoretical models is but a small and specialized part of the writing of medieval history, and although very many historians have worked under their influence, few have been content to formulate all their arguments under the banner of a single model, even though they may be persuaded by the truth of some parts of its reasoning.

The critics of demographically-driven hypotheses frequently make their target all the easier to hit by pinning the label of dogmatic and secular Malthusianism on anyone who believes that the rise and fall of population was a significant force in the promotion of economic and social change. However, the Malthusian/Ricardian model is the most formal and deterministic of all demographic interpretations, and it is inexcusable to confuse an acceptance of the importance of changes in the relative value of land and labour to the economy at large with the belief that the demographic factor was the prime cause of almost all significant economic and social change, or, *a fortiori*, with the expression of faith that population invariably behaved in a Malthusian, neo-Malthusian, or Ricardian manner.

Much more valid are accusations that an excessive attention to demographic factors can lead to the neglect of other powerful

---

[71] The price and wage data are provided in E. H. Phelps Brown and S. V. Hopkins, *A Perspective of Wages and Prices* (1981), 1–59; D. L. Farmer, 'Prices and Wages', *AHEW*, ii. 716–79; *idem*, 'Prices and Wages, 1350–1500', *AHEW*, iii. 431–515.

forces, including a whole raft of legal, social, and political structures and relationships. Although Postan claimed that his research agenda simply did not extend to social structures and relations, and that a failure to consider such matters was not tantamount to denying them, he effectively downplayed the influence of non-economic factors on economic processes, and less reticent neo-Malthusians and Ricardians have explicitly nullified the impact of social and political factors by holding them constant.

But perhaps an even more fundamental weakness of overly rigid versions of the demographically-driven model is that they are heavily reliant on misplaced assumptions of the operation of a free market economy in the Middle Ages. All crude demographic interpretations have at their centre the elemental but mighty economic laws of supply and demand, and they implicitly assume that these laws were permitted to work without hindrance, with the result that changes in the relative scarcities of land or labour resulted in commensurate adjustments in their price. However, although the prevalence of relatively free markets in the factors of production may have been a reasonable assumption for Malthus and Ricardo to make at the turn of the eighteenth and nineteenth centuries, in the Middle Ages the markets in land, labour, and capital were far from free. The powers of lords over most of their tenants extended far beyond the limits of normal commercial relationships; the great bulk of land was held in free or customary tenures, and was generally passed down from generation to generation rather than traded through the mechanism of a land market; much labour was supplied through obligatory labour services, and determined efforts were made by the state to rig the labour market after the Black Death; and anti-usury laws made the charging of interest on loans illegal, as well as unacceptable in religious and social terms. All of this, and much more, meant that the impact of the forces of supply and demand on the creation and distribution of income were mediated through the whole edifice of contemporary social, legal, and political structures. Rising population created pressure for rising food prices and rents and exerted a depressive influence over real wages, but the precise outcome depended upon far more than market forces alone.

Valid assessments of the weight exercised by demographic forces cannot be conducted solely within the terms of conventional population and resources modelling, and a far broader range of factors and forces that influenced economic and social change must be taken into account. But if this is done, the task of determining causality is made far more complex, since any attempt to assess the role of any one of the range of relevant factors must necessarily involve an objective assessment of the weight which should be accorded to all of the others. The dilemma which historians face when they choose to confront rather than avoid this elementary issue may be illustrated by this evaluation of the relative significance of class relations and economic and demographic forces in influencing the trend away from labour rent to money rent, made by R. H. Hilton, a leading Marxist historian:

It could be argued, and of course it is argued, that these trends had nothing to do with the organized and deliberate action of peasant communities but depended simply on such impersonal factors as the supply of land, population trend, the demand for agricultural products and so on. Of course these factors were most important and perhaps the most that one could claim for peasant actions, in the long run, was that they followed, perhaps reinforced, the existing currents of historical change.[72]

The difficulties of successfully establishing any overarching force or set of forces as a constant prime mover are a main theme of this book, and they multiply when the merits of conflicting hypotheses are studied with an open mind. Unfortunately, however, few of those who engage in the relative ranking of the forces for economic and social change are able to be wholly objective in their judgements. It is not without significance that the most vigorous assaults on the

[72] R. H. Hilton, *Bond Men Made Free: Medieval Peasant Movements and the English Rising of 1381* (1973), 234–5.

demographic factor in history, as well as upon explanations dependent upon the growth of markets and trade, have come from those
who are seeking to put other factors in their place. In the forefront
of a long series of such onslaughts have been the proponents of the
pre-eminence of class factors. On the second page of his influential article on the economic development of pre-industrial Europe
Robert Brenner proclaimed:

it is the purpose of this article to argue that such attempts at economic
model-building are necessarily doomed from the start precisely because,
most crudely stated, it is the structure of class relations, of class power,
which determine the manner and degree to which particular demographic and commercial changes will affect long-term trends in the
distribution of income and economic growth—and not vice versa.[73]

Thus, Brenner asserts not simply that the demographic and the
commercialization interpretations of history are irredeemably flawed,
but that the true dynamic is class relations. The agenda of seeking
to prove that there has been a single constant prime mover in history cannot be more clearly stated, and the merits of the case for
awarding that role to class relations is examined in the next chapter.

[73] 'Agrarian Class Structure and Economic Development in Pre-Industrial Europe', in
Aston and Philpin (eds.), *Brenner Debate*, 11.

3

Class Power and Property Relations

In the previous chapter we outlined a series of plausible arguments intended to demonstrate that the key to economic development is to be found in the relationship between population and resources, labour and land, people and the environment, and the economic forces that they generate. This chapter is devoted to an alternative but equally plausible explanation that the key is to be found instead in the social relations and political and legal institutions of society. Whereas population and resources models concentrate on such matters as the density of settlement, soil quality, agricultural yields, rents, prices, wages, standards of living, and population trends, the models discussed in this chapter stress the leading roles played by the contrasting lifestyles and priorities of lords and peasants, the conflictive relations between landlords and tenants, and the institutions of feudalism, vassalage, and villeinage in determining the pace and direction of economic change.

By focusing on the social, legal, and political structures of the Middle Ages, and the attitudes which lay behind their operation, it is possible to construct elaborate models which are the antithesis of those which have the land : labour ratio as their foundation, and the basic laws of economics and demography as their dynamic. From this alternative perspective, it may be argued that the economic forces set in train by changes in the relative scarcity of land and labour did not operate according to theoretical economic laws in a predictable and inexorable manner, but were channelled instead through the existing structures of society, with their customs, cultures, and laws, and their hierarchies of wealth and power, which were capable of draining or boosting the strength of economic forces and even reversing their direction. The prime determinant of the pattern of change and development in societies, and the main source of its momentum, is therefore to be found in the relations between the leading classes and in developments in what are termed the 'mode of production', and not in the operation of economic forces.

The Theory (i): Karl Marx and his Successors

The most coherent and influential models based upon the pre-eminence of social, political, and institutional factors in the shaping of long-term historical processes are those constructed by Karl Marx and his intellectual successors.[1] For Marxists, history is a dialectical process in which the future is shaped by the present, just as the present was shaped by the past, and each distinct era of human development—ancient, oriental, feudal, capitalist—generates from

---

[1] For useful introductions to the theory of Marxism and Marxism in history, see e.g. G. A. Cohen, *Karl Marx's Theory of History: A Defence* (Oxford, 1978); S. H. Rigby, *Marxism and History: A Critical Introduction* (Manchester, 1987); W. H. Shaw, *Marx's Theory of History* (1978).

within itself the conditions which will ultimately transform it. Marxism is also, like Malthusianism, a materialist conception of history which is centred on the economic base of society. Economic activity is the dominant function of any society, and for Marxists the 'production process' is at the heart of the dynamism which drove these vast historical sequences. But this does not mean that economic forces are given pre-eminence in the promotion of social and economic change. On the contrary, in this school of thought societies are categorized according to their class structures, and it is these which determine the ownership of economic and productive resources as well as the manner of their operation. It is the nature of the prevailing social and political framework which determines the level and extent of economic development, and not vice versa. Such interpretations are, therefore, directly at odds with those which stress demographic and economic determinism. As Joseph Stalin put it in the *History of the Communist Party of the Soviet Union,* which is credited to his authorship, 'growth of population does influence the development of society, does facilitate or retard the development of society [but] it cannot be the chief force of development of society'.[2]

Whereas models based on the working of economic forces tend to neglect the influence of non-economic factors, Marxist approaches place them at the centre. But non-economic factors—the social, political, legal, and cultural elements in any society—comprise a vast, varied, complex, and inherently unmanageable collection of variables, and Marxists therefore focus their attention on a limited range, and in particular on the relations between social classes, and the conflicts between them, as the main agent of social and economic change and development. In according the role of prime mover to class structures and class conflict, the part which can be allowed

---

[2] Quoted in E. A. Kosminsky, 'The Evolution of Feudal Rent in England from the XIth to the XVth Centuries', *P&P* 7 (1955), 36. It should be noted that in this passage Stalin allows rather more weight to the demographic factor than does Brenner (see e.g. below, pp. 108, 223–4).

to economic forces has to be commensurately downgraded. Robert Brenner, in a highly influential article which in 1976 relaunched a major and long-standing debate, proclaimed that 'class structures tend to be highly resilient in relation to the impact of economic forces; as a rule, they are not shaped by, or alterable in terms of, changes in demographic or commercial trends'. Because Marxism is a dialectical process, in which modes of production succeed each other in a predictable manner occasioned by struggles between the classes, it follows that 'economic development can only be fully understood as the outcome of the emergence of new class relations more favourable to new organizations of production, technical innovations, and increasing levels of productive investment', and that '[t]hese new class relations were themselves the result of previous, relatively autonomous processes of class conflict'.[3]

Marxists commonly use three conceptual tools in their investigation of the role of economic activity in historical development, each of which is placed firmly within its broader social and political context.[4] First, 'the mode of production', which embraces the whole structure of a society (its laws, customs, cultures, state form, religion, and so on), and which collectively contributes towards determining the form of its economic organization (ancient, feudal, capitalist, etc.). Second, 'the forces of production', sometimes known as the 'means of production', which are anything that is required to make articles of utility, such as natural resources and raw materials, the instruments of production (tools, fuels, technology, etc.) and, of course, labour. Third, 'the relations or social relations of production', which are the relationships between those who own the means of production and those who provide labour.

A crucial element in the 'relations of production' is the manner in which the product, created by the application of labour to the

---

[3] Brenner, 'Agrarian Class Structure and Economic Development', 31, 37.
[4] See R. H. Hilton, 'Introduction', in Aston and Philpin (eds.), *Brenner Debate*, 5–9, for a preliminary discussion of these concepts.

means of production, is shared between the owner and the worker, and in particular the manner in which the 'surplus labour'—that which enriches the exploiting class and not the labourer—is extracted. In the words of Marx, 'the specific economic form, in which unpaid surplus-labour is pumped out of direct producers, determines the relationship of rulers and ruled'.[5] In capitalist society, this surplus is extracted through waged labour, with the 'unpaid surplus' consisting of the difference between the wages which the worker is paid and the value of his or her labour to the employer. In the Middle Ages, the 'specific economic form' was rent, which was paid in labour, kind, or money, and for Marx rent was extracted from the peasantry primarily through the system of serfdom.

Marx, like Malthus and Ricardo, did not accord much importance to improvements in technology and productivity in the promotion of change and development. Although he believed that there is an inherent tendency for the forces of production to advance or develop, he argued that technical change would cause tension in the existing relations of production, and eventually be restrained by them. This basic tenet explains why Marxist historians writing on the thirteenth century have tended to agree with neo-Malthusians that productivity was low and declining. But unlike the latter they find the cause in non-economic factors, and they argue that it is in the social relations of production, the behaviour of landlords and peasants, and, in particular, the social relations of serfdom that the reasons for low productivity and the lack of substantial technical advances are to be found.

In Marx's thought, therefore, significant economic change and development occurs only through a transformation of the relations of production. The dynamic for such a transformation lies primarily in the relationship between lords and peasants, the two prime opposing classes of feudal society. This relationship is essentially

---

[5] Karl Marx, *Capital: A Critique of Political Economy*, ed. F. Engels, 3 vols. (London: Lawrence and Wishart, 1979 edn.), iii. 791.

one of conflict. Conflict is regarded as inevitable, due to the potentially explosive tensions generated by the structural contradictions inherent in the feudal mode of production, which must eventually lead to crisis and transformation.

This process of transformation is commonly called the 'crisis of feudalism', and its onset is usually located in the late thirteenth and early fourteenth centuries. This is, of course, the same time period as the economic and demographic crisis discussed in the previous chapter. However, the 'crisis of feudalism' is a much wider phenomenon and is measured by different criteria. Whereas at heart the economic and demographic crisis is defined by falling output per caput, falling incomes for the masses, and falling population, the feudal crisis was essentially a crisis in the relationships between the two main classes of feudal society. Thus, for Marxists changes in settlement, rents, prices, and incomes are not key indicators of crisis, because the feudal economy can experience the ebbs and flows of economic cycles without necessarily entering upon a process of irreversible social change. In the feudal crisis there is an escalation in social conflict and consequential changes in both the relations and the mode of production. When these processes of change become irreversible, the way is paved for the rise of capitalism.

The Case for the Class Struggle Model

It would be wrong, however, to imagine that there is a single uncontested Marxist interpretation of the crisis and subsequent decline of the feudal system. Differences between Marxists arise not only because of the complexities of historical experience and deficiencies in the evidence it has left, but from the fact that Marx's interest in early periods of history was largely confined to explaining the preconditions of capitalism. Marx did not hand over a working model of the Middle Ages to his successors: he devoted little space to the nature of feudalism, provided no adequate analysis of its internal contradictions, and scarcely discussed the social relations of serfdom.[6] Moreover, the little he did write is by no means unambiguous.[7] The legacy of the sketchiness of Marx's treatment of the feudal period is the heated debates which recur between avowed Marxists, sometimes over the most fundamental aspects of medieval development.

Some of these debates are discussed later in this chapter, but at this stage it is appropriate to concentrate on areas of agreement rather than on differences. The majority of Marxist historians and theorists choose to give prime emphasis to the internal structural contradictions inherent in the feudal mode of production and the struggle over rent between the landlord and peasant classes. Foremost among the structural contradictions are those which arise from the incompatibility of the basic inefficiency of the feudal system of production and the rapidly growing appetites of the landlord classes for revenue. On the one side, there are low levels of productivity of labour and income generation, and, on the other, rapidly rising expenditure on warfare, building, and household consumption. The tensions generated by these contradictions are held to have led to an intensification of the struggle over rent and placed it at the centre of the stage, because the landed ruling class derived the bulk of its income from rent (in the form of cash, labour, and sometimes food) which it extracted from the peasant masses. The conditions of servitude under which the bulk of the peasantry lived meant that the primary determinant of the level of rent that they paid was not the market, the land : labour ratio, or the level of agricultural technology, but the power of the landlord and the ability of the peasantry to resist that power. In the words of Marx 'the property relationship must simultaneously appear as a direct relation of lordship and servitude, so that the direct producer is not free',[8] and it determined the respective shares in the product of the labour of the peasant which the peasant was able to retain and the lord

[6] E. J. Hobsbawm (ed.), *Karl Marx: Pre-capitalist Economic Formations* (1964), 41–4.
[7] Cohen, *Karl Marx's Theory of History*, 83–4.   [8] Marx, *Capital*, iii. 790.

was able to expropriate. The level and the method of extraction of rent depended upon forces which were 'political' rather than 'economic', and which must in the last resort rest upon 'non-economic compulsion'.[9] Since the relationship between landlord and tenant is exploitative, and depends upon 'non-economic compulsion', it is inherently conflictive and ultimately helps to destroy the feudal mode of production and pave the way for the evolution of capitalism.

A broad schematic model of the period between the eleventh century and the mid-fourteenth, fashioned on basic Marxist lines, would have at its heart the belief that the relations of production eventually stifle the ability of the forces of production to develop.[10] The relations of production in twelfth- and thirteenth-century England were dominated by the institution of serfdom and the struggle over rent. Landlords were endowed by the common law and the manorial system with almost limitless rights of exploitation over their dependent peasantry, and so the rent which peasants paid for their land was determined by the will of the lords and not by the forces of supply and demand. In the words of Robert Brenner, serfdom involved 'the direct, forceful, extra-economic controls exerted by the lord over the peasant. Since the essence of serfdom was the lord's ability to bring extra-market pressure to bear upon the peasants in determining the level of rent'.[11]

The strength of the power which English landlords wielded over their tenantry provides a ready explanation for low and declining productivity in the peasant sector before the Black Death, an

---

[9] In the interpretation of these passages, as in so many areas of Marxist scholarship, there is fierce debate as to precise meaning. See e.g. J. E. Martin, *Feudalism to Capitalism: Peasant and Landlord in English Agricultural Development* (1983), 1–26.

[10] In much the same manner as the works of Postan were used in the construction of the basic population and resources model in the previous chapter, the rudimentary model of the English experience sketched over the next few pages draws on the two lengthy articles by Robert Brenner: 'Agrarian Class Structure and Economic Development in Pre-industrial Europe', *P&P* 70 (1976), 30–75; 'The Agrarian Roots of European Capitalism', *P&P* 97 (1982), 16–113; they are reprinted in Aston and Philpin (eds.), *Brenner Debate*, 10–63, 213–327. This is the edition used hereafter.

[11] 'Agrarian Class Structure and Economic Development', 26.

explanation which Marxists believe is glaringly absent from the population–resources model. It was inevitable that 'the lord's surplus extraction (rent) tended to confiscate not merely the peasant's income above subsistence (and potentially even beyond) but at the same time to threaten the funds necessary to refurbish the peasant's holding and to prevent the long-term decline in its productivity', and also that 'the surplus-extraction relations of serfdom tended to lead to the exhaustion of peasant production *per se*'.[12] Moreover, not only did the seigneurial regime ensure that the English peasantry was impoverished and that its ability to farm the land productively and maintain it in good heart was undermined, the restraints which it imposed on the mobility of land and men led to an extreme maldistribution of landholdings by curbing migration to areas with the potential for expansion.

Nor was this all. The manner in which feudal landlords disposed of their incomes greatly exacerbated the harmful tendencies engendered by their modes of surplus extraction. The priorities of their expenditure led to conspicuous and wasteful consumption, including huge households, extravagant buildings, luxuries (many of them imported), and warfare. It can also be argued that the levels of

---

[12] 'Agrarian Class Structure and Economic Development', 31, 33. It should be noted that in his second article Brenner attempted to deflect criticisms of the accuracy of his judgements on English history (see, e.g. J. Hatcher, 'English Serfdom and Villeinage: Towards a Reassessment', *P&P* 90 (1981), 4), by claiming that statements made in his first article, such as that on p. 33, that English lords in the early 14th century 'had an alternative, "exploitative" mode available to them: the use of their position of power over the peasants to increase their share of the product', had been misinterpreted, and that what he had really argued was that 'under similar "objective" economic conditions (demographic or commercial) *either* lords *or* peasants could benefit at the others' expense' ('Agrarian Roots of European Capitalism', 222 n. 11). But this response misses the point. There is no dispute that a central argument in Brenner's article is that, across Europe as a whole, either lords or peasants might gain the upper hand, but what is at issue here is his repeated and unequivocal categorization of England in the 13th and early 14th centuries as a country where feudal lords triumphed and were able essentially to determine the distribution of income (for a range of further quotes telling the same story, see above, p. 73, below, p. 75). Indeed not only does this premiss underpin Brenner's entire interpretation of the English experience in this period, England provides a leading case study for his comparative analysis of contrasting developments in different parts of Europe. If it is withdrawn the case falls. For further discussion of the generic weaknesses displayed by grand historical models when they are forced to confront the realities of particular places at specific times, see below, pp. 200–7.

expenditure of landlords tended to rise inexorably over time because of the growing burdens of retaining private armies, the increasing sophistication of warfare, with its major advances in costly offensive and defensive equipment, the construction of ever greater castles and more magnificent cathedrals, and the progressively enlarged appetites for consumables whetted by advances in the scale and scope of trade. Finally, to complete the vicious cycle of underdevelopment and to return to the deleterious impact of the relations of serfdom, such growing demands for additional income naturally led to ever greater levels of exploitation of the peasantry. For 'the lord's most obvious mode of increasing output from his lands was not through capital investment and the introduction of new techniques, but through squeezing the peasants, by increasing either money rents or labour services.' Thus, English landlords 'generally did not have to improve—to raise labour-productivity, efficiency and output—in order to increase income'. This was because they had an alternative, 'exploitative' mode available to them: the use of their position of power over the peasants to increase their share of the product.[13]

These destructive processes were patently unsustainable and led inexorably towards crisis; a crisis which would strike the masses particularly hard in the first instance, but would ultimately lead to the collapse of the whole feudal system. Thus, in Marxist analysis as in Malthusian analysis, there was an inherent long-term tendency towards crisis. But this tendency to crisis was not a natural fact, explicable by reference to available human and natural resources in relation to an ostensibly given level of technique, it was a crisis of productivity brought about by 'the landlords' extraction of rent and the extreme maldistribution of both land and capital'.[14] Its genesis lay, therefore, not in excessive pressure of population but in the nature of the feudal system, its inherent contradictions and the resultant conflicts between its classes.

---

[13] Brenner, 'Agrarian Class Structure and Economic Development', 31, 33.
[14] Ibid. 33.

Robert Brenner has breathed much new life into the debate between Marxists and non-Marxists, although his work draws heavily
upon an established tradition. The equation of feudalism with serfdom, and the location of the instability and eventual collapse of the
system almost exclusively in the struggle for rent and the destructive
exploitation of the unfree peasantry by their lords, have long been
prominent in leading strands of Marxist thought, as the works of
distinguished Marxists of the 1940s and 1950s exemplify. Dobb in
his highly influential *Studies in the Development of Capitalism*, first
published in 1946, specifically addressed the experience of England
in the Middle Ages, and maintained that it 'was the inefficiency
of Feudalism as a system of production, coupled with the growing
needs of the ruling class for revenue, that was primarily responsible
for its decline'.[15] The increasing demand for revenue, in Dobb's
opinion, stemmed from a growth in the numbers of nobles and
their retinues, the effects of war and brigandage, and the growth of
extravagance and conspicuous consumption. Given that the servile
peasantry was the main source from which the feudal ruling class
derived its income, and the only source from which this income
could be augmented, and given also the 'low and stationary state of
labour productivity of the time, there was little margin to spare from
which this surplus product could be increased'. The inevitable result
for Dobb, was that the demands of the lords either taxed the producers' 'strength beyond human endurance' or reduced their 'subsistence below the level of mere animal existence'.[16] Squeezed by the
low productivity of the manorial economy, and lacking the incentive
to labour because his lord was likely to use any improvement in
output as a pretext for a new exaction, the serf was forced to abandon the land, or threaten to, and migrate to the expanding towns.[17]
Dobb, like the majority of contributors to the debate which followed
the publication of his book, was not a medievalist, and his tendency
to equate feudalism with serfdom is a gross simplification. Similarly,

[15] M. Dobb, *Studies in the Development of Capitalism* (1963 edn.), 42.
[16] Ibid. 43.   [17] Ibid. 46–7.

his assertion that it was the flight of serfs which undermined the power of lords and forced them to make concessions as early as the thirteenth century, well before population began to decline, was also mistaken, as R. H. Hilton noted when he reviewed the book.[18]

For E. A. Kosminsky, an expert on English medieval agrarian history writing in Stalin's Russia, it was important to confront the increasing prominence which was being attributed to demographic factors by Western historians, even those of Marxist persuasion.[19] He tackled the presumption of a Malthusian crisis head-on by questioning whether England in the thirteenth century really was overpopulated, and whether the country's means of subsistence really were insufficient to feed the ever-increasing population. But Kosminsky did not challenge the validity of the evidence which pointed to the miserable economic state of the peasantry, to the extension of cultivation to land unsuited for agriculture, to low wages, and to the general rise in rents, the price of land and foodstuffs. Instead, he claimed the overpopulation was 'relative' rather than 'absolute', and saw it as 'arising not so much from the growth of the population as a whole, as from the peculiarities of the prevailing mode of production'. It was therefore an artificially created crisis, and he speculated that '[p]robably, even given the level of productive forces then prevailing, England could easily have supported a much larger population, if the feudal lords, the feudal church and the feudal state had not sucked the labouring classes dry, if a large part of the arable land had not been occupied by the lords' demesnes, if their cattle had not overcrowded the common pastures, if the lords had not seized common lands for their own use', and if restraints on the freedom of movement of villeins had not limited migrations to less densely settled parts of the country.[20]

---

[18] *Modern Quarterly*, 2 (1947), 268.

[19] See, in particular, his 'Evolution of Feudal Rent' and 'Peut-on considerer le XIVth et le XVth siècles comme l'époque de décadence de l'économie européene', in *Studi in onore di Armando Sapori*, i (Milan, 1957). Hilton is criticized by Kosminsky for 'exaggerating the importance of the decline in population in the 14th and 15th centuries' ('Evolution of feudal rent', 23–4).

[20] 'Evolution of Feudal Rent', 21–2.

Kosminsky, in a similar fashion to Dobb, dealt with the incomes of lords largely in terms of their rent rolls, rather than their demesne profits, and therefore linked the rising expenditure of this class almost exclusively with an intensification of the struggle for rent. But an important aspect of Kosminsky's analysis, neglected by Dobb, is a more detailed examination of the means by which the exploitation of the peasantry could be heightened. Kosminsky argued that the development of the common law in the late twelfth and thirteenth centuries weakened the legal position of the unfree peasantry, and, as the state was strengthened as an instrument of class rule, the manorial system was 'strengthened' to provide a 'regulated and ordered form of exploitation'. Thus equipped with the support of law and the means of local enforcement, thirteenth-century landlords intensified pressure on the servile peasantry, with the object of increasing feudal rent.[21] 'The second half of the 13th and the beginning of the 14th century seems to have been the time of the most intense feudal exploitation of the English peasantry, when feudal rent, whether in the form of labour services or of money rent, reached its highest level.'[22] This change in the relations of production sharpened class conflict, but collective overt resistance by thirteenth-century villeins was largely ineffective, and consequently landlords were able to 'consolidate the feudal economy' and win the struggle for rent. Yet the consequence of this seigneurial victory was a destabilization of the economic base of society and the impoverishment of the masses. In sentiments to be repeated by Brenner some thirty years later, Kosminsky concluded that in these ways 'the feudal mode of production became a brake on the development of the forces of production, exhausting the peasant economy, threatening the peasant himself with physical extinction'.[23]

[21] E. A. Kosminsky, *Studies in the Agrarian History of England in the Thirteenth Century* (Oxford, 1956), 328–54.

[22] Kosminsky, 'Evolution of Feudal Rent', 32.   [23] Ibid. 22.

The case for placing the social relations of serfdom at the heart of social and economic development has been strengthened by the findings of a large body of subsequent research, which has focused on what may be termed the inherently conflictive relationships between landlords and their unfree tenants. This evidence may be interpreted as demonstrating that a three-pronged assault was made on the peasantry by the landlord class between the eleventh and the fourteenth centuries, which entailed the consignment of multitudes of formerly free people into villeinage, a substantial increase in the burdens which the unfree had to bear, and the success of landlords in crushing any resistance. Among the large number of historians who have made substantial contributions to our knowledge of conflict in the countryside of medieval England through the systematic study of documentary sources, R. H. Hilton and his former pupils C. C. Dyer, Zvi Razi, and Ros Faith feature prominently.

For Hilton conflict was 'the principal underlying feature of the relationship between the main classes of medieval society' and 'rural social relationships in the middle ages were characterised by conflict rather than harmony of lord and peasant interests'.[24] Consequently, the struggles which took place over the rents and services owed by peasants and the restrictions which were placed on their freedom of action were one of the most important features of rural life, not just in the later Middle Ages, a period long-renowned for conflict, but during the twelfth and thirteenth centuries as well. In an impressive series of books and articles Hilton has chronicled and interpreted these struggles, which arose from a wide spectrum of disputes over matters of crucial significance to the lives of peasants and the incomes of their lords, including the right of people to enjoy free status and tenure, the exaction and performance of labour services, the levying of tallage, heriot, and merchet, the right to buy

---

[24] R. H. Hilton, *Bond Men Made Free: Medieval Peasant Movements and the English Rising of 1381* (1973), 233–4.

and sell land, and access to common rights, as well as the levels of rent charged by the lord.[25]

It is argued that after suffering at the hands of their new masters at the time of the Norman Conquest, the majority of the English peasantry experienced a further and unprecedented depression in status in the closing decades of the twelfth century and the opening years of the thirteenth.[26] At this time changes in the common law, and in particular the exclusion of the unfree from the protection of the royal courts, led to many who had previously been free or relatively free being cast wholly into the hands of their landlords. Put at its crudest, the evolution of the common law relating to freedom and villeinage was manipulated by the ruling classes in their own interests. Moreover, this loss of legal freedom coincided with major changes in estate management. In particular landlords progressively turned to the direct management of their manors and the farming of their demesnes and away from indirect management and leasing, which in turn entailed the imposition or re-imposition of labour services as well as the establishment of systematic record keeping and managerial bureaucracies whereby the lives of peasants could be regulated more effectively. The cumulative result was that not only did the proportions of unfree in the population rise substantially, so did the weight of their burdens.

Such revolutionary changes, and the severity of the adverse consequences which they brought for the majority of the peasantry, naturally provoked resistance, both at law and by direct action. Between *c*.1180–1220 very many peasants sought in the courts to

---

[25] See, in particular: 'Peasant Movements in England before 1381', *EcHR* 2 (1949), reprinted in E. M. Carus-Wilson (ed.), *Essays in Economic History*, i (1962), 73–90; *The Decline of Serfdom in Medieval England* (1969); *The English Peasantry in the Later Middle Ages: The Ford Lectures and Related Studies* (Oxford, 1975); and *Class Conflict and the Crisis of Feudalism* (1985).

[26] R. H. Hilton, 'Freedom and Villeinage in England', *P&P* 31 (1965). See R. Faith, *The English Peasantry and the Growth of Lordship* (Leicester, 1997), 245–65, for a recent complementary discussion of these issues.

establish their free status, although with scant success, and as the thirteenth century wore on, and landlords imposed ever greater personal restrictions and financial burdens on their villeins, sizeable numbers of disputes and conflicts took place on manors throughout England. A number of such disputes rumbled on over many decades with the peasantry as well as their lords showing themselves to be 'tenacious, even . . . pugnacious' in defence of their interests.[27]

The most sustained struggles in the thirteenth and early fourteenth centuries centred on disputes about the obligations and status of groups or communities of tenants and the exactions of their lords. They normally involved both litigation and occasional direct action, and the better known struggles included those between the prior of Harmondsworth and his villeins, the prior of Bec and his tenants on the manors of Ogbourne, Weedon, and Hooe, the canons of Ottery St Mary and their villeins, the abbot of Leicester and his villeins, and the villeins of Darnhall against the abbey of Vale Royal. The first record in the famously protracted contest between the abbey of Halesowen and its tenants dates from 1243, when an agreement between the abbot and the men of Hales setting out the former's rights and the latter's obligations was enrolled in the proceedings of the court of King's Bench sitting in Westminster. Peace did not last for long, and in 1252 the abbot found it necessary to secure a royal writ close, which granted him the assistance of the sheriff of Staffordshire in exacting tallage from his tenants, as the 1243 agreement allowed. Just three years later a royal inquest reported its findings into a suit brought by the men of Hales against the abbot, and in 1275 yet another inquest reported on a further complaint made by the tenants. Other complaints about the behaviour of the parties and the status of the tenants and the manor peppered the 1280s, and involved direct action and violence as well as

[27] Hilton, *Bond Men Made Free*, 145.

litigation, until in 1286 the abbot finally emerged triumphant, when the royal court declared that 'the tenants are villeins for ever'.[28]

In addition to conflicts such as these over important and fundamental issues, trouble flared up from time to time on many manors over more mundane matters. The alleged misbehaviour of bailiffs and other seigneurial officials provoked some notable confrontations, but the refusal to perform labour services, or the quality of the work done when it was performed, was probably the most common cause of trouble. Hilton has calculated that cases concerning labour discipline were dealt with at 21 sessions of courts held in Ramsey Abbey manors between 1279 and 1311, which resulted in 146 convictions for deliberate non-performance of labour services, as well as others concerned with bad work which may or may not have been deliberate. Sometimes the cases arose from collective refusals, as in 1294 when 26 tenants of Cranfield failed to turn up for the lord's ploughing, or at Houghton, in 1307 when 18 tenants failed to turn the lord's hay when summoned, or in the following year when 15 tenants ploughed their own land after dinner instead of their lord's.[29]

For Hilton, such episodes demonstrate that thirteenth-century 'village life was a continuous series of guerrilla actions by the tenants', and he concluded that 'in many cases the element of class conflict is obvious'.[30] Moreover, in his view, such small-scale collective activities were of 'great importance', since they helped to train the peasants in resistance to oppressive authority and to generate

[28] The most recent study is Z. Razi, 'The Struggles between the Abbots of Halesowen and their Tenants in the Thirteenth and Fourteenth Centuries', in T. H. Aston, P. R. Coss, C. Dyer, and J. Thirsk (eds.), *Social Relations and Ideas: Essays in Honour of R H Hilton* (Cambridge, 1983), 151–67. But see also G. C. Homans, *English Villagers of the Thirteenth Century* (Cambridge, Mass., 1941), 276–84; R. H. Hilton, *A Medieval Society: The West Midlands at the end of the Thirteenth Century* (1966), 159–61.

[29] Hilton, 'Peasant Movements', 82. Further examples of disputes on Ramsey Abbey manors have been collected by J. A. Raftis (see, e.g. *Tenure and Mobility: Studies in the Social History of the Medieval English Village* (Toronto, 1964), 104–9), who places a different interpretation on them.

[30] *Medieval Society*, 154, 155.

'fighting spirit'.[31] Such confrontations can thus be seen as emblematic of the intensity of the class struggle taking place in the English countryside over scarce resources, but for Dobb, Kosminsky, and Brenner they should not be allotted a major dynamic role in economic and social development at this stage in the Middle Ages. Quite simply peasant revolts and resistance were then almost invariably of peripheral significance because lords were all-powerful and the unfree were weak and their resistance was able to be swept aside. The crisis of feudalism, therefore, unlike the succeeding decline of feudalism, was hastened not by direct destructive confrontations between the classes, but instead by the inability of the unfree peasantry to defend their interests against the rising demands of their lords. As a consequence, in England the bulk of the rural population suffered progressive impoverishment from the ever-mounting seigneurial depredations which they had to endure.

In keeping with the key questions on the Marxist historian's agenda, a major thrust of Brenner's work is to approach economic and social development in comparative terms across medieval and early modern Europe as a means of uncovering the preconditions which enabled England to become the first industrial nation. By so doing he exposes what he sees as a fatal flaw in the 'neo-Malthusian orthodoxy', namely that different economic outcomes proceeded from similar demographic experience. In different parts of medieval Europe 'the same upward pressure of population could, and did, lead to changes in the distribution of income favourable to the lords *or* to the peasants'.[32] Whereas English servile peasants in the thirteenth century suffered from the depredations of their lords, in many areas of France where population was also high and rising, customary peasants gained the upper hand at the expense of their lords, with the result that their rents were frozen and their tenancies assumed the status of inheritances. Some English regions of greater freedom,

---

[31] 'Peasant Movements', 82–3.
[32] 'Agrarian Class Structure and Economic Development', 23.

like East Anglia, were able to support higher populations because their inhabitants had lighter seigneurial burdens to bear, but peasants as a whole fared far worse in England because the political power of lords was greater than in France, and 'the extraordinary intra-class cohesiveness of the English aristocracy was . . . manifested simultaneously in their formidable military strength, in their ability to regulate intra-lord conflict, and in their capacity to dominate the peasantry'. By contrast the lack of political unity of northern French feudal lords had led to their relative weakness 'as surplus-extractors during the growth phase of the medieval economy', with the result that their peasants 'achieved effectively full property rights to the customary land'.[33]

It therefore follows that the key variable which determined patterns of development could not have been the rise and fall of population and the economic forces it generated, and was instead 'social-property relationships and balances of class forces'.[34] The prime cause of the early fourteenth-century crisis in England was the dysfunctional seigneurial system rather than any absolute imbalance between numbers of people and the resources available to support them. If expropriation by landlords was the driving force, and rents were determined not by the market but the will of lords, then the inexorable rise of population merely influenced when the crisis occurred. The demographic factor is thus rendered subservient to the class structure, and it is the latter which determines how and to what extent population growth is permitted to exert influence.

Neo-Marxist Variants and their Supporting Evidence

This class-centred model has provided a powerful and durable explanation of twelfth- and thirteenth-century developments and of

---

[33] Brenner, 'Agrarian Roots of European Capitalism', 252–64; quotations on 258, 259, 252.

[34] Brenner, 'Agrarian Class Structure and Economic Development', 23. For a similar comparative analysis of different European regions and similar conclusions, see Dobb, *Studies in the Development of Capitalism*, 33–82. These matters are discussed further below, pp. 108–9.

the causation of the crisis of the early fourteenth century. But much of its strength derives directly from its simplicity, which is achieved not only by denying the significance of economic and demographic forces, but by focusing selectively upon certain parts of the social, political, legal, and ideological components of the feudal system, and interpreting their significance in a particular manner. Even within a Marxist framework there are many alternative readings of the same and similar evidence. There are some Marxists who place considerable weight on changes in the whole mode of production, and thus propose broader and subtler interpretations of the forces at work in medieval society. By so doing they are able to create explanations which are more sensitive to the surviving evidence of the period and which allow more emphasis to be given to the influence of economic, demographic, and commercial forces. But as they draw closer to the complexities of real historical experience, these more flexible and inclusive models inevitably lose much of the brute intellectual strength which cruder versions derive from their simplicity.

The work of Perry Anderson scarcely featured in the 'Brenner Debate', receiving only a single footnote reference, yet it has exerted significant influence elsewhere and is notable for its 'eclectic Marxism'.[35] Anderson accepts many of the arguments used by neo-Malthusians in interpreting the problems of the peasantry in the early fourteenth century as due primarily to overpopulation rather than excessive exploitation, and he lays much less stress than most Marxists on the power exerted by an autonomous class struggle. In particular, he argues that although the resolution of major economic and social crises 'always depends on the intervention of the class struggle, the *germination* of such crises may take all classes by surprise in a given historical totality, by deriving from other structural levels of it than their own immediate confrontation'.[36] But from among the innumerable attempts by Marxist writers to speculate

---

[35] See, in particular, *Passages from Antiquity to Feudalism* (1974) and *Lineages of the Absolutist State* (1974). Anderson's contribution to Marxist historiography is considered in R. J. Holton, The *Transition from Feudalism to Capitalism* (1983), 91–102.

[36] *Passages from Antiquity to Feudalism*, 198.

on the forces which provoked the crisis in the feudal mode of production and eventually brought about its destruction, that put forward by Guy Bois from French sources, and that by Rodney Hilton in his later work from English sources, are notable for their substantial empirical foundations.[37] In these new interpretations the forces for change are held to be the product of far more complex phenomena than merely the struggle between landlords and tenants and the internal contradictions of the feudal system, and substantial weight is placed on changes in the economic and demographic context in which it existed. Most strikingly, and in direct contrast to the highly politicized class-conflict model just outlined, which sees increasingly excessive depredations by the landlord class undermining productivity and plunging the peasantry into poverty, these interpretations maintain that the feudal crisis owed much to the fact that 'in the feudal system the rate of seigneurial levies shows a tendency to *fall*'.[38]

It is almost certainly not coincidental that these sensitive and inclusive models have been formulated by specialist historians who are well versed in medieval sources. From the start of his career in the 1940s, Hilton immersed himself in the archives and set about providing a firm evidential base which would support and, if appropriate, counterbalance, the largely theoretical approaches of Marxist writers such as Dobb and Sweezy. Although he has written on many aspects of medieval social and economic history, Hilton has made a particular contribution to the field of 'the property relations of feudalism', particularly serfdom, which in many important respects parallels that made by Postan to the study of population and resources. Like Postan, he has sought to frame hypotheses 'as a means of ordering the scattered fragments of information', in his

---

[37] See, in particular, G. Bois, *The Crisis of Feudalism: Economy and Society in Eastern Normandy, c.1300–1550* (Cambridge, 1984) and 'Against the Neo-Malthusian Orthodoxy', in Aston and Philpin (eds.), *Brenner Debate*, 107–18; R. H. Hilton, 'A Crisis of Feudalism', *P&P* 80 (1978), reprinted in *Brenner Debate*, 119–37.

[38] Bois, 'Against the Neo-Malthusian Orthodoxy', 115 (our emphasis).

case concerning in particular the character of peasant movements and their role in influencing the course of historical change. Hilton, too, takes care to define his terms of reference, which are less concerned with attempts at individual self-improvement, or with peasant involvement in 'social, political or religious movements whose aims were determined by other social classes', than with 'common action in pursuit of aims which are specific to peasants as a class . . . and aimed at some shift in the position of the peasants as a class'.[39]

Whereas in his earlier work Hilton stressed the overwhelming successes of English lords in substantially increasing the proportions of unfree in the population and the sums which they extracted from them, in his 1982 article on the 'Crisis of Feudalism' he admits that 'the struggles for peasant communities to retain as much as possible of the product of their holdings and to gain as much access as possible to common woods pastures and fisheries . . . was by no means unsuccessful'. Though the degree of success was greater in some parts of France and Germany than in England 'the tendency here too was for the stabilization of labour services and arbitrary exactions such as tallage'.[40] In fact, Hilton now largely follows the thesis developed by Bois in his study of Normandy, and maintains that the exploitation of the opportunities provided by economic and demographic buoyancy rather than the exploitation of the unfree peasantry was the most flexible and dynamic constituent of rising seigneurial incomes in the thirteenth century. The bulk of the ample rise in revenues which both French and English landlords enjoyed over most of the twelfth and thirteenth centuries came not from heavier levies upon individual peasants but from an expansion in the numbers of tenants paying rent and in the amount of land under occupation; from the adoption and expansion of demesne farming in an era of low wages, which yielded a rising stream of bountiful profits from the sales of agricultural commodities at buoyant prices;

---

[39] *Bond Men Made Free*, 61–2.   [40] 'Crisis of Feudalism', 128–9.

and from the increasing exploitation of urban, industrial, and commercial properties and rights, as towns, trades, and manufactures developed and expanded.

Because they examine the system of peasant production from the perspective of the family farm as well as from the relationship between tenants and landlords, both Bois and Hilton assign considerable weight to the importance of such matters as inheritance practices, family relations, mobility, and attitudes to trade, as well as to the demographic regime and the land : labour ratio. Unlike the crude class structure model, the character of the peasant household, its processes of production, and its interaction with the natural environment and the broader economy, are integral and critically important elements. The social relations of production between landlords and tenants, and in particular the struggle over rent, are explicitly acknowledged to take place within the context of secular movements of the feudal economy, namely periods of economic and demographic expansion, stagnation, or recession. Bois and Hilton also acknowledge most of the characteristics which are held to be central to the population and resources model, including, for the generations around 1300, high population densities, declining productivity, and falling peasant incomes, and Bois openly admits that in his work, 'Certain strange convergencies with conclusions of Malthusian inspiration may even be detected'.[41] It was doubtless just such 'convergencies' which persuaded Le Roy Ladurie to assert that Bois's major work on Normandy was imbued with the spirit of Postan and Abel, and their intellectual mentors, Malthus and Ricardo.[42]

But, leaving the question of the Malthusian credentials of Bois to one side, it cannot be denied that his analysis of the genesis of the fourteenth-century crisis in the feudal mode of production, and, more particularly that for England recently proposed by Hilton, are seriously at odds with the conventional old-Marxist case put

---

[41] *Crisis of Feudalism*, 392.
[42] Quoted in Bois, 'Against the Neo-Malthusian Orthodoxy', 107 n. 3.

forward by Dobb, Kosminsky, and Brenner. Bois argues that a prime role was played by an 'evolution in relative economic strength in favour of the peasant . . . [which] generated an erosion of the rate of levy', and Hilton now stresses for England, a 'stagnation of land-owner income derived from peasant rent'.[43] By so doing, of course, Hilton also challenges the stark contrast posed by Brenner between ruthlessly oppressed English peasants and sturdy independent French ones.

Although the implications are not fully developed in their models, for Bois and Hilton the crisis of subsistence faced by the majority of the peasantry must owe far more to the relentless rise of population than Marxist analyses normally allow. Since the burden of peasant rents was relatively fixed, over-exploitation cannot be presumed to have played the leading role in bringing about progressive impoverishment. Indeed, it was precisely the failure of rents to rise which played a large part in creating a crisis of seigneurial incomes. Since the growth in the revenues of landlords depended on the expansion of settlement, increasing numbers of tenants, a bouyant market for agricultural products and thriving towns, the slowing and subsequent reversal of the long expansionary era of the high medieval economy was bound to cause them problems. In the words of Hilton, 'there are good reasons for supposing that the cash incomes of many estate owners were stationary or declining by the early decades of the fourteenth century because of a crisis in demesne profits or because of difficulty in sustaining rent levels, or both', and for Bois the long-term fall 'in the rate of the seigneurial levy' was combined for the first time with a fall 'in the volume of the seigneurial levy'.[44]

As so far described, such a model might appear to contain relatively little mainstream Marxist dogma, nevertheless its authors are at pains to stress the importance of contradictions inherent in

---

[43] Bois, *Crisis of Feudalism*, 397; Hilton, 'Crisis of Feudalism, 132.
[44] Bois, *Crisis of Feudalsim*, 401; Hilton, 'Crisis of Feudalism', 129–30.

the mode of production. They place at the heart of their models the contrasts which existed between almost every aspect of the lifestyles and priorities of peasants and those of feudal lords. The peasants ran their own landholdings as individuals or as members of village communities, using their own resources of cash and labour; their priorities lay in providing for the subsistence of their families using as far as possible family labour. The role of the lords in the production process, by contrast, with the exception of demesne farming, was largely restricted to demands for rent and other charges and services.[45] In the words of Bois, 'hegemony of small-scale production, and seigneurial levy by political constraints . . . were the two major characteristics of the socio-economic system, the foundations of which thus appear contradictory'.[46] In a complementary manner Hilton elaborates on the inconsistency and instability generated by 'a landowning class whose very existence depended on the transfer to it of the surplus labour and the fruits of surplus labour of a class which was potentially independent of it, over which it exercised political, military and judicial power, but in relation to which it fulfilled no entrepreneurial function'.[47]

In a way which is rarely spelt out in any detail, but which must have been extremely powerful and pervasive, the constant tension which existed between these twin pillars of the feudal system acted as the 'deep-seated origin of the dynamic of the system'.[48] The famines, agrarian crisis, and arrival of plague in the first half of the fourteenth century may have ushered in the feudal crisis—they were not the prime cause of it. 'The watershed at the beginning of the fourteenth century is not simply one episode among the many dramatic conflicts between resources and needs that punctuate the history of feudalism. It must be seen at a deeper level, as the beginning of the crisis of a mode of production.'[49] In other words, social factors and class conflict loom larger than economic and demo-

[45] Bois, *Crisis of Feudalism*, 215–60.   [46] Ibid. 391–408.
[47] 'Crisis of Feudalism', 127.   [48] Bois, *Crisis of Feudalism*, 397.   [49] Ibid. 405.

graphic forces in promoting the fatal crisis and determining the course which was to be taken in the later Middle Ages.

The Decline of Feudalism and the Role of Commercialization

It is in the next stages of the historical process that the feudal system enters upon its ultimate demise, to be supplanted by the forces of emergent capitalism. The transition from feudalism to capitalism was a central concern of Marx and the process has been modelled from this perspective on innumerable occasions, with most expositions containing common threads of argument. In the late Middle Ages, a time of deep and prolonged agricultural recession, lords sought to arrest or reverse the fall in their incomes by extracting more from their tenants. This was the so-called 'seigneurial reaction', and it had the effect of gravely exacerbating the tendency towards crisis by provoking the tenants into spirited resistance. In the Normandy of Bois the 'impasse was at once political, institutional, and moral', and since the lords no longer possessed sufficient powers over their tenants, they were driven into warfare and new forms of state taxation as a means of bolstering their finances, which in turn paved the way for a 'proliferation of the machinery of the state, with absolutism on the horizon'.[50] In England, in addition to mounting a reaction using parliament, local government, and their own manorial courts, the nobility and gentry attempted to bolster their incomes by plunder, and engaged in warfare, both in the Hundred Years War with France and later at home in the Wars of the Roses. Most importantly, there was an intensification of class conflict as peasant resistance mounted. The clash of interests between the masses and the elite over serfdom and lordship resulted in the Peasants' Revolt of 1381, while in the longer term the social relations of

---

[50] Ibid. 405–8.

serfdom, which for many historians are the defining characteristic of feudalism, were transformed as unfree tenure and status went into terminal decline. A decisive shift in the balance of power occurred in favour of the peasantry, and, as the position of the lords progressively weakened, the peasantry seized the opportunity to wrest a long series of concessions which ultimately liberated them, and turned them into copyholders, leaseholders, or the occupiers of *de facto* tenancies at will.[51]

While such explanations of long-term change place emphasis on the class struggle, on falling incomes for lords and rising incomes and increased power for peasants and labourers, and occasionally recognize the influence exerted by the attractions of towns for countryfolk and the fall in population, they do not accord much of a role to commercialization. Yet hypotheses and models have been put forward by writers in the Marxist tradition which maintain that the major driving force behind the decline of feudalism and the rise of capitalism lay in the contradictions generated by the development of commerce on the margins of feudalism: not in developments within the feudal countryside but in the conflict between the countryside and towns. The publication of Dobb's class-conflict centred *Studies in the Development of Capitalism* was followed by a wide-ranging debate in which Paul Sweezy stressed that feudalism was founded on self-sufficiency (a 'system of production for use') rather than on commerce (a 'system of production for exchange'), and that it was the expansion of trade, with the concomitant growth of towns and markets, which undermined the feudal system as a mode of production.[52] By so doing, he followed in the footsteps of a notable non-Marxist historian, Henri Pirenne, who in greater detail had pre-

---

[51] For example, Hilton, *Decline of Serfdom*, 28–58; *idem*, 'Crisis of Feudalism', 131–7; Brenner, 'Agrarian Class Structure and Economic Development', 35–6; Dobb, *Studies in the Development of Capitalism*, 48–67; Martin, *Feudalism to Capitalism*, 117–27. See below, pp. 106–20 and 179–82, for further discussion of Marxist interpretations of the later Middle Ages.

[52] Two essays by Sweezy together with those by other contributors to the debate are published in R. Hilton (ed.), *The Transition from Feudalism to Capitalism* (1976).

viously argued that 'the decay of the seigneurial system advanced in proportion to the development of commerce'.[53] For Sweezy the desire of lords for increased consumption goods was frustrated by the inefficiency of the manorial system and its inherent unsuitability for production for sale, which encouraged them to innovate by dismantling the manorial and servile system and developing new types of productive relations better suited to the evolving world of towns and trade. The importance of the non-feudal elements in society is further emphasized by the fact that it was the growth of towns, trade, and industry which provided both the market for agricultural produce, on which the cash incomes of lords ultimately depended, and the wider range of manufactures, semi-luxuries, and luxuries which lords desired.

In a manner which is reminiscent of Adam Smith, the hypotheses of Sweezy and, more recently, of Immanuel Wallerstein, consciously or unconsciously acknowledge a powerful tendency for mankind to 'truck, barter and exchange', and maintain that this natural desire led irresistibly to the progressive expansion of trade, towns, industry, and the division of labour.[54] In this branch of the Marxist tree, which might be termed 'the exchange relations' approach as opposed to the 'property relations' approach,[55] we thus have a primal force for social and economic change which mirrors the belief of Malthus in the innate desire in the human race to copulate and reproduce. Of course, the views of neither Malthus nor Smith are compatible with current mainstream Marxist analysis, and Hilton has recently argued that towns and trade are an integral part of the feudal system rather than being inimical to it.[56] Furthermore for Brenner, this variant, which he terms Neo-Smithian Marxism, is fatally flawed because it sees increases in the income of lords flowing from 'improvements', whereas '[g]iven the inherently forceful nature

---

53 H. Pirenne, *Economic and Social History of Medieval Europe* (1938), 84.
54 In particular, I. Wallerstein, *The Modern World System*, 2 vols. (New York, 1974–80).
55 Holton, *Transition from Feudalism to Capitalism*, 74–9.
56 R. H. Hilton, *English and French Towns in Feudal Society* (Cambridge, 1992).

of the system of surplus extraction—the relationship between lord and serf—the method of "squeezing" must have generally appeared to be the logical, perhaps the only feasible path'.[57]

Yet it is possible that in some respects Sweezy and Wallerstein are closer to the writings of Marx than are many of his critics. Marx held that numerous elements of the feudal mode of production were characteristic of a natural rather than an exchange economy, and that therefore 'surplus-labour will be limited by a given set of wants which may be greater or less, and that here no boundless thirst arises from the nature of production itself'.[58] Marx repeatedly stressed the role of trade and the rise of an exchange economy as main agents in the disintegration of the 'inherently conservative and change-resisting character of western European feudalism': 'Wherever personal relations were superseded by money relations, wherever natural duties gave way to money payments, there bourgeois relations took the place of feudal relations'.[59]

A fuller discussion of the validity of the various versions of a commercialization thesis is best suited to the next chapter, but we may conclude this chapter by making some general remarks about the strengths and weaknesses of Marxist models of economic and social development. Since there are so many disputes about how Marx's writings ought to be interpreted, and about which Marxist hypothesis is the more faithful or deviant, it should be stressed these matters are not our concern and that our assessment of the strengths and weaknesses of prominent Marxist models is restricted to commenting on the extent to which they reflect historical reality and succeed in their attempts to explain the course of economic and social development. We begin our assessment with some general remarks and then consider the main Marxist models as they relate to the periods before and after the Black Death.

---

[57] R. Brenner, 'The Origins of Capitalist Development: A Critique of Neo-Smithian Marxism', *New Left Review*, 104 (1997), 25–92, quote at 43.

[58] Hobsbawm (ed.), *Pre-capitalist Economic Formations*, 46–9.

[59] Quoted in W. H. Shaw, *Marx's Theory of History* (1978), 146.

The Strengths and Weaknesses of Marxist Models

One of the prime strengths of the Marxist approach to long-term economic and social development is that, in contrast to the great majority of models which are based on the relationship between population and resources or on the power of commercialization, it explicitly seeks to provide an analysis of the workings of the whole of society, and not just of the economy. By so doing it opens up the possibilities of constructing a comprehensive overview which maps and measures the multiplicity of interconnections between political, social, economic, legal, cultural and religious institutions, ideologies and practices, and of providing explanations of economic and social change which take them fully into account. Marxist analysis is also commendably ambitious in other ways, most notably in seeking answers to some of the biggest questions which confront medieval historians, and in searching for the roots of capitalism and the origins of industrialization in the fundamental changes in agrarian structure, conditions of tenure, and relations between landlords and tenants, which took place within the Middle Ages.

At the outset, it should be noted that although demographic models and Marxist models are ranged against each other as rival explanations, they do have a number of features in common. Both approaches concur that 'there was a long-term tendency to demographic crisis inherent in the medieval economy',[60] and that the turn of the thirteenth and fourteenth centuries was a crucial period of transition, when population, rents, settlement, and prices ceased to rise. The root cause of this crisis is a matter of dispute, of course, but both Marxists and demographic determinists stress the acute instability of the economic system at this time, and the vulnerability of the mass of the people to famine. Furthermore, neither

---

[60] Brenner, 'Agrarian Class Structure and Economic Development', 31.

approach accords much weight to progress in technology or to the ability of commercial and industrial developments to compensate for the progressive weakening of the agrarian sector.

Most positively, the basic contention of Marxist analysis, that economic forces do not operate in a vacuum but within societies, is self-evidently true. As we have seen in the preceding chapter, approaches to the history of the Middle Ages which adopt the premisses of population and resources modelling, and apply economic reasoning based on changes in the relative scarcity of land and labour, frequently neglect the influence of the broader environment and fall into the trap of assuming that economic and demographic forces had a direct and proportionate impact on the real economy. Marxist thought, by contrast, stresses the distinctiveness of many aspects of the medieval world, not just its economic features, and argues for the importance of non-economic forces in determining economic outcomes. The rise and fall of population, and the increasing and decreasing scarcity of land or labour had to be mediated through social, political, and legal structures and mores which could thwart, impede, divert, or boost their power. The manner in which the medieval economy operated was influenced by the priorities, lifestyles, and consumption patterns of nobility, gentry, and clergy; by the relations of lords and peasants, the nature of serfdom and the means by which the level and form of the rents which the unfree paid were determined; by the relations of town and country, the role of the Crown and the state, and much more besides.

Marxist analysis places special emphasis on the role of friction and conflict, which is ignored or neglected in most other accounts of long-term social and economic development. Changes in the levels of rents, wages, and prices did not come about silently or automatically, as they tend to in economics textbooks. They were changed by the actions of thousands of individuals, and not always as a result of amicable bargaining between them: indeed, economic relationships not infrequently involved differences of interest and on occasion these could turn into direct conflict. It may further be argued that conflict was more likely to occur in a society where a substantial proportion of the population was not free but servile, where a great part of the land was held by custom rather than by leasehold, and where much of the labour employed each year was not hired but rendered as an obligation of tenure. Unfreedom was a subservient status, which carried liability to a panoply of fines and the performance of dues and duties of a personal kind, in addition to the payment of a cash rent. As a result customary rights and obligations commonly loomed larger than supply and demand in the fixing of rents and conditions of tenure, and imposed a rigidity on the positions which landlords and tenants adopted. The exaction of a fine for a breach of seignorial rules, the increase or decrease in the labour services demanded from a tenant, the imposition or rescission of the requirement to pay a heriot on death, to seek the lord's permission to transfer land, to educate a son or marry a daughter, often proved to be far more problematic than merely raising or lowering cash rents in accordance with market values.

The social context of economic processes is also evident in Marxist treatments of productivity and technology. For neo-Malthusians the failure to improve technology or even maintain productivity in the thirteenth and early fourteenth centuries is largely a consequence of the excess of people, whose poverty and ever more desperate quest for subsistence resulted in inadequate levels of investment and the proliferation of harmful agricultural practices. But many of the reasons why landlords failed to invest on a greater scale in measures designed to raise the productivity of land are to be found elsewhere. Judged by the size of their estates, landlords were at least the equal of modern business enterprises, but they ran their affairs with very different objectives. Rather than investing heavily in their economic assets, landlords overwhelmingly used their income to support lavish lifestyles, to demonstrate status and power, to pursue family or national objectives, to buy support and influence. Although demesnes were managed with reasonable efficiency and care was taken with the collection of rents and fines, medieval landlords never invested directly in the holdings of their tenants. If the productivity of peasant holdings had been higher, they would have been capable of yielding higher rents, but such investment as took place in peasant holdings had to come from the surplus resources of the tenants who occupied them, and these were severely depleted by the heavy rents and fines which they had to pay. The priorities of the expenditure of the landlord class lay in consumption: in the maintenance of households and hospitality, in building castles, abbeys, and cathedrals, in securing retainers and fighting wars, rather than in improving yields. In this way economic performance was gravely inhibited by the nature of the feudal system and the social and political structures which were an integral part of it.

The encompassing of such a comprehensive agenda, however, multiplies the difficulties of assessing the relative contributions of each of the multifarious sectors, and impedes the drawing of clear historical patterns. Thus, broad though the range of factors ostensibly considered by Marxists might be, relatively few are commonly accorded significant independent weight. Installed at the heart of most Marxist models are the social relations of serfdom, and prime emphasis is normally placed upon what are seen to be the 'inherently conflictive relations' between landlords and their unfree tenants. But there was far more to medieval society, culture, politics, and economics than the conflictive relations between its classes, and, in the life of the lay and ecclesiastical aristocracy and gentry, relations with tenants had to take their place alongside the vicissitudes of government and the rules of law, the burdens and penalties of war, dynastic fortunes, royal benevolence and malevolence, and religious beliefs and priorities. Nor were the lives of medieval English peasants continually dominated by relations with their landlords: they had lands to farm, families and neighbours to deal with, and religion to think about. Family structures, inheritance practices, farming systems, village and manor communal facilities, prevailing peasant attitudes to consumption, sale, and accumulation, are but a few of the elements which, in addition to the simple availability of resources, helped to determine the health of the agricultural base of society and the direction in which it moved. Marxists attempt to counter criticisms of the neglect of these and other such elements by claiming that they do take them into account, but in practice if they are included in Marxist analyses it is invariably done only in order to demonstrate their subservence to the main dynamic forces of the class struggle and destructive social dysfunction.

The Class Struggle before the Black Death

The overwhelming emphasis placed in Marxist models of English development on the conflictive relationship between landlords and their unfree tenants—the social relations of serfdom—in determining the course which history took may also be misplaced for even more fundamental reasons. On the one hand, it overstates both the proportions of unfree in the population and the contribution which they made to seigneurial revenues, thereby exaggerating the significance of class struggle, and, on the other, it underestimates the contribution of other sources of revenue, in particular the profits of demesne farming, thereby understating the importance of fluctuations in the prices of agricultural commodities and labour. It is likely that not more than three-fifths of all rural tenants were unfree in later thirteenth-century England and that, if we may judge from the broad swathe of eastern and midland England covered by the Hundred Rolls survey, they held only around 30 per cent of the land. Therefore, when account is taken of rural subtenants and the landless, as well as of townsfolk, the gentry, nobility, and clergy, then fewer than half of the households in England were unfree.[61] The liability of the unfree to perform unpaid work on the lord's demesne on a regular weekly basis is taken in most analyses to be the conventional hallmark of villeinage and the source of most

[61] Rigby, *English Society in the Later Middle Ages*, 40–5; Hatcher, 'English Serfdom and Villeinage', 6–7; E. King, *England, 1175–1425* (1979), 50.

potential disputes, but it was a burden borne by only a minority of the unfree and its significance declined even further as the thirteenth century drew to a close. Constructing a model of economic development founded almost exclusively on serfdom and villeinage is therefore self-evidently flawed.

If the scale and influence of villeinage and serfdom is often exaggerated, the frequency and severity of class conflict in the English countryside before the mid-fourteenth century seems also to have been overstated. For Hilton, episodes of rural discontent and friction between lords and tenants recorded in the manor courts create the impression that thirteenth-century 'village life was a continuous series of guerrilla actions by the tenants'.[62] Moreover, in his view, even small-scale collective activities helped to train the peasants in resistance to oppressive authority by generating 'fighting spirit'.[63] However, an objective assessment of the nature and significance of peasant disputes with their lords is by no means a straightforward matter. The statement made by Marc Bloch, that peasant revolts were as inseparable from the seigneurial regime as strikes are from large capitalist enterprise is frequently quoted in this context, but it does not take us far.[64] Are strikes in our society a major weapon in a destructive class struggle or merely one of a range of processes by which disputes are resolved? Certainly, the deprivations of freedom inherent in villeinage and serfdom were resented, along with the baseness of many of the fines and obligations which the unfree had to bear, and so too was the payment of rents which ate into a peasant's ability to subsist. It was irksome for the unfree to have to perform labour services on their lord's land when they would rather be working on their own holding, and it is not surprising that the work that was done was sometimes inadequate, either through lack of care or lack of skill. But what type of

---

[62] Hilton, *A Medieval Society*, 154.   [63] 'Peasant Movements', 82–3.
[64] 'la révolte agraire apparait aussi inséparable du régime seigneurial que, par exemple, de la grande enterprise capitaliste, la grève': M. Bloch, *Caractères originaux de l'histoire rurale française* (Paris, 1935), 175.

behaviour and what degree of conflict of interest turns disputes into confrontation, and confrontation into class struggle?

Hilton would see 'conflict as the principal underlying feature of the relationship between the main classes of medieval society',[65] a view shared by Kosminsky, Brenner, and Martin among many others. But, J. A. Raftis and historians of the so-called 'Toronto school', who have specialized in the detailed study of English rural communities, take a directly contrary position. Instead of seeing the countryside peopled with peasants who lived in manors and whose lives were dominated by struggles with their landlord, they have found villagers for whom day-to-day relations with neighbours and the local community loomed far larger than occasional dealings with their lords, which were in any case rarely antagonistic.[66] In such a world conflict between peasants loomed larger than conflict between peasants and lords. Thus, whereas for Razi the opposing interests of peasants and lords meant that 'they coexisted in a constant state of tension and conflict rather than harmony', for DeWindt, Britton, and Rafis 'conciliation was more common than conflict'.[67]

Such disagreements are difficult to resolve because they flow from fundamentally different conceptions of the manner in which medieval rural society operated, which leads historians to make contrasting interpretations of the same evidence, sometimes even when

[65] For example, Hilton, *Bond Men Made Free*, 233.

[66] For example, J. A. Raftis, *Tenure and Mobility: Studies in the Social History of the Medieval English Village* (Toronto, 1964); *idem*, *Warboys: Two Hundred Years in the Life of an English Medieval Village* (Toronto, 1974); E. B. Dewindt, *Land and People in Hollywell-cum-Needingworth* (Toronto, 1972); E. Britton, *The Community of the Vill: A Study in the History of Family and Village Life in Fourteenth-Century England* (Toronto, 1977). Z. Razi, 'The Toronto School's Reconstitution of Medieval Peasant Society: A Critical View', *P&P* 85 (1979), provides a critique of the methods used in these studies and an alternative interpretation of the evidence which they rely on. For a recent conspectus very much along the traditional 'Toronto school' lines, see J. A. Raftis, *Peasant Economic Development within the English Manorial System* (Montreal, 1997).

[67] Razi, 'The Toronto School', 153. For recent contributions which concentrate on conflict, see P. Franklin, 'Politics in Manorial Court Rolls: The Tactics, Social Composition, and Aims of a Pre–1381 Peasant Movement', in R. M. Smith and Z. Razi (eds.), *Medieval Society* (Oxford, 1998); I. Hargreaves, 'Seignorial Reaction and Peasant Responses: Worcester Priory and its Peasants after the Black Death', *Midland History*, 24 (1999), 53–78.

it relates to small individual incidents. But an assessment of the significance of the role of conflict should in part rest upon matters which ought to be susceptible to quantification. Namely, how frequently did conflicts arise, and how severe did they tend to be? Yet no sophisticated quantification of unrest and conflict has so far been undertaken, and consequently judgements about the prevailing relations between landlords and peasants, and whether or not they constituted class conflict, and if so whether that conflict was destroying the feudal system, depend on moral or subjective stances.

Those who have set out with the intention of collecting examples of quarrels and disputes between villeins and their lords have not found it difficult to amass a fair number of instances. But how is the significance of such examples to be determined? One method is to place them in the context of the thousands of documents which survive for the thirteenth and early fourteenth centuries, and if this is done their numbers are apt to look somewhat sparse, even allowing for the fact that very many conflicts may not have found their way into the records. Another is to assess their scale, and when this is done the majority are shown to involve individuals or small groups rather than substantial numbers. Moreover, the character of even the larger disputes was commonly restrained and litigious, with both sides displaying a considerable regard for legal procedures; violence between the parties occurred only rarely before 1381, and when it did it was almost invariably small in scale.

The twenty-one cases involving labour discipline on the Ramsey estates which were noted above, were garnered by Hilton from more than 200 rolls of court proceedings, which thus average out at a mere one such case in every ten court rolls.[68] What is more, most of these episodes were distinctly small in scale, and some were decidedly trivial, as well as being occasionally amusing: as when Hugh

---

[68] The surviving court rolls are listed in the bibliography of Raftis, *Tenure and Mobility*, 289–99. Some cases are discussed on 104–9.

Walter's son was fined at Shillington for impeding the work of the lord by lying at the head of a ridge while a field was being harvested, or when Robert Crane of Broughton was discovered playing 'alpenypricke during the lord's work', and duly fined.[69] This is hardly the stuff of class warfare. Even the significance of the strike at Broughton in 1291, when all the customary tenants 'in contempt of the lord, and especially as in his presence, withdrew from the great autumn boon works leaving their work from the ninth hour until evening . . . [because they claimed] they had not received bread in the amount that by custom they had the right to receive', is open to sharply differing interpretations.[70] From Razi's perspective it was 'a general strike', an act of collective resistance to oppressive exploitation by the abbot of Ramsey,[71] while from another viewpoint it might be taken to indicate that the Broughton villeins, far from being downtrodden, possessed a good measure of sturdy independence and a willingness to insist on their rights and to strike on a point of principle not of necessity; in this instance over the weight of a loaf of bread worth less than a penny. Moreover, the punishment the miscreants received from the abbot for their act of defiance in his presence was a fine rather than the imprisonment or eviction one might expect in a bitter class war.

Such independence and dogged defence of perceived rights is exemplified to an even greater degree in the grander struggles. But, though such protracted disputes feature prominently in the literature, there were actually relatively few of them, and the majority were confined to a handful of estates in the hands of religious houses. Moreover, some singular threads run through such struggles, most notably the manner in which the conflicts were characterized by litigation rather than violence, and in particular the ubiquity of appeals by tenants to have their manors declared to be 'ancient demesne'.

---

[69] F. W. Maitland, *Collected Papers*, ed. H. A. L. Fisher, 3 vols. (Cambridge, 1911), ii. 369–80.

[70] Raftis, *Tenure and Mobility*, 108; Britton, *The Community of the Vill*, 168–71.

[71] Razi, 'Toronto School', 153–4.

Only rarely were such claims proved to be valid, but ancient demesne status was a prize worth seeking, for it gave tenants legal protection against demands by their lords for increased or disputed rents and services.[72]

Despite the considerable attention given to class conflict in accounts of the twelfth and thirteenth centuries, it is only after the Black Death that it begins to play a major role in leading traditional Marxist models. Before that event, the crucial element determining the character of economic and social change is the excessive amounts of rent which the powerful landlord class extracted from the unfree. But, the level and flexibility of villein rents have received scant scrutiny from most Marxists, notwithstanding the importance which they attach to it in destabilizing the agrarian economy and promoting crisis. In the old-Marxist schema, propounded by Kosminsky, Dobb, and Brenner, although concepts of 'extra-economic coercion' and 'exploitation' loom large, there is scarcely any systematic analysis of what the prevailing rent levels actually were.

We are told that the transfer of rent from the unfree to their lords ultimately depended upon force rather than economic laws, and was therefore feudal in nature, but scant attention is paid to such vital matters as at what level rents constituted exploitation, and at what level they were damaging to the economy. Marx asserted that all property is theft, and it may therefore be considered that all rent payments, however low, were exploitative and harmful because they took resources away from those who were relatively or absolutely poor and gave them to the rich. But to follow this line of thinking is to adopt a moral and political position, rather than an objective and economic one,[73] and in any case this sentiment is not a major constituent of the argument adopted by Brenner and others.

---

[72] A manor was held to be ancient demesne if it could be shown to have been in the hands of the king at the time of Domesday Book. The rents and services of tenants of ancient demesne manors were immutable.

[73] In a similar fashion Dyer asserts that it cannot be maintained that 13th-century 'serfs were not weighed down with particularly heavy burdens . . . in view of the obvious resentment of many serfs to their condition' (C. Dyer, *Everyday Life in Medieval England* (1994), 2).

Inherent in their case is that lords, through the legal and coercive powers which they possessed over the unfree, forced up rents and charges to levels which were artificially high and damaging to the peasantry. In this way the contribution of rising population and growing land scarcity to low and falling peasant incomes is minimized.

But, as has been noted earlier, recent work favours the conclusion that unfree rents, far from being higher than market rents, actually failed to keep pace with rising land values, and that consequently the weight of the seigneurial burdens on individual tenants fell in real terms in the inflationary and land-hungry conditions of the long thirteenth century.[74] Custom, bolstered by the spirited resistance put up by the unfree, exercised a powerful restraint on the behaviour of lords and therefore on endeavours to increase the rents and dues of the unfree (the obligations of free tenants being, of course, largely fixed under common law). As a consequence, the poverty of the rising numbers of free as well as unfree peasants would seem to owe more to the fewness of their acres, the high price of food, and the inadequate level of wages and employment, than to 'squeezing' by their lords.[75] It is a relatively easy task to demonstrate, in theory and practice, that most smallholders at the turn of the thirteenth and fourteenth centuries could not afford to pay any rent at all without threatening their subsistence, but that the peasant elite with landholdings of 30 and 40 acres and more could prosper even while paying high rents and entry fines.

It is also worthy of special note that the notion of the relentless squeezing of the peasantry by their lords, propounded for the English case by a long line of Marxist writers culminating in Brenner, is at odds with the views of Marx himself. Marx did not portray serfdom as a system which facilitated limitless exploitation and conveyed inevitable immiseration. On the contrary, in a neglected passage in

[74] For recent discussions of the causes and severity of poverty at the turn of the 13th and 14th centuries, see: R. H. Britnell, *Commercialisation of English society*, 2nd edn. (1996), 126–7 and M. Bailey, 'Peasant Welfare in England, 1290–1348', *EcHR*, 2nd ser. 51 (1998).

[75] Hilton, 'Crisis of Feudalism'; Bois, *Crisis of Feudalism*; Hatcher, 'English Villeinage and Serfdom'.

Capital, Marx professes himself convinced that the serf could 'acquire independent property or, relatively speaking, wealth', despite the fact that 'all his surplus-labour *de jure* actually belongs to the landlord'.[76] Displaying a perceptive grasp of the culture of the period, Marx goes on to argue for the 'dominant role' of 'tradition', 'custom', and 'usage' in regulating relations between lord and serf in feudal society, which tended to transform rent into a 'constant magnitude'. Marx identifies three main sources of the strength of 'tradition' which limited the demands placed on the unfree. First, 'here as always it is in the interests of the ruling section of society to sanction the existing order as law and to legally establish its limits given through usage and tradition'. Second, 'such regulation and order are themselves indispensable elements of any mode of production, if it is to assume social stability and independence from mere chance and arbitrariness'. And, third, the existing forms, through mere repetition continuing for some time, became entrenched as custom and tradition and then were finally sanctioned as an explicit law.

The Class Struggle after the Black Death

The fourteenth and fifteenth centuries pose severe problems for Malthusian-type models because, in stark contradiction of the normal relationship specified by Malthus, long-term population decline persisted in the face of an abundance of land and sharply rising living standards. But the era is no less difficult to incorporate into models constructed by Marxists. Hypotheses framed from this perspective cannot allow much significance to the collapse of population, and must instead attempt to account for the major changes of the era—the decline of serfdom, the demise of feudalism, and major progress towards capitalism—by contradictions and tensions generated within the feudal system, and the class conflict which resulted from them.

[76] *Capital,* iii. 793–4.

Most Marxist accounts, however, provide sweeping critiques of these processes, and deal in generalizations and abstractions that fail to fully engage with the swelling mass of evidence which is now available on what was actually happening in the later fourteenth and fifteenth centuries. Thus, for Kosminsky the success of peasants in gaining more land at lower rents and, most importantly, 'freedom against their oppressors', was to be ascribed to the fact that peasant demands 'corresponded to the whole course of social development of feudal England. Serf production had begun to hamper the productive forces of medieval society.'[77] According to Bois, in Brenner's writings on these matters 'theoretical generalization always precedes direct examination of historical source material', and the medieval source material he uses has almost invariably been collected by others.[78] Certainly, in the course of his two very lengthy articles in which the special development of England is the main focus, Brenner pays scant attention to specific historical events, to the contents of manorial records, or to the chronology and scale of population decline. In fact, to all intents and purposes Brenner's analysis leaps from the so-called 'seigneurial reaction' of *c.*1350–80 to the middle of the fifteenth century, when 'in much of western Europe, the conditions making for crisis finally receded, and there was a new period of economic upturn'.[79] He tells us that the economic and social changes of the later Middle Ages in Western Europe stemmed directly from the inability of lords to strengthen serfdom in the face of the relatively greater strength of Western peasants,[80] and that in England the peasantry won their freedom 'through flight and resistance', which ensured the decline of serfdom and a long-term fall in rents.[81] But so rarefied are these abstractions that neither of them would attract much dissent, even from adherents to a strict demographic determinism. This is because the key questions

---

[77] Kosminsky, 'Evolution of Feudal Rent', 26.
[78] Bois, 'Against the Neo-Malthusian Orthodoxy', 110 and n. 9.
[79] 'Agrarian Roots of European Capitalism', 270, 274.
[80] Ibid. 277.   [81] 'Agrarian Class Structure and Economic Development', 46.

of why lords lacked the ability to enforce their wills and why peasants possessed both the desire and the ability to flee, are not adequately addressed.

Adopting a comparative method, Brenner makes much of the fact that, although the population declined at a broadly similar rate across Europe, not all regions and countries experienced the same social and economic outcomes. For example, serfdom faded rapidly in England as lords found it impossible to resist the demands of their tenants, whereas in parts of Eastern Europe more powerful lords successfully imposed serfdom on previously unfree populations.[82] Such contrasting outcomes, Brenner claims, not only demonstrate the independent primacy of class relations they throw doubt on whether 'demographic change can be legitimately treated as a cause'.[83]

However, these claims are false.[84] The fact that the demographic factor was not as predictable nor as influential as Malthusian models assume it to have been, neither denies a major role to late medieval population decline, nor makes class relations the sole significant dynamic variable. Brenner's claims can also be shown to be false by applying his own comparative analytical method to the contrasting experience of England before and after *c.*1300. In the twelfth and thirteenth centuries, according to the old-Marxist case, lords had the upper hand, and substantially increased both their power over the unfree and the incomes which they received from them. In direct contrast, in the fourteenth and fifteenth centuries the balance of power shifted decisively against landlords: peasants gained the upper hand,

---

[82] 'Agrarian Class Structure and Economic Development', 35–47; 'Agrarian Roots of European capitalism', 275–84.

[83] 'Agrarian Class Structure and Economic Development', 21. In his response to challenges to his denial of any significant power to the collapse of population, Brenner retreated and claimed instead that he meant that the rise and fall of population has an impact on social and economic development 'only in connection with specific, historically developed systems of social-property relations and given balances of class forces' ('Agrarian Roots of European Capitalism', 213). See the discussion in Rigby, *English Society in the Later Middle Ages*, 139.

[84] The merits of Brenner's contentions are discussed further below, pp. 223–7.

their incomes rose while those of their lords fell, and serfdom disappeared, as eventually so too did the the whole feudal system.

But why did the two periods exhibit such contrasting characteristics? Why did the balance of power between the classes shift so dramatically? Why, as in Brenner's own schema, was the crisis in seigneurial revenues so great and the power of the peasantry so strong in the century and a half after 1350, when the power and income of lords had been immense before *c.*1300 and they had triumphed with ease over a weak and impoverished peasantry? What had changed? In order for Brenner's model to establish its validity, these sharply contrasting situations would have to be solely due to changes which occurred independently in the structure and power of the two conflicting classes. No such case has ever been made in detail, nor can it be made with any degree of plausibility. The starkly contrasting land : labour ratios of the two periods must form part of the reason for the transformation. It would seem undeniable that the abundance of alternative landholding and employment opportunities almost everywhere in the Late Middle Ages played a significant part in determining the outcome of the multitudes of bargains made in the manors and villages between peasants and the agents of landlords. As much as Brenner may assert that class structures 'as a rule . . . are not shaped by, or alterable in terms of, changes in demographic or commercial trends',[85] it is simply not credible that the English fifteenth-century experience of plunging rent levels, loosening conditions of tenure, and a decisive shift in the balance of power between lords and tenants, did not owe much to economic recession, the scarcity of tenants, and a severe and long-term slump in the demand for land. Nor is such a conclusion weakened by the fact that, at a somewhat later date and in another country, a different body of lords had the power to tighten their hold of their peasantry.

[85] 'Agrarian Class Structure and Economic Development', 12.

The severity of the threat which epidemic disease poses to the coherence of Marxist models was eventually acknowledged by Brenner in his second essay. But he did so only in a brief series of insubstantial postulations, in the course of which he questions whether plague should be regarded as 'wholly exogenous', and suggests there was a causal link between plague and famine, and then between famine and war, and thus between class factors and plague.[86] Armed with this hypothesis, Brenner goes on to see increased mortality flowing from an 'aristocratic reaction', by which lords sought to recoup their fortunes 'through aristocratic reorganisation to squeeze the peasants and to wage intra-feudal warfare more effectively'. These actions, he claims, 'tended to cause further disruption of the peasant productive forces, leading to additional demographic downturn'.[87]

By these means Brenner tries to turn Malthusian and Ricardian arguments on their head and absorb plague, war, and population decline into his model, not as independent variables but as consequences of the class struggle. He invites us, against a great weight of current medical and demographic theory and practice, to see the massive fall in late medieval population flowing from pre-existing endogenous social tendencies. However, it is hard to see the relevance of his contentions to later medieval England. While the ravages of war may have played some part in explaining the dismal demographic experience of those areas of France which were pillaged and brutalized by rampaging English and French armies, the Wars of the Roses had little lasting impact even on the populations and economies of the regions where it was most fiercely fought.

Nor is the case for placing class structures and class relations at the heart of the dynamic process of long-term historical change much more adequately made. It is indisputable that demographic decline is neither a sufficient nor universal explanation, but if we wish class conflict to be the prime mover it faces equally formidable problems. Is class conflict in the later Middle Ages much more than the

---

[86] 'Agrarian Roots of European Capitalism', 267–8 n. 97.   [87] Ibid.

processes by which changes in the value of land and labour were translated into new levels of rents and wages and altered conditions of tenure and employment? What determined the extent, pitch, and persistence of class conflict? Why did conflict increase to the point where it destroyed serfdom in some places and intensified it in others? These are crucial questions which are seldom addressed directly.

We may agree with Brenner that the

outcomes were not arbitrary, but rather they tended to be bound up with certain historically specific patterns of the development of contending agrarian classes and their relative strength in the different European societies: their relative levels of internal solidarity, their self-consciousness and organisation, and their general political resources—particularly their relationships to the non-agricultural classes (in particular potential urban class allies) and to the state (in particular whether or not the state developed as a class-like competitor of the lords for the peasants' surplus).[88]

Such factors, and many others, have to be taken into account in fabricating answers, but presented in this way they are items on an agenda for research and analysis rather than solutions to key problems.

Brenner's description and analysis of the reasons for the relative weakness of the late medieval English aristocracy are scarcely more substantial. 'The English aristocracy may, for a certain period, have compensated to some extent through war overseas', but eventually even war ceased to pay.

As a result of the class-wide crisis of seigneurial revenues, neither the crown in relation to its magnate followers, nor the magnates in relation to their lesser landed class followers, possessed the economic resources, the necessary 'glue', to cement the old intra-aristocratic alliances, which had formed the basis for aristocratic and, ultimately, monarchical strength and stability in England.[89]

At first sight these and similar statements might appear to signal the breadth and richness of the factors which have been taken into

[88] 'Agrarian Class Structure and Economic Development', 36.
[89] 'Agrarian Roots of European Capitalism', 292–3.

account when formulating this version of the class relations model, but in reality they are less the concluding remarks to a long and detailed consideration of all the surviving evidence than a list of some of the range of potential determinants of the class power of the aristocracy. As such we are not offered an explanation, but a mere listing which begs far more questions than it answers.

The intensification of the class struggle in the later Middle Ages is a central component of most Marxist interpretations, and the strength and assertiveness of peasants and the weakness and self-destructiveness of the landlord class normally assume the prime dynamic roles in the shaping of events. Whereas peasant movements and protests in the thirteenth and early fourteenth centuries were overwhelmingly defensive, with individuals and communities appealing to custom and seeking to resist increased demands from their lords, or trying to gain special exemptions from unfree status or some of the burdens attaching to it, the next phase is held to be far more aggressive. 'Throughout Western Europe in the later middle ages, peasant revolts were transformed from localised movements limited in scope and aimed at altering only the balance of the relationship of community and lord to regional and large-scale revolts concerned more with the transformation of social relationships.'[90] Rising aspirations and confidence brought peasants into conflict with the state as well as with individual landlords in country after country. In England the unfree fought to overthrow serfdom, and to occupy the land on lower rents and with fewer obligations and restrictions on their freedom.

In addition to stressing the strength and cohesiveness of the peasantry in their struggles against landlords, Kosminsky strove to explain the falling rents and abundant land in the countryside by large-scale migration into the towns, and the acreage thrown onto the market by the abandonment of demesne farming, and he attributed the fall in the prices of agricultural commodities to a growth

---

[90] Martin, *Feudalism to Capitalism*, 74.

of agricultural productivity rather than a contraction in demand. In other words the economic conditions prevailing in late medieval England were caused by anything but the fall in the numbers of people. The collapse of demesne farming and the improvement in the position of peasants and labourers, 'can [all] be explained without recourse to the hypothesis of a substantial and long-drawn-out decline in England's population or to "Malthusian" speculations'.[91]

Kosminsky's account goes further than most in remorselessly denying significance to the demographic decline and economic contraction experienced by late medieval England, but its central line of reasoning has been widely adopted. In the immediate aftermath of the Black Death (*c.*1350–1380), it is commonly argued, conflict was fuelled by the aggressive manner in which lords sought to maintain or even enhance their revenues in defiance of the deteriorating economic environment. To this end lords mounted a 'seigneurial or feudal reaction' by using to the full the legal powers which they possessed over their unfree tenants. In this they were backed up and augmented by the authority of the state, which legislated to prohibit wage increases and provided machinery for enforcement, and offered the assistance of the sheriff and his posse to discipline unruly peasants. On the manor, lords strove to enforce the performance of labour services, sometimes at an increased level, to manipulate the land market in their favour and maintain the level of rents, to restrict mobility, to compel the unfree to take up vacant holdings and on the old conditions, and to fine their villeins, often at exorbitant levels, for all sorts of things, including asserting their freedom, transferring land, failing to maintain their buildings, trespassing with their animals, marrying, migrating, and brewing.[92] As a result of this concerted reaction, which Dyer has called a 'second serfdom',[93] landlords were

---

[91] 'Evolution of Feudal Rent', 27.

[92] Accounts of the ongoing rural struggles are given in Hilton, *Decline of Serfdom*, 37–43 and C. Dyer, 'The Social and Economic Background to the Rural Revolt of 1381', in R. H. Hilton and T. H. Aston (eds.), *The English Rising of 1381* (Cambridge, 1984), 19–36.

[93] Dyer, 'Background to the Revolt of 1381', 25.

able to keep their incomes very close to their pre-plague levels. But it was at the cost of sharply increased tension, which flared up in the later 1370s, and again on an even more spectacular scale in the Peasants' Revolt of 1381.[94]

Although few important consequences flowed immediately from the Peasants' Revolt, and the charters of freedom which the rebels had extracted in London were swiftly revoked, the class struggle continued unabated on thousands of manors throughout the country, and 'a strand of open and self-conscious opposition to seigneurial control' is evident,[95] which took expression in refusals to take up land on servile terms or perform demeaning services, or to pay unpopular dues or rents which were considered exorbitant. By the mid-fifteenth century villeinage had largely ceased to exist in England and land was held cheaply on flexible terms. The conclusion to which this line of reasoning ineluctably leads is that this transformation occurred as a result of the fierceness and cohesiveness of peasant resistance to lordship and the weakness of English lords.[96]

On the other hand, important and deep-seated as the opposing interests of landlords and tenants undoubtedly were for much of the time, the evidence of destructive class conflict is by no means as unequivocal or as abundant as Marxists would have us believe. Systematic analysis, in a precise historical context, is rarely applied to defining the nature and circumstances of actions which render them part of a class war rather than instances of conflicts of interest. There is a good case for believing that conflicts of interest were intensified in the later Middle Ages, but outside of the 1370s and 1380s large-scale disturbances are more notable for their absence than their occurrence. The fifteenth century did experience a few instances of well-organized collective action by tenants to improve

---

[94] For the large-scale rural disturbances in the mid-1370s, see R. Faith, 'The "Great Rumour" of 1377 and Peasant Ideology', in Hilton and Aston (eds.), *The English Rising of 1381*, 43–73.

[95] Dyer, 'Background to the Revolt of 1381', 30.

[96] Martin, *Feudalism to Capitalism*, 72–8, 117–26.

their conditions of tenure, and a classic case occurred on the estates of the bishop of Worcester in the mid-1430s during a vacancy of the see. When the customary fine of *recognitio* was levied for the arrival of the new lord, the king, not a single tenant on any of the manors of the estate paid a penny towards it, and they jointly threatened to 'surrender their holdings into the hands of the same king if the said recognition or any part of it was levied'.[97] But such 'battles' rarely involved any form of direct action and are characterized more by negotiation than by resort to violence.

Immense though the significance of the decline of serfdom was for English history, it faded away in a prosaic fashion through the passage of time and a series of thousands upon thousands of small bargains. The long fifteenth century was characterized far more by an infinity of individual and small-scale deals and accommodations between tenants and landlords, or rather their local part-time officers, than by open class warfare. The abandonment of demesne cultivation meant that labour services, one of the hallmarks of villeinage, were no longer required, and also inevitably led to the scaling-down of the bureaucracy which had accompanied large-scale farming. Fewer officers on or visiting the manor meant, in turn, that the lord's hold over his tenants was weakened, and with it his ability to counteract the destructive force of a declining land market. Inexorably, along with the straightforward reduction of rents, came the dropping of the burdens of serfdom resented by the peasantry: the lifting of the requirement to pay a heriot on this holding, the ending of the liability to pay merchet on that, eventually brought about the widespread tenure of land, often for terms of years, in return for a simple payment of cash.

The parameters within which this tenurial struggle was conducted in England were in place soon after the arrival of the Black Death, and probably set long before, when lords sought to use persuasion,

---

[97] C. C. Dyer, 'A Redistribution of Incomes in Fifteenth-Century England?', *P&P* 39 (1968), quote at 201.

legislation, and the power of their manorial courts rather than direct action and violent methods to defend their class interests. For a variety of reasons which are rarely elaborated, English lords did not pursue the violent option (perhaps it was never even thinkable to do so), and because they had no recourse to brute force they found themselves having to pay considerable heed to market forces. In fact, greater and lesser landlords displayed a notable lack of class solidarity in the manner in which they managed their estates in the later fourteenth and fifteenth centuries. They competed with each other for tenants as well as labourers by taking in migrants and varying the rent packages which they offered. Employers repeatedly broke the statutes of labourers, but were rarely fined for paying excess wages; landlords whose officials took in the runaway villeins of other lords were subject to no penalties; and little external assistance was made available to lords to assist them in the recapture of their runaways.[98] Because landlords lacked the willingness and capacity to act cohesively as a class, the potential for sustained class conflict was lessened. In the slack land market which generally prevailed from the closing decades of the fourteenth century onwards, most peasants seriously dissatisfied with their lot did not have to engage in protracted struggles with their lord: if better terms were on offer elsewhere they could simply move away.

Flight was a much stronger weapon than any that landlords possessed. 'Around 1400 on nearly all Ramsey [abbey] manors, the trickle of emigrants burst into a veritable flood. The exodus was largely illegal.'[99] In many west midlands villages three-quarters of the surnames of the inhabitants changed every 40–60 years, as families died out and people moved around in order to take advantage of the abundant opportunities furnished by the availability of

---

[98] In these and other crucial respects the weapons available for the enforcement of serfdom in late medieval England were notably less effective than those available to the masters of servile workers in 17th- and 18th-century Scotland (B. F. Duckham, 'Serfdom in Eighteenth-Century Scotland', *History*, 54 (1969)).

[99] Raftis, *Tenure and Mobility*, 153.

land and work.[100] In order to keep his lands as fully occupied as possible a lord had to reach an accommodation with his tenants, since any attempt to restrain them by force or to recapture runaways was ultimately futile. Even Thomas Hatfield, bishop of Durham from 1343 to 1381, could not arrest unwelcome change, despite mounting a feudal reaction with exceptional force, backed up by extraordinary powers derived not simply from his ownership of one of the largest estates in the country, but from his palatine authority which enabled him to use local government officers to enforce his estate policy.[101]

Whether we term these innumerable deals, threats, bargains, disputes, and occasional resorts to direct action a class war or a variant on a universal relationship between tenants and landlords is of far less significance than our assessment of the context in which the demise of serfdom and declining seigneurial incomes took place, and the strength of the various forces which helped to determine the outcome. Despite the implicit or explicit assumptions of most Marxists, the struggle between landlords and their tenants manifestly did not take place in a vacuum isolated from the influence of dramatic falls in the numbers of potential tenants and the value of land, it was intimately connected to them. Economic and demographic trends and fluctuations generated powerful forces for change, and lords and tenants naturally sought to protect their interests by attempting either to thwart these forces or to take advantage of them. The nature of the outcome, of course, depended on the relative strength of these economic and social forces, and a lot more besides. The seigneurial reaction of the immediate post–Black Death decades has sometimes been portrayed as an example of brute class power successfully flying in the face of economic adversity, when 'increasing seigneurial extra-economic pressures on and controls over the

---

[100] *AHEW*, iii. 17–18.
[101] R. H. Britnell, 'Feudal Reaction after the Black Death in the Palatinate of Durham', *P&P* 128 (1990).

peasants . . . [resulted in] the maintenance of rents at old pre-plague levels, sometimes well into the 1380s on various estates around the country—despite the drastic demographic decline',[102] and when there was 'exploitation of the peasants in excess even of the bad days of the thirteenth century'.[103]

But the reality is not so starkly one-sided. Brenner would see coercion and conflict in the aftermath of the Black Death, and a dramatic tightening in the lords' control over peasant mobility: 'serf-dom was still the order of the day, and they had every intention of enforcing it'.[104] But J. A. Raftis, the author of *Tenure and Mobility* the only supporting source which Brenner quotes, refutes this interpretation of his work, terming it 'incorrect on all counts', and instead he stresses the prevalence of a climate of compromise and cooperation.[105] The relative peace in the countryside during the third quarter of the fourteenth century, and the financial success which landlords enjoyed, was underpinned by the high prices which agricultural produce fetched and the persistence of a healthy demand for land.[106] Much has been made of the ruthless exploitation involved in the 'milk[ing] of large sums of money through the manorial court' from villein tenants,[107] but the great majority of such fines were extracted from thriving richer peasants with large landholdings, who were tied to the manor by the considerable resources they had invested in farming and buildings. Less affluent and more mobile tenants had to be treated far more lightly or they would simply run away.

Nathaniel Forster wisely noted when questioning the merits of imposing corn bounties and other measures to depress the wages of the masses in 1767, that 'Providential calamity leads to harder work and greater industry. Artificial oppression leads to minds being

---

[102] Brenner, 'Agrarian Roots of European Capitalism', 271.
[103] J. L. Bolton, *The Medieval English Economy, 1150–1500* (1980), 213.
[104] 'Agrarian Class Structure and Economic Development', 27.
[105] Raftis, *Peasant Economic Development*, 128, 214.
[106] J. Hatcher, 'England in the Aftermath of the Black Death', *P&P* 144 (1994).
[107] Dyer, 'Background to the Revolt of 1381', 36.

agitated and inflamed.'[108] Tension between tenants, their lords, and hence the class struggle, was at its greatest when the land market slumped and lords fought against market forces in an attempt to sustain customary rents and conditions of tenure which had been rendered excessive. The enforcement of legislation designed to prevent wages soaring to market levels by tying them to the rates prevailing immediately before the Black Death had provoked much resentment and resistance almost from the day of its inception. Is it mere coincidence that it was when grain prices collapsed in the mid-1370s that tenants first rose up en masse in rebellion against their landlords across broad swathes of southern England and, in the words of the Commons' petition of 1377: 'withdraw the services and customs due to their lords . . . and have made alliance together to resist the lords and their officials by force'?[109]

The class struggle fed on changing market conditions, and was profoundly influenced by their strength and duration: as population continued to fall and agricultural recession bit ever harder landlords naturally sought to shore up their revenues while tenants sought to obtain easier terms. Just as the labour legislation had been introduced in 1349 'because a great part of the people and specially of the workmen and servants has now died in this plague',[110] so the escalating scarcity of tenants played a major part in dragging the land market down. Families deserted their holdings and migrated because they were confident they could obtain more attractive land or employment elsewhere. Vacant holdings, falling agricultural prices, and the lack of people willing to take up the land on more exacting terms lay behind rent reductions and the abolition of servile dues. In the longer run the most successful lords were pragmatists who took care to fashion their policies in accordance with

[108] Nathaniel Forster, *An Enquiry into the Cause of the Present High Prices of Provisions* (London, 1767), 60.

[109] The petition is printed in R. B. Dobson, *The Peasants' Revolt of 1381*, 2nd edn. (1983), 76–8. See also Faith, ' "Great Rumour" of 1377'.

[110] The Ordinance of Labourers, 1349, printed in *English Economic History: Select Documents*, ed. A. E. Bland, P. A. Brown, and R. H. Tawney (1914), 164–7.

prevailing economic and social conditions. This is not to say that the class power of landlords and tenants and the actions they took were derived wholly from market forces, simply that attempts to construct arguments which ignore or minimize the significance of demographic and economic factors fly in the face of both evidence and common sense.

It is not only non-Marxists who find ingenious gyrations in order to avoid confronting the obvious wholly unconvincing. Bois allows considerable weight to the collapse of population in his models of economic and social change in medieval Normandy and Europe, although as he frankly acknowledges: 'this can make the various demarcation lines between Malthusian and Marxist approaches more difficult to discern.'[111] Rodney Hilton is equally dismissive of attempts to fashion arguments from the perspective of the class struggle alone, and proclaims that 'It would be an utterly blind historian who would ignore the demographic factor in the shaping of the economic and social developments of the period'.[112] Here we have a statement as powerful in its rejection of the class struggle as the sole, supreme, and independent prime mover in history as that made by Postan on the limitations of demographic forces. But, encouraging as such ecumenical statements may be, we must beware of the temptation to restrict the list of the prime influences on the course of historical change to class relations and population. As we have seen above, other Marxists have propounded equally pluralistic views by stressing the power of the 'exogenous' factor of commercial development. The modelling of the impact of this force is the subject of the next chapter.

---

[111] Bois, 'Against the Neo-Malthusian Orthodoxy', 118. It should be noted that Bois is consciously (but inexcusably) using the terms 'Malthusian' and 'neo-Malthusian' in an extremely loose fashion, to include 'any model in which the principal determinants are in the last resort of a demographic order' (ibid. 107 n. 2).

[112] Hilton, 'Crisis of Feudalism', 131.

4

Commercialization, Markets, and Technology

Having looked in some detail at demographic and class-based analyses of historical development, it might appear incontestable that the leading forces driving change in the medieval economy are to be found in the overwhelmingly dominant agricultural sector and in the relations between those who owned the land and those who worked it. But such assumptions have long been open to vigorous challenge. The notion that things inevitably improved and advanced over time has always attracted many adherents, and it was natural that historians looking back from the industrializing, urbanizing world of the nineteenth century, with its global trade, powerful empires, and sturdy institutions, should be tempted to view history as the march of progress from murky origins in a primitive, rural, self-sufficiency to its glorious efflorescence in the present. It was also to be expected that key elements in the world in which they wrote should dominate the agenda for the study of the past—the use of money, the rise of the middle classes, the advance of technology, the growth of towns, trade, and industry—and for these elements to be seen as the main forces which in the past had propelled the world towards the present. Setbacks in the long march of progress were rare and temporary, and the advances that were made provided a springboard for the next leap upward.[1]

It was the early dominance of these simple, optimistic, and unilinear accounts of historical development focused on the 'Rise of the Market' which helped to provoke the emergence of the models considered in the previous two chapters. The neo-Malthusian and Marxist traditions question whether the advance in many sectors of history was progressive and cumulative rather than staged or cyclical, and whether commercial and industrial development was a cause rather than a consequence of changes elsewhere in the economy and society. In a brief but influential critique published in 1944, Postan scorned the resort which historians frequently made to ill-defined notions such as 'the rise of a money economy', and the 'rise of the middle classes', when seeking to explain complex phenomena or fill in gaps in their knowledge. Thus we are told, he complained, 'if towns grew in the eleventh and twelfth centuries, this was due to the rise of the middle class', and if the labour services of villeins were commuted into cash in the fifteenth century, this was due to the rise of the money economy.[2]

Ironically, matters have now turned full circle and it is the dominance of models of a Malthusian and of a Marxist kind, which stress the restraints to growth inherent in pre-industrial economies, that have encouraged scholars to reconsider the role of market incentives and commercialization in easing or even releasing these restraints. Research into the medieval economy of England in recent years has increasingly focused on commercial activity and tech-

---

[1] W. Cunningham (1849–1919), one of the modern fathers of the subject of economic history, entitled his major work *The Rise of English Industry and Commerce*, and defined economic history as 'the study of material progress'. Adam Smith, long before him, saw history as 'the progress of opulence'.

[2] 'The Rise of a Money Economy', reprinted in Postan, *Medieval Agriculture and General Problems*, 28–40 (quote on 28).

nical progress, and the ways in which they interacted with population growth and social change. Local, regional, and sectoral studies of these themes have multiplied and produced a mass of new evidence, to which increasingly advanced methods of presentation and analysis have been applied.[3]

The result has been a distinct widening of the perspectives from which the economy has to be viewed, which poses a serious challenge to the credibility of the essentially 'stagnationist' models outlined in Chapters 2 and 3. But despite the antiquity of some of the intellectual pillars supporting the role of commercialization, and the ambitious and abstract nature of some of the current modelling, the assessment and assimilation of the new evidence is still at a formative stage. In contrast with the maturity of the leading Marxist and population–resources models, which have been refined to a high level of exposition and coherence over many decades, most of the historians working on the significance of commerce and technology have so far operated within a looser conceptual framework and are far from producing comparably taut and rigorous models. These considerations have necessitated the adoption of a somewhat different structure for this chapter, with more space being devoted to surveying the rapidly expanding evidentiary base, and rather less to analysing a wide variety of loosely connected and partly-formed theoretical models.

All models which stress the benefits arising from the growth of exchange and specialization owe a great debt to Adam Smith, who formulated an extremely powerful and durable exposition of the

---

[3] For recent general historical accounts, see R. H. Britnell, *The Commercialisation of English Society, 1000–1500*, 2nd edn. (Manchester, 1996); E. Miller and J. Hatcher, *Medieval England: Towns, Commerce and Crafts, 1086–1348* (1995); J. Masschaele, *Peasants, Merchants and Markets: Inland Trade in Medieval England, 1150–1350* (Basingstoke, 1997). For recent conceptual and theoretical accounts, see K. G. Persson, *Pre-industrial Economic Growth: Social Organisation and Technical Progress in Europe* (Oxford, 1988); G. Snooks, 'The Dynamic Role of the Market', in R. H. Britnell and B. M. S. Campbell (eds.), *A Commercialising Economy: England 1086–c.1300* (Manchester, 1995); G. W. Grantham, 'Espace privilégies: Productivité agraire et zones d'approvisionnement des villes dans l'Europe preindustrielle', *Annales ESC* (1997), 695–725.

manner in which commerce stimulates economic growth through the operation of free markets. Human society has an innate propensity to 'truck, barter and exchange one thing for another', and if this drive is allowed to proceed unfettered it will lead to a virtuous cycle of improvement, in which each individual pursuing his or her own interests will, as if 'led by an invisible hand', promote the benefit of the whole of society. The exchange of goods and services facilitates the division of labour, specialization, inventiveness, and the accumulation of capital, and all serve to raise productivity and promote economic growth.[4]

When ideas as powerful as these are applied to the medieval economy, they encourage the contention that commercial development and technical progress in the twelfth and thirteenth centuries were capable of offsetting, perhaps even reversing, any tendency towards diminishing returns to land and labour. Expressed simply, the expansion of trade and the development of towns and industry generates not merely additional employment, which helps to absorb the surplus labour of the countryside, but promotes increases in productivity by supplying incentives to producers and by facilitating specialization of production and the greater division of labour, thereby reducing both the costs of production and the costs of buying and selling. Further improvements in productivity also flow from advances in knowledge and techniques, which occurred in all areas of economic life from the selection of the seed which a peasant farmer chose to sow, and when and where he chose to sow it, to the manner in which a merchant kept account of his purchases and sales. Moreover, these improvements tended to be cumulative and, once acquired and found to be beneficial, were only rarely lost or abandoned. Although there were few epoch-making leaps forward, evolutionary advances over long periods of time progressively transformed many areas of economic and social life.

---

4 See, in particular, *An Inquiry into the Nature and Causes of the Wealth of Nations*, which was first published in 1776. The quotes are taken from the edition prepared by R. H. Campbell and A. S. Skinner, 2 vols. (Oxford, 1976), i. 25, 456.

A growing population is a powerful stimulus for commercial development and technical progress. Denser settlement improves communications and access to markets, reduces transport costs, increases the opportunities for economies of scale, and encourages specialization. Rising numbers also promote improvement and invention in a variety of ways, the most direct being the simple fact that more people mean more potential inventors. There is also the stimulus provided by the price mechanism and the profit motive, which will thrive in times of expansion. As population presses upon resources so prices will rise, and rising prices mean greater incentives for suppliers to produce for the market: demand will call forth its own supply.

Therefore, rather than viewing the inexorable rise in population as a negative force doomed to outrun employment and subsistence, it may be argued that it was the very rise in the density of settlement and the increasing populousness which stimulated trade, specialization, and inventiveness. Population levels have soared over the centuries, but so has the ability to feed them. Indeed, data extracted from a vast sweep of history going back to the era of hunters and gatherers can be used to suggest that technical change and economic growth have been fastest in regions of high population densities. Thus, it may be argued, the rate of increase in output in the medieval economy was similarly capable of exceeding the rate of increase in the numbers of people, with the result that in the long thirteenth century standards of living rose rather than plunged. According to hypotheses such as these, population growth in the High Middle Ages triggered technological changes in agriculture and commerce which weakened and ultimately broke the spiral of diminishing returns to land—and even to labour, some may claim.

Both Malthus and Ricardo painted pessimistic canvases which stressed the propensity of demand to outstrip supply, but here the emphasis is placed on the stimulus provided by rising demand, and its ability to generate positive feedback in the economy. Once markets began to expand they created possibilities for production on a larger scale, which tended to increase output and to reduce the unit costs of production of many commodities by encouraging specialization and the division of labour. This in turn stimulated a further growth of markets and division of labour which fed on itself, and by so doing promoted yet further growth and development, very much as Adam Smith maintained that it would. The theoretical arguments for the ways in which market incentives can trigger a more efficient use of resources can be crudely categorized as follows.

The Theory

Improvements in Agriculture

At the most basic level, the very processes of production will result in a succession of small but cumulative advances in technique and method simply because the endless repetition of acts such as cultivating the land, rearing livestock, fashioning artefacts, or making tools, will eventually suggest improvements to the workers who perform them. Thus, society has an inherent, endogenous, tendency to generate technical know-how, which is then added to its stock of knowledge to be built on by future generations.

It is important, therefore, that this inherent capacity to improve should not be underestimated, even in relatively simple economies. But what determines the extent to which this potential is converted into achievement? What encourages or discourages the spread of technical knowledge among more people and a broader cross-section of society, and what encourages or discourages the implementation of that knowledge? It is one thing for knowledge of a technique to exist and another for that technique to be commonly applied, and it is here that population and the relationship between numbers of people and quantities of resources are held to play a vital role. The dispersal of better techniques throughout a pre-industrial economy depends not just on the knowledge which producers have about them but on the incentive which they have to adopt them, both of which are determined principally by population pressure. Rising population exerts pressure on resources which in turn increases the demand for goods and services, thereby creating the incentive to adopt innovations. Rising population also increases the density of settlement, which results in greater and more efficient contact between peoples and places, and which in turn facilitates the spread of knowledge. By contrast, if the pressure of population is low or falling, incentives to adopt improvements are reduced and the spread of ideas is inhibited.

This reasoning is most obviously applicable to agriculture. Land and food become more scarce when population rises, and farmers will respond to this scarcity by increasing output on the farm. This could be achieved by ploughing up more acres of pasture and by reducing the amount of land left fallow each year, although both courses of action would be liable to raise the spectre of declining yields. But by adopting better technology, raising levels of invest-ment, and improving systems of land management farmers might postpone the onset of diminishing returns to land. Moreover, under conditions when labour is becoming ever cheaper and more abun-dant, the most beneficial strategy of all might be for farmers to adopt a progressively land-saving bias by substituting the abundant factor (labour) for the scarce factor (land). In other words, by investing more time and effort on farming their land, in the form of more weeding, ploughing, manuring, tending, of livestock, and so on.

Yet the adoption of a progressively more labour-intensive agri-culture cannot, by itself, provide the solution to the adverse effects of population pressure. For, although the application of more and more labour may well maintain or increase the productivity of each acre of land, eventually it is likely to result in the falling productivity of each day of labour. If there are no additions to capital, each further day of labour performed on the same area of land will ulti-mately result in a progressively diminishing increment to the yields of the holding.[5] If all other things are held constant in the economy at large, it must follow that declining marginal labour productivity in agriculture would eventually constrain the economy's ability to absorb a rising population without inducing a fall in standards of living.

However, a growing availability of alternative employment outside the farm could help to offset or even reverse this decline. As we noted in Chapter 2, every pre-industrial economy has a range of non-agricultural occupations, which serve the needs of the masses as well as the rich. Even where the primary concern of most producers is to meet their own subsistence requirements, few production units will be entirely self-sufficient in all goods and services. A modest peasant household will have some dependence on trade and exchange, and will have to make purchases, however small and infrequent, of iron, leather, hardwood, salt, and suchlike. At the most rudimentary level, non-agricultural employment opportunities can make labour in an agrarian economy more productive by providing work during those times when it is not possible to be fully employed on the farm. Although labour productivity might be relatively high in the busy periods of the farming year, the lack of productive work during slack periods serves to depress overall labour productivity. Many agricultural tasks—especially in grain production—are seasonal, and require concentrated effort only for certain periods of the year; the maximum length of the working day on the farm depends upon the hours of daylight, which likewise vary with the seasons; and the tending of livestock requires a varying commitment during the working day which frequently leaves farmers with periods of time on their hands. Thus, in addition to the casual employment that could be obtained by working on other farms, craftwork could readily be undertaken by smallholders in the home, if it was available—carding and spinning wool, working wood, plaiting baskets, and so on. Most basic medieval crafts used cheap and

---

[5] Diminishing returns to labour under such conditions are, of course, a central plank in population and resources modelling (see the discussion above, pp. 23–4).

easily obtainable raw materials and few required expensive or sophisticated equipment, therefore many people could turn their hands to
some sort of by-employment. Some landholders acquired the ability
to practise one or more skilled or semi-skilled secondary occupation
—such as carpentry, tiling, thatching, smithing, or weaving—which
shaded through greater specialization into those craftsmen who supplemented their earnings by farming a plot of land.

England in the High Middle Ages was, of course, far from being
a primitive subsistence economy where production and exchange
merely serviced the essential requirements of farming communities.
She possessed thriving industries, towns, and trades which offered substantial scope for employment, specialization, and the enhancement
of the productivity of labour. Adam Smith stressed the benefits of the
division of labour, and proclaimed that 'the greatest improvement
in the productive powers of labour, and the greater part of the skill,
dexterity, and judgment with which it is any where directed or applied,
seem to have been the effects of the division of labour' and that
'so far as it can be introduced, [it] occasions, in every art, a pro-
portionable increase of the productive powers of labour'.[6] Thus,
workers who concentrate on a particular craft or trade, or who
specialize in a specific part of the production process, will be more
efficient and productive than those who split their time and expertise between a variety of pursuits. The specialized producer, or the
specialized unit of production, will become more dextrous in the performance of its task, and thus reduce the time taken to complete it.
'[T]he certainty of being able to exchange . . . encourages every man
to apply himself to a particular occupation, and to cultivate and to
bring to perfection whatever talent or genius he may possess for that
particular species of business'.[7] Familiarity with the task will stimulate improvements in the techniques of production by encouraging
both the introduction and the spread of innovations, thus further
increasing the rate of technical progress and productivity gains.

---

[6] *Wealth of Nations*, ed. Campbell and Skinner, i. 13, 15.　　[7] Ibid., i. 28.

The potential for gains from the division of labour in agriculture, however, was acknowledged by Smith to be limited. Farm work involves a wide range of tasks, many of which are seasonal and relatively unskilled, which limits the scope for the division of labour even on large farms. Thus, the same workers are likely to have to perform different tasks on a daily or weekly basis and in accord with the passing seasons, which necessitate moving from threshing to ploughing, to weeding, to mowing, and then to reaping. Some small additional scope for labour specialization on the farm may lie in the employment of craftsmen to fulfil its non-agricultural require-ments, such as the repair and maintenance of buildings, and of wooden and metal tools and farm equipment. But, then again, such productivity gains may prove to be illusory, since the farmer may well find it more profitable to undertake such tasks himself during the inevitable periods when he is confined indoors and has no other work to do, especially in inclement weather and long winter evenings.

In fact the greatest gains in pre-mechanized agriculture were likely to come not from the division of labour but from specialization by a farm or a region in the production of particular commodities. The more primitive the market and transport facilities the more the farmer, both peasant and lord, will be driven towards producing as much as possible of what he needs to consume. A wholly self-sufficient farmer must produce his own bread and fodder crops, and rear a range of livestock for the purposes of consumption and traction, regardless of the soil and climate with which he has to contend. Growing crops or raising animals which are not well-suited to the local environment naturally depresses yields, while the productivity of labour on the farm may also suffer from having to perform too wide a range of tasks. In contrast, an efficient marketing and trans-port system would enable a farm or region to specialize in producing the particular range of commodities to which its resource endow-ment, location, or expertise are best suited, and it would thereby enjoy higher mean productivity.

Urbanization and Improvements in Commerce

An obvious manifestation of an expansion in commercial activity and a greater division of labour is the growth of towns, for towns are peopled with specialists who gain their livelihoods from trade, manufacturing, and the provision of services. The correlation between the growth of occupational specialisms and the growth of towns is based on the self-evident advantages gained by specialists who congregate together: an arrangement which is more attractive to consumers and more convenient to suppliers, and thus liable to reduce production and transaction costs. Likewise, there are clear advantages for specialists to settle in places where raw materials are locally available; where market institutions are well-developed; where they can pursue their trade free of feudal intrusions; and where they are afforded a degree of physical protection from military invasions.

Just as specialization and commercialization in agriculture is stimulated by the growing demand for agricultural produce generated by the development of towns and industries, so the development of towns and industries depends fundamentally on the performance and fortunes of agriculture. A growth in non-farm employment diminishes the proportion of the population producing its own food, and so agriculture must be capable of creating a surplus sufficient to feed those who specialize in other activities. Consequently, it may be argued that the level of urban development in an economy can be taken as a rough measure of the extent to which the division of labour—and by extension labour productivity in the economy as a whole—has progressed.[8]

Cities stimulated the commercialization of agriculture, and the relationship between concentrated urban demand and rural land use was fruitfully explored as a theoretical model by Johann von Thünen in the early nineteenth century.[9] Not surprisingly von

---

[8] For example, by Persson (*Pre-industrial Economic Growth*, 76–7).
[9] P. Hall (ed.), *Von Thünen's Isolated State* (1966).

Thünen found that the closer a city was to a farming region the greater the degree of commercialization and intensification of production that region experienced, and that self-sufficiency and extensive production increased with distance. However, he also went on to analyse how distance from the market determines the type of crop that was produced as well as the intensity of the agricultural system. Thus, high levels of urban demand will lead to the formation of a series of zones of rural land use in the hinterland of the town, where certain crops will be produced near the market (under relatively intensive agricultural systems) while others will be produced further away from the market (under relatively extensive agricultural systems). From this, von Thünen postulated an 'ideal' distribution of agricultural production, based on theoretical concentric rings of specific types of product around the market. For example, perishable goods must be delivered to consumers quickly, while for products whose weight and volume is high relative to their value the point will soon be reached at which transport costs will equal profits. In both cases these goods will have to be produced close to the market. By contrast, transport costs are a relatively small part of the total costs of goods that are low in bulk and high in value, and thus they can be produced at a greater distance from the market.

If this model is applied to the main products of the medieval economy, then one might expect bulky goods such as fuel and fodder crops and perishable goods such as dairy produce to be produced close to a main urban market. The next few 'zones of production' would be devoted to the production of bread and malting grains under farming systems which decrease in intensity as distance from the market increases, and in the furthermost zones there would be stock-rearing, and the production of industrial crops, and so on. Von Thünen's work is a theoretical statement about the potential impact of markets on land use, and there is no claim that in practice such zones would be perfectly formed and perfectly observable upon the ground. The zones will only become clearly established with appropriate levels of urban demand, and will become less well defined if that demand is not sustained. The clarity of von Thünen's production zones will also be modified in reality by the physical environment, which locally may be unsuited to the production of a particular product or the adoption of a particular farming system. Nor do markets exist in isolation, and any one locality might be affected by the competing demands of various local, sub-regional, and regional markets for different goods. Similarly, his model assumes constant transport costs, but in practice there exist lines of lower transport costs, such as rivers or mountain passes, which would distort the zones of production on the ground.

At the most fundamental level von Thünen's model usefully emphasizes the impact of economic and commercial forces on agriculture, as opposed to the environmental/demographic or social/structural forces beloved of the other models. It also provides a clear framework with which to assess, and perhaps explain, local and regional differences in agricultural output and organization. Of course the relevance of von Thünen's work to pre-industrial economies in general, and to medieval England in particular, depends upon an assessment of the prevailing levels and concentration of urban demand. But it does lend conceptual force to the intuitive and empirically supported notion that an economy which is significantly influenced by market forces will exploit its resource base more efficiently, and thus be better placed to absorb a rising population, than one which is not.

The Evidence

This general and largely theoretical discussion has identified the wide range and potency of the economic improvements which might flow in the Middle Ages from advances in the techniques of production, the division of labour, the specialization of production, and commerce and urbanization. Yet, as we have seen in Chapters 2 and 3,

historians stressing the power of the relationship between population and resources, or the primacy of class factors and property
relations, have not conceded much significance to them. While the
proponents of these interpretations acknowledge that trade and
the urban sector expanded, and that some technical advances did
occur, their firm overall conclusion is that the cumulative importance of such non-agrarian developments was strictly limited, since
the economy as a whole remained overwhelmingly underdeveloped
and subject to diminishing returns.

   The disagreement between historians owes much to the nature
of the evidence, which permits considerable variations in the assessment of the influence and importance of commercialization. Indeed,
how does one measure the extent and impact of trading and commercial activity within a pre-industrial economy, when the source
material offers little hard quantitative information about such central issues as the dimensions of internal trade, urbanization ratios,
labour productivity, and the availability of non-agricultural employment? Since it is not possible to quantify commercialization in the
Middle Ages with any pretence of precision, historians are forced to
rely upon a range of inexact and imprecise measures. They do, however, agree broadly that the most valid indicators of commercialization in the medieval economy are the extent of the division of
labour in the countryside, the development of urbanization and
marketing institutions, the extent of the use of money and credit,
the extent of regional specialization of agricultural production, and
its varying intensity, and progress in transport. It is now time to
review the evidence which survives for each of these areas, paying
particular attention to the advances in knowledge which have been
gained in recent years.

The Rural Division of Labour

The existence of an abundance of smallholders in late thirteenth-
century England—comprising perhaps a half of the total population

—is widely accepted by historians, but its significance is disputed. Malthusian and Marxist models would interpret this state of affairs as clear evidence of a mounting economic crisis, but it has also been taken to indicate the impressive scale of the economic development which had taken place. The fact that many people were able to support themselves with by-employments demonstrates a growth in the volume of industrial and commercial activity in the rural economy as well as outside. Recent studies have pointed to the impressive range of occupations which became progressively available in the thirteenth-century village, and in the words of one recent commentator 'changes in occupational practice were so numerous in thirteenth-century society as to transform it'.[10]

Larger villages, particularly those with weekly markets, possessed a wide variety of traders and craftsmen offering basic goods and services. The retailing of bread, ale, meat, and fuel was commonplace, and resulted in specialist as well as part-time processors of these commodities: bakers, cooks, brewers, millers, butchers, charcoal-burners, and suchlike. Indeed, commercial ale production in some places was tantamount to a 'brewing industry', sustaining poorer families in particular.[11] Shoemakers, tailors, weavers, and dyers were not uncommon, and smiths and carpenters could be found even in small villages. A wide range of occupations were practised even in essentially rural areas: in the Wiltshire tax returns of 1332 occupational surnames indicate that men, and occasionally women, were working in forty different crafts, in addition to millers, clothworkers, and smiths, while in Cambridgeshire thirty crafts were listed in 1279.[12]

In regions where the resource base was particularly diverse, the scale of opportunities for employment off the landholding could be even greater. Deposits of tin, lead, iron, and coal frequently

---

[10] Britnell, *Commercialisation of English Society*, 81.

[11] E. Britton, *The Community of the Vill* (Toronto, 1977), 87–7.

[12] Miller and Hatcher, *Towns, Commerce and Crafts*, 128–33; Britnell, *Commercialisation of English Society*, 79–81.

boosted local employment in mining and smelting, while common rights over heaths, moors, woods, and fens encouraged the development of a variety of pastoral, craft, and industrial pursuits. An example from the fenland edge of Huntingdonshire conveys a sense of the potential of such regions for occupational diversity: peasants were variously engaged in fishing, fowling, peat-digging, sedge and reed cutting, pastoral activities, and the transporting of goods and people on the busy fenland waterways.[13] Fenland villagers here were drawn into a regional labour market, and were regularly prepared to travel between seven and ten miles for employment.[14] The abundance and range of employment prospects in such villages 'may well have been a vital factor in the survival of . . . families during the first half of the fourteenth century'.[15] As a consequence of such opportunities, and the incidence of fertile soils, the recorded population density of the northern fenland in the later thirteenth century was very high and the average holding size very low. But in some regions it was the prevalence of poor soils which successfully stimulated the diversity of employment. In the Breckland of East Anglia arid and acidic soils provided little scope for intensive arable or pastoral farming, yet villagers carved a living from a variety of pursuits, including the collection of fuel and building materials, textile manufacturing, poaching, horse rearing, and the preparation of animal skins. As a consequence the individual wealth of Breckland's residents was actually greater than in nearby villages on better soils.[16]

Although by far the greater part of non-agricultural employment in the countryside was devoted to providing goods and services to local markets and consumers, an increasing number of rural areas

---

[13] A. R. DeWindt, 'Redefining the Peasant Community in Medieval England: The Regional Perspective', *Journal of British Studies*, 26 (1987), 163–207.

[14] S. A. C. Penn and C. Dyer, 'Wages and Earnings in Late Medieval England: Evidence from the Enforcement of the Labour Laws', *EcHR*, 2nd ser., 43 (1990), 363.

[15] Britton, *Community of the Vill*, 92.

[16] M. Bailey, *A Marginal Economy? East Anglian Breckland in the Late Middle Ages* (Cambridge, 1989), 158–99.

by the early fourteenth century were specializing in the manufacture of goods for sale in distant markets, including overseas. A concentration upon cloth production is evident in certain villages and small towns of Norfolk, Suffolk, Wiltshire, Somerset, and Gloucestershire, while in the West Riding of Yorkshire, especially around Sheffield and Rotherham, commercial metalworking as well as clothmaking was to be found. There were concentrations of tinners on the moorlands of Devon and Cornwall, of lead miners especially in Derbyshire, Durham and Northumberland, and the Mendips, and of iron-miners, iron-workers, and charcoal-burners in the Forest of Dean and the Kent and Sussex Weald.[17] The existence of diversified and specialized employment opportunities in the rural areas of medieval England is not to be doubted, although it is equally evident that they were not available in abundance everywhere.

Urbanization and Improvements in Commerce

There is a mass of direct and indirect evidence which points unerringly to the rapid expansion and growing sophistication of commercial activity in the two and a half centuries between the Norman Conquest and the Black Death, which complements that available for the growth of industrial production. Major advances in markets and transport occurred in response to the requirements of those who sought to buy and sell goods and move them from place to place. A growing population provided a powerful stimulus simply by multiplying needs, and flourishing trade led to the establishment of additional markets, the improvement of roads and tracks, the building of bridges, and the clearing of rivers for navigation. The proliferation of markets and fairs is a central facet of the commercialization of medieval England, but technological advances were also achieved in the methods by which goods were transported and

---

[17] Miller and Hatcher, *Towns, Commerce and Crafts*, 410–11.

transacted. The efficiency of trade depends on the means available for matching buyers and sellers, for ensuring payment for goods supplied, enforcing quality control, and standard weights and measures. Trade is fostered by security as well as trust, and travel needs to be safe as well as cheap. Developments in these and related matters of regulation and law and order, which abounded in the central Middle Ages, constituted real technological breakthroughs and led to substantial reductions in what economists call search costs and transaction costs, and thus stimulated yet further commercial development.

While it is possible to exchange goods and services by barter, and to pay rents in produce and labour, any substantial advance in commerce is dependent on the use of money. As trade develops so will attitudes to money, and the use of money will become more widespread and persistent as the need for it and confidence in it grows. Trade thrives on an adequate supply of coin maintained to a steady standard and provided in appropriate denominations, which was England's fortunate experience from William I to Edward III, when the money supply rose much faster than the numbers of people and the rate of inflation, and the quality of the coinage was well-maintained. Current opinion suggests there may have been no more than £25,000–37,500 in currency circulating in the realm in the late eleventh century, but that by the early thirteenth century there was around £250,000, and by the early fourteenth century around £1,000,000. This would have meant a doubling in the real value of money per head between 1086 and *c.*1300, even after allowing for a threefold increase in population and a fourfold increase in prices.[18]

Commerce also relies on the provision of credit, not just in the form of cash loan advances but, perhaps even more importantly in the Middle Ages, in delayed payments for goods purchased or

---

[18] N. Mayhew, 'Modelling Medieval Monetisation', in Britnell and Campbell (eds.), *Commercialising Economy*, 55–77; R. H. Britnell, 'Commercialisation and Economic Development in England, 1000–1300', in Britnell and Campbell (eds.), *Commercialising Economy*, 12–14; Miller and Hatcher, *Towns, Commerce and Crafts*, 396–7.

services rendered. The expansion in the availability of credit and manifold improvements in the means by which it could be obtained facilitated dealings at every level from great merchants operating on a national or international scale to ordinary people when they acted intermittently as buyers and sellers. Thus, the growth in the supply of coin and credit, and perhaps also the gentle rise in prices which eased the burden of debt, combined to provide a distinctly favourable environment for the growth of transactions, local, regional, and national, and a rise in economic activity.[19]

England became progressively integrated into the trading networks of Europe in the generations after the Norman Conquest, and the scale and value of her overseas trade multiplied. By the 1300s the value of annual imports reached perhaps around £200,000 and exports around £300,000. The most secure statistics show that at this time the fleeces of eight million sheep worth *c.*£250,000 were exported each year, and 20,000 tuns of wine (each containing 250 gallons) worth a total of £60,000, were imported.[20] Even more informative for our purposes is evidence of the growth of domestic trade, and in particular of the number and size of English towns and the number and distribution of markets, together with improvements in the legal and institutional framework within which trade took place. The latter was a major achievement of the period, for the growth of regulations and rules, implemented, extended and enforced by the Crown, landlords and towns themselves, provided greater security for commercial activity.

The number of settlements which might plausibly be termed towns multiplied from around 120 in 1086 to perhaps as many as 500 in the early fourteenth century, and while lots of these places were very small and had distinct rural as well as urban characteristics, the numbers of larger towns also grew rapidly. In the early fourteenth century there may have been nearly twenty provincial towns with

---

[19] Mayhew, 'Modelling Medieval Monetisation', 74–5.
[20] Miller and Hatcher, *Towns, Commerce and Crafts*, 210–15.

populations in excess of 5,000, compared with only four in the late eleventh century, and perhaps fifty market towns with populations in the 2,500–5,000 range. Growth was no less pronounced at the top of the urban hierarchy. It has long been thought that in the early fourteenth century London's population was of the order of 50,000, and that around 15,000 persons lived in each of the three largest regional centres—Norwich, Bristol, and York. But recent estimates would place the capital's population at 80,000 or even 100,000, and that of Norwich in 1333 at around 25,000.[21]

If sustainable, such upgradings would have important implications for estimates of the proportion of Englishfolk who lived in towns rather than in the countryside. Previous assumptions that little more than one in ten lived in towns in the early fourteenth century would be clearly untenable, and are perhaps more applicable to Domesday England. But if around 3 per cent of the nation's population lived in the four largest towns in the early fourteenth century, and a further 6 per cent resided in England's leading one hundred towns, then townsfolk may have comprised by *c.*1300 one in every six or seven of the population. Indeed, it has recently been claimed on the basis of tax assessments that the true figure was one in five.[22]

It was within towns that the most pronounced specialization and division of labour could take place, and once again this was a process which surged forward in the course of the twelfth and thirteenth centuries, reflecting especially a growing sophistication in the economic and social structure of larger towns. London advanced the furthest, of course, and its lay subsidy roll of 1332 indicates that the taxpaying citizens alone engaged in well over a hundred distinct occupations. Town registers of the admissions of

---

[21] Britnell, *Commercialisation of English Society*, 115; *idem*, 'The Towns of England and Northern Italy in the Early Fourteenth Century', *EcHR*, 2nd ser., 44 (1991), 21–4; Miller and Hatcher, *Towns, Commerce and Crafts*, 274–5.

[22] C. Dyer, 'How Urbanised Was Medieval England', in J.-M. Duvosquel and E. Thoen (eds.), *Peasants and Townsmen in Medieval Europe: Studia in Honorem Adriaan Verhulst* (Gent, 1995), 169–83.

freemen in the later thirteenth and early fourteenth centuries reveal some 60–70 occupations in Winchester and Norwich, and almost 100 in York.[23] Although Durham was a town of moderate size, it was a major ecclesiastical centre, where more than fifty trades are noted in the records in *c.*1300, including scriveners, lawyers and doctors, parchment makers, goldsmiths, locksmiths, spicers, and vintners.[24] Registers of freemen do not, of course, reveal the range of skilled, semi-skilled, and unskilled occupations practised by the unenfranchised masses. At the other end of the spectrum specialization often ran very deep, especially in the textiles, leatherworking, and victualling trades. It is common to find in textile production in the larger towns not only a range of craftsmen and women concentrating on the various stages of manufacture, from spinners, dyers, weavers, and fullers, to shearmen and tailors, but specialists in the making of particular types of cloth, or items of clothing, linen, or haberdashery. The process advanced so far in London that by 1300 there was a cushion-maker and a wimple-maker. This increasing division of labour reflected the growth of consumer demand, but it was also encouraged by technical innovation, which made available basic machines and pieces of equipment which were suited to particular processes, like the fulling mill and the spinning wheel which became more widespread in the thirteenth century.

At the bottom of the urban hierarchy, it was also the wide variety of craftsmen which distinguished the innumerable small towns from villages. The inhabitants of semi-rural Linton (Cambs.) engaged in at least fifteen different crafts in 1279, while those of High Wycombe (Bucks.), Thame (Oxon.), and Highworth (Wilts.) had a couple of dozen or more.[25] Occupational specialism was most frequently encountered in the retailing of foodstuffs (for example, bakers, brewers, butchers), and simple task distinctions could often

---

[23] Miller and Hatcher, *Towns, Commerce and Crafts*, 324–5.

[24] M. Bonney, *Lordship and the Urban Community: Durham and its Overlords, 1250–1540* (Cambridge, 1990), 148.

[25] Miller and Hatcher, *Towns, Commerce and Crafts*, 128–9.

be found in the leather trade (tanners, skinners, and saddlers) and the cloth trade (weavers and tailors). However, this evidence must be balanced against a realization that the limits to task specialization are also readily apparent in small towns, for the number of specialists was small and it is also doubtful whether they found regular work in their nominated trades. For example, those metalworking tasks undertaken in the larger towns by wheelwrights, harrow-makers, and locksmiths, would often have been undertaken lower down the urban scale by the ubiquitous and jobbing 'smith'.

The growth in the number of weekly markets was even more impressive than that of towns. By the eve of the Black Death there were probably more than 1,500 licensed markets located in the towns and villages of England, of which two-thirds had been established after 1200.[26] Even if some of the market charters granted by the Crown merely formalized existing arrangements, the undoubted net effect was a large increase in the number and range of rural marketing outlets. The establishment of franchises allowed the landlord to channel local trade through markets, and to profit by levying tolls and charging rents for stalls and shops. Yet it also offered benefits to producers and traders, by providing a safe, reliable, and fixed meeting place for the purpose of trade, and a framework of rules, regulations, and legal protection within which to conduct it.[27]

The proliferation of markets therefore reduced search and trans-action costs, decreased the potential risks inherent in trading with relative strangers, and allowed information about commercial opportunities to circulate more freely. These local developments particularly favoured the lower orders of rural society, whose confidence and ability to produce for the market was enhanced. Peasants commonly sought commodities such as iron, tools, coarse fabrics, fish, tar, and salt from dealers in these small market communities,

[26] R. H. Britnell, 'The Proliferation of Markets in England, 1200–1349', *EcHR*, 2nd ser., 33 (1991), 209–21.

[27] Britnell, *Commercialisation of English Society*, 79–101.

and there was a reciprocal trade in small quantities of grains, vege-
tables, or livestock, which might have enabled poorer peasants to
supplement their subsistence economy. The peasant elite, those with
farms of 20 acres and more, had to be market-oriented simply because
they produced more than their families could consume, but evidence
is forthcoming which suggests that they capitalized on their opportunities. Raftis has remarked on the impressive wealth of virgaters
in Huntingdonshire, and Biddick has deduced from the evidence
of tax assessments that there was a high degree of responsiveness
to the market among the substantial peasantry of late thirteenth-
century Bedfordshire.[28] At the other end of the spectrum, among
the smallholders and cottagers, the need to obtain cash for rents
and other seigneurial dues may have forced the sale of crops in local
markets, even if this was food which was needed for the subsistence
of their families or their livestock or for seed-corn. Thus, access to
markets could exert a powerful influence over the sources and
gradations of wealth in village societies, stimulating the polarization
of peasant society. In Biddick's words, 'marketing chains forged links
that socially separated groups in [English] villages. The influence of
commercial production and regional markets could help to shape
the development of village communities, thereby challenging the
dominance of demographic and structural forces.'[29]

Thus, the volume of traded goods rose strongly in the twelfth
and thirteenth centuries in many small towns and rural markets, and
it is highly likely that the proportion of total production which was
traded rose also. Furthermore, it has recently been argued that
rural markets became enmeshed within increasingly regular and
sophisticated regional trading networks, to the extent that 'the

---

[28] J. A. Raftis, *Peasant Economic Development within the English Manorial System*
(Stroud, 1997), 11–17; K. Biddick, 'Medieval English Peasants and Market Involvement',
Journal of Economic History, 45 (1985), 823–31; Masschaele, *Peasants, Merchants and Markets*,
33–54.

[29] K. Biddick, 'Missing Links: Taxable Wealth and Stratification among Medieval English
Peasants', *Journal of Interdisciplinary History*, 18 (1987), 297.

ever-deepening interdependency between town and country . . . was one of the principal achievements of the entire period . . . [and] contrary to what many historians have said and thought, markets that found their clientele chiefly among the poorer peasants living within a few miles of the site do not typify the commercial economy of the period'.[30]

A recent calculation reckons that *c.*1330 most of England's wool production was sold and perhaps up to a third of its grain.[31] By providing incentives to increase production, easier access to markets could also encourage investment in the land and lead to improvements in technique and management, on peasant farms as well as those of the gentry and nobility. The most powerful influences for investment and improvement in agriculture were felt in the vicinity of towns, whose populations generated consistent and sometimes substantial demand for food and other farm products. London, of course, exerted by far the most powerful influence of all, and the capital's requirements have been calculated by Galloway and Murphy at 1 million bushels of grain and 100,000 tons of fuel every year. They go on to argue that London's voracious appetite for agricultural produce created zones of production broadly along the lines suggested by von Thünen, although they emphasize the importance of transport-cost distance rather than crow-fly distance in the formation of these zones. Thus, good water transportation along the coast enabled eastern Norfolk and coastal Sussex to supply London with grain, while closer but landlocked regions were less capable of supplying the metropolis. Vital wood fuel—bulky and low in value— was commonly supplied from an area within 15–40 km of the city, while cheese and butter was sent from the Essex marshlands and the Stour valley.[32]

---

[30] Masschaele, *Peasants, Merchants and Markets*, 73–188, 161, 212.

[31] Britnell, *Commercialisation of English Society*, 123.

[32] J. A. Galloway and M. Murphy, 'Feeding the City: London and its Hinterland', *London Journal*, 16 (1993), 3–14; Galloway, Keene, and Murphy, 'Fuelling the City', 460–70.

The reconstruction of the agricultural geography of medieval England is still in its infancy, but suggestive and innovative research has attempted to sketch its broad outlines. In particular it is argued that the intensity and consistency of the demands generated by thriving urban centres had a major impact on land use and productivity in their hinterlands. Not surprisingly the influence of the appetite of London for food and fuel left the most indelible mark on the regions which supplied it. Campbell and Brandon have detailed the intensive arable farming practised in the late thirteenth century on certain demesnes in east Norfolk and coastal Kent and Sussex which supplied urban markets, notably London. Here, through the use of copious amounts of labour on land where fallows were significantly reduced and crop specialization relatively pronounced, yields were high and constant by medieval standards, and were achieved with no sign of the soil exhaustion predicted in other models of development.[33]

The same ingredients are held to be evident—though in lesser quantities—across areas of the Home Counties and East Anglia where mixed farming predominated. Grain was less dominant in these regions, the arable land was cropped with intermediate intensity, and greater emphasis was placed upon pastoral farming, especially the intensive exploitation of dairy herds. By implication it is assumed that the farming of the peasantry in these advanced areas was similarly intensive, flexible, and productive, encouraged by the relative freedom which they enjoyed.[34] The belief that farm enterprise reflected von Thünen's model of land use more than Ricardo's has been encouraged, namely that it was not simply the quality of the

[33] P. Brandon, 'Demesne Arable Farming in Coastal Sussex during the Late Middle Ages', *Agricultural History Review*, 19 (1977), 113–36; B. M. S. Campbell, 'Agricultural Progress in Medieval England: Some Evidence from Eastern Norfolk', *EcHR*, 2nd ser., 36 (1983), 26–46.

[34] B. M. S. Campbell, 'Land and People in the Middle Ages: 1066–1500', in R. A. Dodgshon and R. A. Butlin (eds.), *An Historical Geography of England and Wales* (1990), 89–92; B. M. S. Campbell, K. C. Bartley, and J. P. Power, 'The Demesne Farming Systems of Post-Black Death England: A Classification', *Agricultural History Review*, 44 (1996), 142–54.

soil but its location which determined its product, value, and the extent of its exploitation.[35]

A potential has thus been revealed for innovative farming methods in parts of medieval England. Evidence from the turn of the thirteenth and fourteenth centuries reveals that farms in some regions responded positively to the incentives created by high and rising demand and were able to raise the productivity of the land. This is a prospect which is either neglected or explicitly denied in other models of change and development, although its broader significance is open to dispute.[36]

Transport

The pace and extent of urban development and agricultural specialization are clearly dependent upon the efficiency of transportation. Efficient transport networks reduce the time and costs of moving goods to market and improve the flow of information about the state of markets among potential producers; inefficient transport results in high costs which seriously reduce the incentive for farmers to supply wider markets and add to the prices which consumers have to pay, and thus can constrain trade and the growth of the urban sector.

While there is scant evidence of large-scale capital investment or technological leaps in medieval transport, and the maintenance of rivers and roadways was largely left to local initiative, the tenor of recent research strongly suggests that there were significant

[35] Or, in the words of Campbell: 'It is hard. . . . not to attribute considerable influence to the role of market-determined economic rent in the articulation of regional farming systems' (*Agricultural History Review*, 40 (1992), 68).

[36] For example, it has been claimed that the existence of the knowledge of how to raise yields means that there were no agricultural restraints to economic development at this time. But both yields and the intensity of agricultural methods remained low or modest over most of the country, and the consequence of raising the productivity of the land by the use of labour-intensive techniques was inevitably the lowering of the productivity of labour. See below, pp. 163–5.

improvements in the course of the twelfth and thirteenth centuries, and that the costs of moving most goods around the country did not prove a major restraint on the progress of commercialization and urban development.[37] A good water transportation system was especially beneficial, because the carriage of goods by river or coast was many times cheaper than overland, and it is no coincidence that almost all the leading English towns were exceptionally well-served by coastal or inland waterways. It has recently been argued that hitherto the scale of improvement in the inland river system of England has been seriously underestimated, and that many rivers were navigable to higher points than previously realized, with the effect that by *c.*1300 few places were more than 15 miles from a navigable waterway.[38] Certain well-favoured locations developed into major inland ports, as Henley did in the course of the thirteenth century, collecting grain and other produce for shipment down the Thames for the London market, while on the edge of the East Anglian fenland more sophisticated wharf facilities were constructed at a variety of inland ports.[39] Consequently, bold claims can be made for the role of cheap and easy water transportation in stimulating urban growth and commercial development in the twelfth and thirteenth centuries.

At the same time, even places with excellent water communications relied heavily on overland routes to reach markets and suppliers, and the majority of the newly-founded towns and village markets were either landlocked or situated by rivers which provided only limited access. Improvements are evident in overland transport in the twelfth and thirteenth centuries, and its growing weight and importance is reflected by the large number of trading sites, formal

[37] Masschaele, *Peasants, Merchants and Markets*, 189–212.

[38] J. F. Edwards and B. P. Hindle, 'The Transportation System of Medieval England and Wales', *Journal of Historical Geography*, 27 (1991), 123–34.

[39] R. B. Peberdy, 'Navigation on the River Thames between London and Oxford in the Late Middle Ages: A Reconsideration', *Oxoniensia*, 61 (1996), 321–5; Campbell, Galloway, Keene, and Murphy, *Medieval Capital and its Grain Supply*, 47–55; S. Oosthuisen, 'Isleham: A Medieval Inland Port', *Landscape History*, 16 (1994), 34.

and informal, which sprang up on arterial roads. A fifteen-mile stretch of Ermine Street in north-east Hertfordshire, for example, had nine licensed markets, and some settlements, such as Caxton (Cambs.) were redeveloped in a more advantageous position on a major routeway.[40] Research into medieval bridges is in its infancy, but enough is known for bridge-building to be seen as an integral component of the commercial advances of the era. Substantial and well-built bridges appear to have replaced fords and ferries on the upper reaches of most English rivers during the Middle Ages, and a concern for bridge maintenance is prominent in royal records.[41]

The most significant development in overland transport was the growing use of horses for traction in the twelfth and thirteenth centuries in preference to oxen. The pace of this change varied according to region and to social group and, in Langdon's opinion, the trend was most pronounced in south-eastern England and among the lower orders of society. In the late thirteenth century around three-quarters of all peasant beasts of burden in East Anglia are thought to have been horses, a considerable expansion since the late eleventh century.[42] As the horse is approximately twice as fast as the ox, a peasant employing horse traction might expect substantial benefits in haulage. Although horses were relatively expensive to keep because they eat far more than oxen, they facilitated a movement to more intensive farming, particularly on lighter soils, as their greater speed in ploughing and harrowing released labour to work on other agricultural tasks. Moreover, because the use of horses rather than oxen doubled the distance which could be covered in a given time, or halved the time which a task took, their adoption clearly helped to reduce transport costs and raise labour productivity. Langdon emphasizes in particular the importance of the horse in

---

[40] C. Taylor, *Roads and Tracks of Britain* (1979), 129–30.

[41] D. F. Harrison, 'Bridges and Economic Development, 1300–1800', *EcHR*, 2nd ser., 45 (1992), 240–61.

[42] J. Langdon, *Horses, Oxen and Technological Innovation: The Use of Draught Animals in English Farming from 1086 to 1500* (Cambridge, 1986), 61, 204–5.

improving access to the market and in widening market opportunities for peasant producers, and thus raising the velocity of goods and money in circulation. He concludes that: 'The rise of horse-hauling and the growth of the market in England occur so closely together as to be almost simultaneous. In any case, it appears they were mutually reinforcing, particularly as horse-hauling was specifically geared to a more active and fast-paced economy.'[43]

The Strengths and Weaknesses of Commercialization Models

This brief review of recent research has highlighted the mounting evidence of substantial commercial and technological progress in medieval England, but it has also revealed how difficult it remains to quantify the extent of commercialization and to measure the impact which it had on the course of economic and social development. Consequently, the implications of these advances are debatable, and they may be used to support a range of contrasting and conflicting conclusions. Were the increases in output and productivity which flowed from them sufficient to offset the potentially adverse consequences of population increase, or did they merely serve to ameliorate temporarily some of the pressure on resources? While it is undeniable that the 'stagnationist' assumptions underlying many Malthusian and Marxist models have been made to look increasingly untenable, it is by no means established that commercialization should be identified as the most dynamic force in medieval European history.

If we accept that the English population peaked at an impressive 6 or 7 million in *c.*1300, then it follows that it could only have reached such a size with the assistance of considerable advances in output

---

[43] Ibid. 272, 286.

and productivity. But some would go further and argue that such advances were cumulatively more powerful still, and that commercialization permitted the growing population before 1348 to maintain or perhaps even to raise its standard of living. The increasing division of labour and greater specialization of production evident in England between *c.*1000 and *c.*1350 created a vastly more flexible and efficient economy, which both stimulated rapid population growth and coped admirably with it. According to Persson, the economy experienced 'a trajectory [which was] a self-sustaining growth process',[44] and for the exuberantly optimistic H. E. Hallam, population pressure brings technological advance and wealth, and he claimed that in eastern England in particular, 'a forward-looking and wide-awake society had developed . . . [and] free and expanding societies in the past have never feared Malthus'.[45]

The welfare of the mass of the population is central to this debate but, because it is not possible to reconstruct peasant household budgets with much degree of accuracy, there are widely differing assessments of the contribution which sales of produce and non-farm employment made to peasant incomes. A pessimist would conclude that nearly half of England's population in the later thirteenth and early fourteenth centuries was extremely susceptible to natural or personal calamity, because the availability of non-agricultural incomes, and the profits of petty commodity production and exchange, were barely sufficient to enable the very high proportions of people with little or no land to subsist in normal years. By contrast, an optimist would view the prevalence of smallholders and landless not as a sign of stress but as confirming the substantial degree of commercial development and occupational adaptation which had occurred since the mid-twelfth century in both the countryside and urban centres, and would see the development of commodity exchange in rural areas as a beneficial trend, rather than as indicative of a

---

[44] For example, Persson, *Pre-industrial Economic Growth*, 72.
[45] *AHEW*, ii. 1007–8.

desperate search for the means to avert a growing vulnerability to dearth.

Hence, it is vitally important to make a balanced and rounded assessment of the evidence which has survived, and it is time to note some caveats and reservations of the body of fact and argument which we have briefly reviewed in a broadly favourable light above. For example, for all the instances of the division of labour in the countryside, occupational specialism did not carry the same connotation in the medieval village as it does in modern times. Almost everyone in the village sought to hold at least a plot of land, and even those people known as brewster, carpenter, tailor, webster, and so forth often turned their hands to other work, as and when they were able to secure it. In addition to these named 'specialists', there were a multitude of villagers who occasionally pursued a wide range of mainly agricultural tasks, many of them semi- and low-skilled. Profit or mere survival encouraged the pursuit of all available sources of income, and workers in the thirteenth and early fourteenth centuries displayed great flexibility in order to capitalize on opportunities in a wide variety of trades and jobs.

This point leads to the heart of the debate on the significance of smallholdings and by-employments in the pre-plague economy. The widespread existence of craft and casual work is indisputable, but the key issue is the degree to which the availability and regularity of work matched up to the needs of those who sought it. Unfortunately, this is a question to which there is no straightforward answer, and defining the extent to which smallholders were able to benefit from marketing their produce is similarly elusive. Neither the regularity with which peasants used rural markets, nor the extent to which rural markets channelled produce into regional markets, can be known with any certainty. The growing influence of the market undoubtedly led some peasants to sow and sell crops for the income that they could gain, and this encouraged a more specialized and efficient use of resources. But the vast majority of peasants were smallholders whose farms were inadequate for subsistence, whose ability to follow such beneficial strategies was severely curtailed and for whom the need to raise money for seigneurial dues deprived their farms of capital as well as their stomachs of food.[46] Commerce in the medieval village could therefore carry very different connotations to commerce in modern times.

An abundance of evidence proves that local trade was commonplace and that there was significant inter-regional trade, but unfortunately the sources often need to be squeezed very hard before they can be made to reveal anything about their relative strength and persistence. It is one thing to demonstrate the existence of trading links between regions, but quite another to be able to prove that they were both regular and substantial. Once again, therefore, there is ample scope for historians to draw different conclusions. Whereas Masschaele believes that the growth of weekly markets reveals the emergence of sophisticated regional trading networks, and an 'ever-deepening interdependency between town and country',[47] the majority of historians continue to believe that it primarily reflects a multiplication of highly localized marketing activity among petty food retailers, craftsmen, and smallholding farmers.[48]

A significant body of recent work increasingly stresses the crucial influence for the modernization of the medieval economy generated by the proliferation of towns and the increase in the proportions of the population living in towns. Despite the greatly enhanced attention which the non-agrarian sector has received over the last couple of decades, and the mounting claims for the significance of the role which it played, Dyer still believes that 'the importance of English towns has been underrated'.[49] But the divisions between town and country should not be made more stark than they actually were. To a very considerable extent the common

---

[46] Britnell, *Commercialisation of English Society*, 121–3. [47] Above, p. 144.

[48] M. Bailey, 'The Commercialisation of the English Economy', *Journal of Medieval History*, 24 (1998), 297–311.

[49] Dyer, 'How Urbanised Was Medieval England?', 183.

run of small market towns sprang from their local rural environments rather than providing an alternative to them. Large numbers of their inhabitants continued to engage in agricultural activities on a part-time basis, and many urban economies continued to be dominated by intensely local trade and agrarian-based activities. Even in towns appreciably higher up the urban scale, local trade continued to predominate and agrarian-based occupations remained vitally important. Similarly, attempts to push up the proportions of the population of who lived in 'towns' rather than the 'countryside' are subject to the same and additional reservations. The most recent attempt would put the urban population of early fourteenth century England at 20 per cent, a far higher figure than any previous estimate, and one which is comparable with the highly urbanized regions of the Netherlands and northern Italy.[50] But this estimate is necessarily based on listings of taxpayers rather than listings of population, which could reflect in a distorting fashion the inclusion of rural areas which were taxed along with neighbouring boroughs and the unsurprising fact that there were disproportionately larger numbers of richer people in the towns than in the countryside.

The progressive achievements of agriculture have been stressed in much recent work, but they must be kept in proportion. The most impressive yields were gained in a few regions highly favoured by soils, climate, and access to large markets. Thus, areas such as eastern Norfolk and coastal Sussex represent the vanguard of agrarian achievement and, supported as they were by exceptional factors, they were untypical of medieval agriculture as a whole. Farming elsewhere was less stimulated by commercial forces and less intensive. The dominance of common field arable systems normally meant that grain production and livestock rearing were less intensive, and yields less impressive, while the sheer extent of the common field arable frequently severely limited the quantity and quality of

[50] Ibid. 173–8.

available grassland, and resulted in low stocking densities.[51] It is in 'ecologically circumscribed common field' regions such as these that the balance between arable and pasture was most precarious by the end of the thirteenth century, and the pessimism about the onset of diminishing and perhaps decreasing returns most relevant. In other parts of England, especially in the natural uplands of the south-west, the Welsh border, and the Pennines, the balance was less precarious but the intensity of farming was even lower.

Clearly, the economic and social complexion of English regions was highly varied, and consequently there was no uniform response to the demographic and commercial changes of the Middle Ages. We find areas of low arable and pastoral productivity, where change had been relatively slow and population pressure relatively light, as well as regions where land productivity was high, and local specialization of production was pronounced. Those areas of medieval England where agrarian advance was most pronounced tended to exhibit similar characteristics: a dense population, a fluid manorial and social structure, flexible field systems, and good water transport to substantial urban markets. In crowded eastern Norfolk, where labour inputs were relatively high, such agricultural efficiency helped to sustain a population which subsisted on ever smaller holdings. There are shades here of the theories of Ester Boserup, who contended that in pre-industrial economies population pressure would stimulate technical change in agriculture.[52] It should be noted, however, that the high levels of land productivity recorded in eastern Norfolk were achieved largely by the use of labour-intensive methods of farming, such as weeding, marling, and manuring, rather than through any revolutionary innovations in agricultural technology.

Advances in transportation and communications were also more selective and less boundless than they are sometimes portrayed.

[51] Campbell, 'Land and People', 95–7.
[52] For example, E. Boserup, *Population and Technology* (Oxford, 1981).

Although real improvements took place in both water and overland transportation, in most areas of economic activity England remained a series of distinct regions rather than a nation. Most significantly, variations in grain prices from region to region could be substantial, indicating that markets for basic foodstuffs in England remained localized and poorly integrated. The great bulk of the commercial output of grain and fodder crops was sold to local markets in most parts of England, and the evidence of manorial accounts indicates that, even in years of high prices, grain did not often travel far overland. Only those locations with ready access to water transport, or with a large town close by, could hope to participate in wider grain markets. Water carriage was far cheaper than overland carriage, but it was not without its limitations.[53] Prominent inland waterways as well as lesser ones were liable to obstruction or were periodically impassable, and a recent work, otherwise enthusiastically supportive of the growth in the scale and sophistication of England's trade in the twelfth and thirteenth centuries, has concluded that, whatever the improvements in inland waterways, riverine transport remained twice as expensive as coastal transport due to the problems caused by river obstructions and seasonal variations in water levels.[54] Finally, although cheap for compact and costly items like wool, cloth, tin, and wine, road transport remained expensive for low priced bulky goods. While livestock could be moved long distances on the hoof for little cost, the overland carriage of bulky, low-value commodities like fuel, lime, marl, and stone was prohibitively expensive over all but the shortest distances.

Although the data does not exist to measure changes in the real cost of carriage over time, there is good reason to believe that improvements in the transport system did result in a fall in the unit costs

[53] Bailey, 'Peasant Welfare', 234–6; J. Langdon, 'Inland Water Transportation in Medieval England', *Journal of Historical Geography*, 19 (1993), 1–11; Galloway and Murphy, 'Feeding the City', p. 11

[54] J. Masschaele, 'The Transport Costs of Medieval England', *EcHR*, 2nd ser., 46 (1993), 273.

of carrying goods to and from markets in the course of the twelfth and thirteenth centuries. When this achievement is combined with the well-documented reduction in search costs and the risks of trade, then it is certain that transaction costs also fell in real terms. The greater the fall in transaction costs the more it follows that factor and commodity markets could have undergone a transformation, with wide beneficial implications for the economy as a whole. But if, despite the fall, transaction costs still remained relatively high, then the significance of the improvement would seem to lie primarily in enabling the economy to accommodate the rapidly increasing flows of goods. Inevitably, the sources do not provide a definitive answer.

The Abstract Modelling of Commercialization

Since we lack precise information on a wide range of crucial areas, those who seek to model the impact of commercialization on England's economic development have to make a number of essentially subjective judgements and assumptions about key economic facts. These speculations are then integrated into a theoretical framework and, in some cases, into mathematical equations which seek to predict overall economic performance. It is perhaps not coincidental that the more theoretical and abstract approaches, which are relatively unhampered by the complexities and contradictions of the actual evidence, tend to arrive at the firmest conclusions. Notable among the more recent of such attempts to model the impact of commercialization on the English economy between the eleventh century and the early fourteenth, are those of Karl Gunnar Persson and Graeme Snooks. Both present extremely positive outcomes, which are in direct conflict with the main assumptions and conclusions of neo-Malthusian and Marxist interpretations.

Whereas the pessimism of the demographic model stems from the presumption that population growth must eventually result in diminishing returns, Persson's model stresses that 'population growth endogenously creates countervailing forces to diminishing returns'. A 'dynamic model' is thereby substituted for a 'stagnationist model'.[55] As we have seen, there can be no dispute that such countervailing forces were at work in many sectors of the economy, but Persson's optimism about the eventual outcome for living standards stems from his belief that the strength of the beneficial effects of technological progress in agriculture, of the increase in the urbanization ratio, and of the loosening of seigneurial and feudal restraints, were more than sufficient to overwhelm any deleterious tendencies in the economy stemming from the increasing numbers of people. As a consequence, instead of suffering in a Malthusian and Ricardian fashion from the pressure of excess population, the per capita income of Englishmen and women actually rose. Persson is therefore able to conclude 'that the demographic interpretation cannot be upheld as a general model for European history, and its validity for English economic history can also be challenged'.[56]

Persson also launches a fierce assault on Marxist models. We have seen that Brenner, following in the tradition of Dobb and Kosminsky, argues that the intensification of exploitation of the English peasantry through the institution of serfdom deprived them of the resources with which to farm efficiently and resulted in 'technological retardation', which eventually destabilized the economy and led to crisis in the early fourteenth century. But for Persson one of the beneficial effects of a combination of a rising population and a commercializing economy was a loosening of feudal bonds and, eventually, the dissolution of the manor. Developments between *c.*1000 and *c.*1300, in particular the advance of monetization and trade, and the growth of population and the

---

[55] Persson, *Pre-industrial Economic Growth*, esp. 67–88.   [56] Ibid. 78.

increasing demand for land, made lords aware that they were in possession of marketable assets, and since under these market conditions they did not have to coerce their serfs to hold land or enforce labour services, 'the cash nexus replaced personal obligations'. Moreover, the whole beneficial process was self-reinforcing. Persson, like Brenner, believes that the manor was an inherently inefficient productive unit, but in his view its early decline stimulated yet more improvements in specialization and technical change, thereby creating the impetus for the further erosion of customary relations. Hence, he argues that during the twelfth and thirteenth centuries the lifting of many servile obligations not only allowed the bulk of the English rural population a greater degree of personal freedom, it made them more productive. As they were now more mobile, and increasingly paid their dues in cash rather than labour services, peasants had greater freedom of time and action to respond to 'demand conditions and (to be) technologically adaptive'. Further gains to overall efficiency also stemmed from the fact that serfs now willingly held land on customary terms, which were normally below market levels, and that whereas 'social factors' (feudalism) had once been essential to bind them to the land, now 'real factors' (land scarcity and population pressure) held them there. Thus, demographic growth fuelled, and in turn was fuelled by, changes in property relations and commercialization: these were interactive and interdependent rather than conflicting processes, and ultimately they substantially raised productivity and economic capacity.[57]

Persson's interpretation of the thirteenth-century English economy is therefore fundamentally different from that of Marxists, in both his description and his explanation of the main economic developments. He also draws attention to a logical flaw in the basic assumptions of traditional Marxist models concerning the early fourteenth-century crisis, namely that it was a crisis brought about by the distribution of income rather than by the level of total income that the economy produced. Whereas Brenner would see

---

[57] Persson, *Pre-industrial Economic Growth*, esp. 65–7, 82, 88.

the source of the crisis in the excessive rate of feudal levies which enriched the lords and starved the peasantry, Persson stresses that 'a change in the distribution of income in favour of peasants will not divert the economy from its long-term equilibrium'.[58] This is because, if population is behaving in a Malthusian fashion, a reduction in the amounts of rent and other charges borne by tenants would only lead to a temporary increase in their incomes, since higher incomes would stimulate further population growth which would in turn depress incomes again.

The hypotheses of Snooks offer strong support to a number of Persson's conclusions.[59] In fact Snooks provides an even more exuberantly optimistic vision of the achievements of England's economy under the stimulus of a high and rising population, by claiming that in real terms the total output of the economy (Gross Domestic Product: GDP) rose more than sevenfold between Domesday Book (1086) and the turn of the thirteenth and fourteenth centuries. As a consequence, after taking account of the increase in population, real GDP per head virtually doubled. Of course, such figures are extremely speculative, since they are derived from a combination of mathematical modelling and raw data drawn from Domesday Book projected forwards to Gregory King's famous estimates dating from the late seventeenth century. According to Snooks, the prodigious achievements revealed by his computations rested in large part on a significant 'growth in the size and efficiency of commodity and, especially, factor markets, that promoted a more effective allocation of resources . . . [and] the growing involvement of the unfree peasantry in them', with the result that 'population, natural resources, technology, economic organisation and real GDP per capita all interacted with each other in a positive fashion'.[60]

If one accepts the proposition that commercialization was a powerful, self-perpetuating beneficial influence on the medieval

[58] Ibid. 75.
[59] Snooks, 'The Dynamic Role of the Market', 27–54. Similar arguments are deployed in Snooks, *Economics Without Time*, 238–55.
[60] 'Dynamic Role of the Market', 51, 54.

economy, then it follows logically that major economic shocks and turning points would not have been caused by endogenous forces, such as overpopulation or social crises, but rather by exogenous or chance events. The more successful the economy was in coping with the rise in population, and responding positively to its stimulus, the less case there is for seeing the early fourteenth-century economy beset by an internally generated 'systemic' crisis. Thus, it had to be the chance occurrence of freak weather conditions which was responsible for the devastating famines and agrarian crises of 1315–22, and equally fortuitous was the arrival of the exceptionally virulent disease which caused the Black Death and subsequent epidemics, and owed little or nothing to the economic and social condition prevailing in the regions which it visited. Persson therefore maintains that 'the hypothesis of a general crisis in the early fourteenth century caused by overpopulation cannot be upheld'.[61]

Commercialization models such as these furnish an explanatory framework for the mass of recent research which points unerringly to the positive impact of trade and urbanization on the medieval economy. Indeed, by demonstrating that demographic, commercial, and institutional changes could interplay and interact beneficially in a mutually reinforcing and immensely powerful fashion, they can provide a salutary antidote to excessively stagnationist approaches to pre-industrial economies. Yet, for all the boldness of their overarching interpretations, a gulf exists between the thrust of this modelling and the available evidence. At the heart of these models lie estimates, equations, and selective economic theory rather than solid empirical data. Snooks constructs his model around his own highly contentious conjectures of a dramatic growth in England's GDP and real income per head during the early medieval centuries. His transmutation of Domesday data on manorial values into output figures, and thence into the GDP of England, provides the essential underpinning of his assertion that England subsequently experienced rates of economic growth which rivalled those of the

---

[61] *Pre-industrial Economic Growth*, 86.

early decades of the Industrial Revolution. Yet, if the output of Domesday England is placed at an appreciably higher level, which is where most medievalists believe it should be, the extraordinary rate of subsequent growth disappears.[62] However, this does not exhaust the problems with Snooks's modelling. Major difficulties for the consistency of his hypotheses are created by his belief that, in stark contrast to the preceding era, growth had virtually ceased by the end of the thirteenth century and went into reverse in the early fourteenth, and, what is more, that it did so because 'population growth began to outrun the supply of natural resources and/or methods of using them more productively'.[63] This is a frankly neo-Malthusian explanation of the early fourteenth century 'crisis', and it sits incongruously alongside Snooks's enthusiastically Smithian interpretation of the preceding era. But he does not attempt to resolve the paradox, and we are offered no explanation of how an endogenously generated crisis of subsistence happened around 1300 when, according to his own estimates, the level of per capita income was almost twice as high as it had been in the late eleventh and twelfth centuries, which he sees as an era of remarkable economic and demographic growth.

Persson's analysis does somewhat less violence to logic and the world as most medievalists would understand it, but his methodology remains problematic. It is one thing to accept the potential benefits and efficiency gains which could derive from increasing specialization, shifts in the distribution of income, increasing returns in urban production, and technical progress, but quite another to conclude with certainty that these forces were able to offset entirely the harmful effects of the increasing density of population in medieval England. Persson attempts to prove his hypothesis through mathematical equations and economic modelling, but despite their superficially objective appearances the outcome of such abstract procedures is in no way impartial. In fact the product of his formulae depends

---

[62] See e.g. the criticisms of Snooks's estimates and the counter-proposals offered by Mayhew and by Dyer in Britnell and Campbell (eds.), *Commercialising Economy*, 195–8.
[63] 'The Dynamic Role of the Market', 53.

crucially upon the relative weightings which he assigns at the out-set to the variables which they incorporate. Deciding what those weightings should be is a subjective exercise which ultimately draws on guesswork, and the author of the statistical appendix to Persson's work admits with disarming frankness that choosing which weight-ings to apply is 'a question which a priori reasoning cannot answer'.[64] Many others who adopt a similar mathematical approach also con-fess to this fundamental problem, but most remain distinctly coy about its full implications for the viability of their conclusions.

Unfortunately, a priori reasoning on this scale is rarely informed by a close acquaintance with the complex and rapidly growing body of detailed evidence which is emerging on medieval England. Nor are the deficiencies of a highly generalized approach merely restricted to the medievalist's familiar litany of local variations. Coherent models demand powerful assumptions and straightforward linkages, but in the real world relationships and feedback are often far more complex and difficult to predict. Even the assumption so fundamental to these commercialization models, that population growth stimulates economic development, does not hold true in all circumstances. In practice a gap often existed between the broad economic incentives created by population growth and the econo-mic reality faced by individual producers and consumers. In their enthusiasm to stress the overall stimulus which demand gave to economic development, proponents of commercialization tend to overlook the existence of constraining forces on supply and the oper-ation of negative feedback in various sectors of the economy.

Regardless of the incentives created by population growth, great farmers often chose to follow political, social, and religious rather than economic priorities, and problems of capital scarcity and unstable product prices often resulted in small farmers adopting risk-averting production strategies. Such behaviour was often entirely appropriate for those who adopted it, but harmful for the economy

---

[64] *Pre-industrial Economic Growth*, 103.

at large and it helped to create bottlenecks to agrarian progress. The premiss that the demands from large towns could stimulate agricultural productivity in those regions which supplied them is wholly acceptable, but it does not follow from this that the overall productivity of English agriculture was raised substantially by such stimuli, still less that there were few constraints to growth in the agricultural sector as a whole. One obvious major constraint was the scarcity of large towns. Grantham has recently argued, in an extended hypothesis which in some ways complements the work of Persson and Snooks, that the level of urban demand constituted the major determinant of economic development in pre-industrial Western Europe, and that towns with populations of up to 250,000 could have been supplied without difficulty by direct marketing of produce by the farmers in their hinterlands.[65] But despite the crucial part which it plays in his argument, he pays insufficient attention to the question of what constrained the further growth of the urban sector, except to suggest briefly that expansion was primarily limited by disease.[66] Yet the reasons why the populations of modern towns are so much larger than those of medieval towns, extend far beyond matters of food supply and health. Excessive concentration on growth and development and a failure to explore adequately the restraining forces on key elements in economy and society render some interpretations open to charges of uncritical optimism.

The Empirical and Eclectic Modelling of Commercialization

Historians well acquainted with the documents of the Middle Ages have also been committed to assessing the nature and impact

---

[65] Grantham, 'Espace privilégies', 695–725.   [66] Ibid. 700–3.

of commercialization on England, and to testing the theoretical models of Smith and von Thünen. B. M. S. Campbell's contribution has been especially notable, and he has pioneered investigations into the vital role played by great cities as 'forcing grounds of commercial agriculture'.[67] In conjunction with researchers on the 'Feeding the City' project, he has demonstrated that the growth of London in the twelfth and thirteenth centuries furnished a concentration of demand which stimulated the intensification and commercialization of agricultural production in its hinterland.[68] Additionally, from his research into demesne farm accounts at the production end of the supply chain, Campbell has been able to show that in some parts of medieval England the productivity of land could rise to impressive levels when operating under the right conditions.[69]

Campbell's work therefore constitutes an important addition to knowledge, but its significance is capable of misinterpretation. The ability to attain strikingly high yields on certain demesne farms does not prove that the overall performance of medieval agriculture was far higher than we had previously thought, still less that there were no significant agricultural restraints on medieval economic development.[70] The bumper yields found on some demesnes in eastern Norfolk, and in a few other highly favoured locations, demonstrate what could be achieved when the exceptional stimuli of high and consistent demand met with a wholehearted response from the owners of farms which enjoyed perhaps the most propitious soils and climate for grain production in England. But they do not provide any basis for arguing that our estimates of average land productivity in medieval England should now be raised: the returns from

[67] B. M. S. Campbell, 'Measuring the Commercialisation of Seigneurial Agriculture *c.*1300', in Britnell and Campbell (eds.), *Commercialising Economy*, 136.

[68] Campbell, Galloway, Keene, and Murphy, *Medieval Capital and its Grain Supply*.

[69] The findings are summarized in Campbell, 'Land and People'.

[70] S. R. Epstein has argued that 'recent improvements in methods of measurement have substantially raised earlier estimates of pre-modern agricultural productivity' (*The Late Medieval Crisis as an 'Integration Crisis'*, LSE Working Papers in Economic History, 46 (1998), 5).

hundreds of demesne farms demonstrate conclusively that it remained relatively low.[71]

The existence among farmers of the requisite technical knowledge to raise grain yields and output is of far less significance for
productivity than the extent of its adoption. There were a multitude of reasons why average yields did not approximate more closely
to the high levels achieved in a few places, which had far more to
do with the broad structure of English society and economy than
with knowledge of agrarian practices. Contrary to the assumptions
of some historians, the maximization of yields was only rarely the
prime aim of farmers, and rightly so, for commercial farmers pre-
ferred high profits to high yields and the two did not necessarily go
hand in hand. There was little that was secret about the beneficial
effects on the size of the harvest of regular and thorough weeding,
of marling, of collecting and digging in manure, or of breaking up
the large clods of clay before sowing. But it was equally well known
how very labour intensive and expensive such practices were, even
in an era of low wages. Hence, they were employed selectively rather
than universally. Routines which could have raised yields substantially were unlikely to be pursued unless they were cost-effective,
and this was dependent upon market stimuli. This is precisely why
there is a positive correlation between advanced agriculture and urban
demand. Furthermore, most of the routines applied to raise land
productivity tended to do so at the expense of labour productivity
on the farm, even in the most successful regions. In other words,
the highest yields depended upon cheap labour, and therefore were
the fruit of poverty rather than a solution for it.

Although it may be true to conclude that 'as an agent of change
commercialisation possessed a momentum of its own',[72] the limits
to the achievements it fostered in the Middle Ages must be appraised

---

[71] A prodigious quantity of data on demesne yields has now been amassed. A useful
summary of its implications is given in Rigby, *English Society in the Later Middle Ages*, 94.

[72] Campbell, Galloway, Keene, and Murphy, *Medieval Capital and its Grain Supply*, 10.

critically. Simple theories of the importance of urban demand in stimulating agricultural improvements and commercial attitudes are not borne out by the evidence, which reveals instead that practice was frequently neither straightforward, consistent, nor readily explicable in such terms. Though high and consistent demand might be a necessary stimulus to heavy investment and the application of costly techniques, it was certainly not an essential prerequisite of efficient farm management. The owners and managers of poorly located farms also tried to make the best of them. Moreover, even within the ambit of large towns many demesne farmers resisted opportunities to dispose of their produce on the market, using it instead to feed their households. Nor was the impact of commerce invariably rewarding, for there are strong reasons for supposing it could create grave risks and consequent liabilities for smallholders.[73]

We must also be careful not to overestimate the scale of urban demand. It is true that 'during the thirteenth century major centres of market demand began to emerge, and the commercial opportunities that these offered clearly induced many producers to become more actively and selectively involved in the market',[74] but such centres were few in number and touched a small proportion of farmers. Location was of vital importance, but even the influence of London must be put into context. Although the capital, with a maximum population of 100,000 around 1300, was much bigger than any other city in the realm, it was also much smaller than it was to become in the late seventeenth century, when it is thought to have contained some 600,000 people, comprising over 11 per cent of England's total population. Since the impact of the bloated capital's appetite on the nation's agriculture at this later date has been a matter of dispute, we must clearly beware of exaggerating the influence which it could have exerted four centuries earlier when

---

[73] Campbell, 'Measuring the Commercialisation', 154–62, 185–92; Bailey, 'Peasant Welfare', 232–3, 237–45.

[74] Campbell, 'Measuring the Commercialisation', 193.

it was only one-sixth of the size.[75] Moreover, we know that the influence of lesser but still sizeable towns did not extend very far beyond their walls. For example, it is thought that Colchester, with a population of around 3,000 in the early fourteenth century, drew its food from within an eight-mile radius, and that even within this area it did not dominate supplies.[76] England's population was overwhelmingly rural, and the bulk of urban dwellers lived in towns smaller than Colchester. It was inevitable, therefore, that 'it was in the countryside rather than the towns that the bulk of demand was concentrated, with the result that the market for agricultural produce remained fragmented and dispersed'.[77] Such considerations help to place in a broader perspective Grantham's recent attempt to make urban demand the prime force propelling medieval agricultural technology forwards at a rapid pace.

Sustained, large-scale, urban demand may have been necessary to produce the maximum stimulus to raising agricultural productivity, but the absence of a nearby urban market did not mean that farmers lacked the motivation to make profitable use of their land. They may not have had the incentive to maximize yields at all costs, but they did have an incentive to cultivate their lands in a businesslike and flexible manner which responded to local market conditions and to changes in the relative prices and yields of different crops and livestock. The manor of Hinderclay (Suffolk) was landlocked, outside the normal range of any urban market, and the intensity of agricultural production on its demesne was relatively low, but in the early fourteenth century it was managed with considerable efficiency and with the local market firmly in mind.[78]

---

[75] J. Chartres, 'Food Consumption and Internal Trade', in A. L. Beier and R. Finlay (eds.), *London, 1500–1700: The Making of the Metropolis* (1986), 168–96. Chartres concludes that 'While stressing, therefore, the growth of London [from 1600–1750] as a potent force in the commercialisation of agriculture it was not a magic wand' (p. 184).

[76] R. H. Britnell, *Growth and Decline in Colchester, 1300–1525* (Cambridge, 1986), 43–7.

[77] Campbell, 'Measuring the Commercialisation', 193. See also D. L. Farmer, 'Marketing the Produce of the Countryside, 1200–1500', in *AHEW*, iii. 329.

[78] D. Stone, 'Medieval Farm Management and Technological Mentalities: Evidence from Hinderclay', forthcoming.

Britnell's contribution to our knowledge of the commercialization of medieval English society is as weighty as Campbell's, yet his assessment of its impact is more cautious. While documenting in detail the benefits which flowed from the proliferation of markets, from record-keeping and the legal and regulatory environment of trade, the growth of urban populations, the expansion of the money supply, and improvements in transport, Britnell retains a sharp eye for limitations. He stresses that the urban, technical, and occupational advances of the Middle Ages were not continuous, and that the gains attendant upon them were unevenly distributed both socially and regionally. Further, by the mid-thirteenth century the major improvements in agrarian productivity, urbanization, and marketing had already been attained, and there were few additional significant advances in the succeeding decades when population pressure peaked. Commercial and technical change in pre-plague England undoubtedly enabled some communities to absorb more people, but it could not prevent a fall in the standard of living of the majority before the Black Death.[79]

A proper understanding of the nature, efficiency, and quality of medieval England's commercial infrastructure is central to any assessment of the extent of economic development, and its implications for welfare, particularly before the Black Death. The growing number and sophistication of commercial institutions in the twelfth and thirteenth centuries did not signify a commensurate growth in free and equal access to the market, because legal controls over trade in the Middle Ages were not intended to secure cheap and ready participation for as many as possible. Rather their object was to extend and protect the control of commercial activity, including monopolistic trading rights, for the profit of a few beneficiaries, and this inevitably restricted the scale of any reduction in the transaction costs of marketing for most producers. Commercial activity was free of neither restrictions nor inequalities.

---

[79] For example, Britnell, *Commercialisation of English Society*, 123–7.

Furthermore, we can also usefully distinguish between 'compulsory' and 'voluntary' involvement in the market. Many peasants sold part of their produce in order to obtain the necessary cash for rents, fines, and taxes, as opposed to engaging 'in commerce for the sake of the profits they could earn'. Hence, for them 'the sale of produce was often detrimental to their consumption and investment, and consequently to the productivity of their farming.' There is considerable truth in the proposition that the growth of rural markets reflected in part a system of involuntary, or 'forced', marketing, where many transactions were driven by neither free market forces nor a desire to be more efficient or productive. Moreover, if we compare the plethora of small markets and fairs in medieval England with the leaner, and less 'public', marketing system of later centuries, then we might well conclude that the former is a quantitative system of marketing and the latter a qualitative system.[80]

It has been noted in other chapters how difficult it is to formulate models which can be applied with equal cogency to the contrasting conditions of the earlier and the later Middle Ages, and commercialization models are no exception. Logic demands that because population growth is seen as the power which drives commercial expansion, demographic collapse ought to bring commercial retrenchment, when the self-sustaining forces of commercial progression are transformed into self-sustaining forces for regression. And this is precisely what some theorists claim to find occurring after 1350: namely declining labour productivity in towns, a rise in the price of urban goods relative to agrarian goods, a retreat into rural self-sufficiency, a fall in the rate of innovation, and, even, a pronounced fall in GDP, not only in aggregate but in per caput terms.[81]

But, once again, history did not obey theory. There is a mass of evidence which is not compatible with the assumption that

---

[80] Ibid. 120–3, 161–71; Bailey, 'Commercialisation', 306–7.
[81] Persson, *Pre-industrial Economic Growth*, 87–8; Snooks, *Economics Without Time*, 256–64.

a simple linear relationship existed between long-term flows in population and the rate of technological change and urban growth and contraction. Although there are abundant signs of falling production and trade in the century and a half after the Black Death, there is no reason to believe that output fell faster than population, that a smaller proportion of output was traded, that a smaller proportion of the population lived in towns, or that the quality of England's commercial infrastructure declined significantly. On the contrary, many historians would argue that commercial progress continued to be made, and, of course, the later Middle Ages is remarkable for its exceptionally high living standards. The improved purchasing power of the masses strengthened the demand for a range of basic consumer goods, which led to a greater degree of commercialization in their manufacture and distribution. Increased specialization can also be found in many branches of agriculture, as peasant farmers were able to shed the subsistence and risk-aversion strategies that they had been forced to adopt before the onset of plague.

The Early Fourteenth-Century Crisis Revisited

Finally, we must return to the big question of whether the basic character of the English economy was transformed by the commercialization which took place before the mid-fourteenth century, and in particular whether the economy had been endowed with the capability of springing the Malthusian trap, and supporting high and even rising levels of population without disastrous consequences? The most optimistic modellers would argue that it had, and that the acute instability of the early fourteenth-century economy resulted from chance blows from the outside inflicted by war, taxation, climatic deterioration, and, ultimately, plague. On the other hand, an awareness of the constraints to economic development in medieval

England and of the extent of regional variations in economic experience must caution even dedicated proponents of commercial progress against employing simplistic models as explanatory tools for economic change. Rather than identifying one primary mover, the general importance of changes in population, commerce, and property relations in driving economic change must be acknowledged, along with pronounced regional and temporal variations in such influences. In a recent contribution Campbell explains economic change in the late thirteenth and early fourteenth centuries by a combination of extreme disruptive forces (such as war, excessive taxation, climatic change) which precipitated environmental degradation and ecological decline.[82] Similarly, stress must be placed upon the limitations of the market in the Middle Ages, and in particular the lack of concentrated urban demand across most of England which acted as a barrier to further dramatic improvement and specialization in agriculture.

Most historians now readily acknowledge that commercial activity played a significant part in medieval economic development, with the result that 'traditional notions of a peasant economy based on the unitary family economy [have been replaced by] . . . a more hybrid concept, based on mixed semi-commercial pastoral and cereal husbandry, lightly capitalised marketing, and industrial and craft enterprises'.[83] However, those who emphasize the benefits of commercialization are sometimes tempted to neglect the fortunes of the poorer strata of society, who were a substantial and growing proportion of the population in late thirteenth- and early fourteenth-century England, and they fail to give full weight to the evidence that agrarian production among the landless and smallholding peasantry took the form of an increasingly precarious economic

[82] B. M. S. Campbell, 'Ecology Versus Economics in Late Thirteenth and Early Fourteenth-Century English Agriculture', in D. Sweeney (ed.), *Agriculture in the Middle Ages: Technology, Practice and Representation* (Philadelphia, 1995), 76–108.

[83] K. Biddick, 'Malthus in a Straightjacket: Analysing Agrarian Change in Medieval England', *Journal of Interdisciplinary History*, 20 (1990), 631.

dualism, which was acutely vulnerable to disruption by a range of factors. The extent of the benefits bestowed by technical progress, urbanization, specialization, and diversification, especially around 1300, must not be overstated. They were regionally and socially specific, and it would be unwise to regard commercialization as an economic or social panacea in medieval England.

Perhaps the most balanced judgement on the impact of commercialization in the central Middle Ages is to conclude that it played a major role in enabling the population to rise to a level which was not to be reached again until the later eighteenth century. This was indeed a striking achievement, but it falls 'far short of representing the decisive transformation of the economy which would have been required to postpone indefinitely the adverse consequences of the progressive reduction in the amount of land per head available to the rural majority of Englishmen'.[84] In this context, it may be instructive to consider the implications of a local study of the manor of Coltishall, located in north-east Norfolk, one of the most commercialized and economically precocious regions of England, where the yields of demesnes were prodigiously high, where by-employments were readily available, and where the inhabitants enjoyed considerable personal freedom. Yet, despite all these advantages, Coltishall failed to exhibit the boundless economic benefits of commercialization which some of the more optimistic modellers believe were widely available throughout England. On the contrary, in Coltishall in the first half of the fourteenth century 'all the classic features of land hunger were present, notably farm fragmentation, morcellation, immiseration and a mounting vulnerability to harvest failure'.[85] The doleful experience of even this exceptionally well-located and well-endowed manor is a salutary warning that the benefits of commercialization were not limitless and did not provide a

[84] Miller and Hatcher, *Towns, Commerce and Crafts*, 402.
[85] B. M. S. Campbell, 'Population Pressure, Inheritance and the Land Market in a Fourteenth-Century Community', in R. M. Smith (ed.), *Land, Kinship and Life-cycle* (Cambridge, 1984), 127.

universal solution to the poverty of the masses. More than that, it suggests that a growing dependence on the market could carry potential liabilities and risks for a high and rising proportion of the population in an economy where land was scarce, prices were likely to fluctuate dramatically, and loanable funds were chronically short.

5

The Importance of Time and Place

It should be clear by now that all of the three main models used to explain economic and social development in the Middle Ages have weaknesses as well as strengths. In this chapter we focus on their weaknesses, both specific and generic, and seek to explore these failings from three different perspectives. The first exposes the difficulties which emerge when the models are applied to the later Middle Ages as well as to the earlier. The second reviews a few of the wide range of alternative models which have been proposed, since every alternative model is in itself a statement of the inadequacies of the others. And the third perspective seeks to test the validity of the assumptions and methods of each of the major supermodels by applying them not to the history of the whole of medieval economy and society but to a particular element within it, in this case serfdom in England.

The Later Middle Ages

In the preceding chapters much more space has been devoted to examining attempts to model the economy of the era between the Norman Conquest and the Black Death than that of the later Middle Ages. In part this was done in order to make our task more manageable, not least because the stark contrasts between many leading characteristics of the twelfth and thirteenth centuries and those of the fourteenth and fifteenth centuries make it difficult to incorporate both eras into the same narrative. But the balance also reflects the priorities of the models themselves, which focus on the long period of expansion which culminated in the decades preceding the Black Death. None of the leading models devotes an equivalent amount of attention to the later Middle Ages. In the event, however, this relative neglect proved providential for the modellers, since England in the later fourteenth and fifteenth centuries is an even more testing environment for models of long-term economic and social change than the preceding era.

As we have seen, both neo-Malthusian and Marxist analyses place great emphasis on the progressive impoverishment of the mass of the peasantry in the thirteenth century and on a decisive change occurring in the path of economic and social development before the Black Death. From the perspective of the former approach, the agrarian crises and demographic setbacks of the first half of the four-teenth century are the inevitable consequence of over-expansion. While from the perspective of the pre-eminence of class conflict, they are the inevitable consequence of a prevailing system which impoverished the peasantry by excessive exactions, denied the agricultural base essential investment and innovation, and distorted patterns of income and expenditure by the extreme concentration of wealth in the hands of feudal magnates and the Church.

In neo-Malthusian modelling, the decisive reversal of population growth well before 1348 is the predictable outcome of the long centuries of rising population which preceded it. But the length and scale of the ensuing demographic malaise, which by common consensus spanned the greater part of two centuries and resulted in the loss of perhaps two-thirds of the population, is far less easy to accommodate within the same explanatory framework. The fact that the collapse of late medieval population appears to have owed so little to movements in living standards and so much more to the ravages of disease, worsens the predicament, since external influences such as plague cannot be allowed much significance without severely weakening the explanatory power of neo-Malthusian models.

Living standards and the availability of land are the primary regulators of the level of population in neo-Malthusian analysis. According to the logic of the 'high-pressure version' of the model, the crisis of the early fourteenth century was essentially a crisis of production and subsistence, in which levels of output were insufficient for the excessive numbers of people it had to sustain. Under such conditions, mortality would rise and scythe back the population until, after an appropriate reduction in numbers and elapse of time, competition for land, work, and food would abate, living standards would rise and mortality fall. Thereby the decline in population would be brought to an end and be reversed. But this hypothetical sequence is in stark contrast to the actual experience of the fourteenth and fifteenth centuries, when population plummeted precipitously and an increasing abundance of land and sharply improving real wages failed to bring a halt to long-term decline. If anything, the 'low-pressure' variant of the Malthusian model is an even worse fit. For if population were being regulated primarily by prudential checks to the birth rate, we would expect setbacks in total numbers to have been relatively modest, as delays in marriage and restrictions on family size would slow the rise in population to a halt well before the economy was plunged into a prolonged and severe crisis.

Malthus did not put a time frame on the 'perpetual oscillation' which he projected between the upswings and downswings of population and, although he admitted that the phenomenon was less regular in real life than in theory, he certainly did not contemplate irregularities on the scale of the later medieval downswing. Precisely what would have happened to the course of England's population if the Black Death had not intervened is a question to which no categoric answer may be given, but on the basis of the evidence currently available it seems probable that the early fourteenth-century decline had slowed before 1348, and may have been halted or even reversed.[1] If this were the case, such a sequence would seem to fit the character of the oscillations envisaged by Malthus, as indeed does the experience of England in the later seventeenth century, when, after more than a century of growth, population fell by at most 10 per cent and then stagnated for around fifty years.[2]

In a rather half-hearted attempt to fit the later medieval evidence into a Malthusian and Ricardian framework, Postan suggested that overcultivation and under-manuring in the thirteenth century had inflicted long-term damage on the arable heartlands of England, and that this lowering of the productive capacity restrained the ability of the population to recover in the fifteenth century. But this interpretation runs directly counter to the cheap food and adequate harvests which characterize the era, and the inability of Postan to explain the experience of the late Middle Ages in terms consistent with the parameters applied to the twelfth and thirteenth centuries highlights a profound weakness in his model. A more promising explanation of the persistence of demographic decline and stagnation after 1350 is offered by Le Roy Ladurie's willingness to allow more and more room in his overtly Malthusian model to specifically epidemic and, as he terms them, 'biological' factors. He suggests that 'side by side with properly and traditionally Malthusian factors' one must allow

---

[1] For recent discussions, see R. M. Smith, 'Demographic Developments in Rural England, 1300–1348: A Survey', in Campbell (ed.), *Before the Black Death*, 25–77; Miller and Hatcher, *Towns, Commerce and Crafts*, 419–21.

[2] Quinquennial estimates of the size of England's population at this time are given in E. A. Wrigley and R. S. Schofield, *The Population History of England, 1541–1871: A Reconstruction* (1981), 528–9.

space for 'strictly epidemic causality'.[3] This may well be true, but any advance in the acknowledgement of the power of exogenous disease in the form of plague and other lethal afflictions must cause a commensurate retreat in the strength of the case for imposing a Malthusian framework on the medieval and early modern European experience. In the event, such liberalization does far graver damage to Ladurie's Malthusian explanatory framework than he is prepared to admit.

We must conclude, therefore, that population often did not behave in a Malthusian fashion. It would seem impossible to deny that epidemic disease played a significant role in the contraction of England's population from probably over 6 million at its peak in the early fourteenth century to little more than 2 million at its trough in the fifteenth century,[4] and that as a consequence it must be included as a major element in the pattern of causality which determined the contraction of the economy, the abandonment of aristocratic demesne farming, the decline of serfdom, and the rise of leasehold and copyhold tenures at the expense of unfree customary tenures. To stress the power of autonomous disease in shaping the course of later medieval economic and social development is, however, far from denying that society and economy was not subjected to pressures of a Malthusian or neo-Malthusian type. The essential logic behind the proposition that population growth will be stimulated by high living standards and eventually inhibited or reversed by hardship and poverty is inescapable. However, such relationships

---

[3] 'A Reply to Robert Brenner', in Aston and Philpin (eds.), *Brenner Debate*, 102–3.

[4] Attempts have been made to argue that it was low fertility rather than high mortality which drove population lower in the late Middle Ages and restrained it from recovering. Speculations on the processes by which fertility might have been depressed have included: improved employment prospects for women and an increase in the proportions of the population employed as servants, which led to delayed marriage and an increase in celibacy; and family limitation within marriage which stemmed either from the desire to defend the rise in living standards or from the reluctance to bring children into a disease-ridden world. However, even if low fertility were shown to be the driving force behind the demographic decline and stagnation (which is disputed in Bailey, 'Demographic Decline'), it would still be the case that the whole process of falling fertility was set in motion by exceptionally high mortality.

between population and resources were far from being the sole or consistent prime movers behind change and development because they were not free to operate unhindered, and other powerful forces and events frequently intervened. Those who favour a demographic explanation of the events of the later Middle Ages are thus faced with a choice between a coherent and universally applicable theoretical model, on the one hand, and the untidiness of historical reality on the other.

Those who would espouse an exclusively socio-political explanation are confronted with a similar dilemma. Brenner attempts to sidestep the massive threat posed by the role of disease to his version of the Marxist model by dealing with it only in passing, and largely in conjectural footnotes. In a series of asides he questions whether the plague was 'wholly exogenous', and clutches at straws by hypothesizing that plague followed outbreaks of famine, and that the eventual decline of the incidence of plague was linked to the improved nutrition of the masses.[5] Ironically, if such speculations were shown to be true, they would lend considerable support to the Malthusian interpretation, which is precisely the intellectual enemy which Brenner is striving to defeat. In reality, however, his musings have little substance because they run counter to the overwhelming weight of both medical and historical evidence. A more popular fallback position for Marxists is to deny a major causal role to disease by asserting that the collapse of population precipitated by the Black Death of 1348–50 only affected the timing of a crisis of feudalism which was in any event inevitable because of the inexorable operation of internal destructive forces. But for this line of reasoning to constitute a satisfactory answer requires the acceptance of the dubious proposition that the crisis of feudalism would have taken essentially the same form and have had essentially the same consequences for the long-term development of history whether or not population had declined, whether the decline had been sudden and steep or

---

[5] Brenner, 'Agrarian Roots of European Capitalism', 267–8 n. 97.

prolonged and shallow, or whether it took place in the seventeeth century instead of the fourteenth and fifteenth.

A central concern of Marxist historiography is to explain the transition from feudalism to capitalism, which involves defining what constituted the crisis of feudalism, and establishing how long it lasted and what its consequences were. But which particular crisis constituted such a turning point? In European history at least three general crises of feudalism have been identified: with one in the seventeenth century and another in the nineteenth, as well as the one beginning in the early fourteenth century which has been analysed in previous chapters. In order to assess the significance of the medieval crisis, it is necessary to examine whether a decisive shift towards a more capitalistic economy and society took place in the later fourteenth and fifteenth centuries. Such a shift would have involved, among other things, an expansion of towns and an increase in their dominance over the countryside, a growth in the scale of the units of production of both agricultural and industrial goods, the decline of serfdom and of peasant producers, the rise of wage labour, and the emergence of a new spirit of innovation and accumulation.

However, while some developments in the later Middle Ages would seem to indicate a shift towards the foundation of a more capitalistic society and economy at this time, many others would not. Although some parts of the urban sector may have fared relatively better than the countryside in the recession of the later Middle Ages, the scale of the advance in the role of towns was far greater in the two centuries before 1300, and while the growth of rural industry outside the confines of the gild system might be seen as a step towards capitalism, the fifteenth century saw a widespread and substantial retreat from large-scale commercial farming, even among the peasantry. An essential part of the genesis of capitalism is the demise of villein tenure and the rise of a landless proletariat, divorced from the means of production, who live by selling their labour. But, while villeinage gradually dissolved, both the numbers and the proportion of landless labourers shrank as a consequence of the collapse of population and the easy availability of land. The swelling of the ranks of a landless proletariat and the rise of the yeoman farmer were primarily developments of the succeeding centuries. Moreover, the depressed economic conditions prevailing during much of the fifteenth century were distinctly unfavourable for capital accumulation and the growth of business enterprises, and consequently it is difficult to detect any enhanced spirit of acquisitiveness among the merchants, minor landlords, or wealthier peasantry.[6] On the contrary, the scale of operations of the leading merchants in many important trades sank very substantially below the levels seen in the fourteenth century; the wool and tin merchants of the fifteenth century, for example, were mere minnows compared with their far richer and more powerful predecessors.[7]

Of course, this is not to deny that the later Middle Ages did experience some developments which were crucial pre-conditions of the ultimate transformation of rural England. Most notably, the rural population was no longer tied to the land or to the payment of rents and obligations at levels determined by custom rather than competition. Not only did rents fall, contractual tenancies advanced at the expense of customary, largely at the behest of the peasantry. From the Marxist perspective these transformations in personal and tenurial status were the product of a crisis in the long-standing conflictive relations between lords and peasants which came to a head in the fourteenth century. But it is difficult to account for the transformation of the balance of power between landlords and tenants without the dramatic shift in the relative scarcities of land and labour brought about by the collapse of population. Consequently, some Marxists have attempted to incorporate depopulation into their

[6] Hatcher, 'The Great Slump', 257–62; R. Britnell, 'Commerce and Capitalism in Late Medieval England: Problems of Description the Theory', *Journal of Historical Sociology*, 6 (1993), 365–7.

[7] E. Power, *The Wool Trade in English Medieval History* (Oxford, 1941), 104–23; J. Hatcher, *English Tin Production and Trade before 1550* (Oxford, 1973), 68–75.

explanations, but as Bois has frankly acknowledged: 'this can make the various demarcation lines between Malthusian and Marxist approaches more difficult to discern'.[8]

Nor are the commercialization theses which are routinely applied to the early Middle Ages necessarily any easier to mould into a shape which fits the experience of the later Middle Ages. As we discussed in Chapter 4, if it was the increasing density of population which acted as the engine driving commercial progress and the more efficient use of resources, then it follows that with demographic collapse the mechanisms should have been thrown into reverse, with negative instead of positive feedback creating the conditions for self-sustaining retrenchment. Most of the proponents of the bountiful benefits of commercialization have failed to address this issue, but Persson has no doubts that the fall in aggregate income and demand brought about by population contraction would have led to a decline in urban labour productivity, and thence to a rise in the price of urban goods relative to agrarian goods. These adjustments would in turn have encouraged peasants to diminish their work effort and lead the countryside to retreat into self-sufficiency. Additionally, 'epidemics, wars and the contraction and disappearance of settlements would have caused repeated disruption to the transmission of knowledge and technical innovation between social groups, geographical areas and generations of people.'[9]

But history perversely refuses to follow the straightforward path predicted by theory, and the experience of the later Middle Ages proved far more complex than such simple pessimistic predictions admit. Aggregate levels of commercial activity certainly fell and the number of formal marketing outlets diminished, but the commercial infrastructure remained more or less intact, and the shortage

---

[8] Bois, 'Against the neo-Malthusian Orthodoxy', 118.
[9] Persson, *Pre-industrial Economic Growth*, 87–8. For Snooks, who prefers to rely on economic theory rather than the abundant historical evidence, the later Middle Ages are a time of *falling* living standards (*Economics Without Time*, 256–64).

of labour stimulated the adoption of labour-saving measures in many sectors of the economy. Efficiency gains also arose from the weakening of the ability of landlords to control the location and operation of markets for their own interests. The redistribution of income down the social scale stimulated demand for a wider range of basic consumer goods, the production and distribution of which became more commercialized. Industry flourished in many parts of the English countryside, and the products of a rural textile industry penetrated overseas markets. But the proportion of people living in towns probably did not decline, and the share of national wealth residing in towns almost certainly increased. The widespread advance of pastoral farming at the expense of arable in the later Middle Ages also led to increased specialization, as farmers were able to shed the subsistence and risk-aversion strategies which had been necessarily adopted before the plague and to abandon the costly growing of bread grains on unsuitable soils. On an abundance of land formerly devoted to crops, sheep were reared for their wool and meat and cattle for their meat, dairy produce, and hides, while on lighter poorer soils new activities emerged, such as commercial rabbit rearing.[10] Greater specialization in the growing of crops is also notable, most particularly barley to serve the expanding market for more and better ale,[11] but also flax, hemp, and saffron.[12] In fact there is a host of evidence which is not readily compatible with the assumption that a simple linear relationship existed between long-term flows in population and the rate of technological progress and regress, or urban growth and contraction.

[10] B. M. S. Campbell, 'Commercial Dairy Production on Medieval English Demesnes: The Case of Norfolk', *Anthropozoologica*, 16 (1992), 110, 114; Britnell, *Commercialisation of English Society*, 195–6.

[11] Bailey, *A Marginal Economy?*, 237, 238.

[12] *AHEW*, iii. 232, 234, 260; J. Lee, 'The Trade of Late Fifteenth-Century Cambridge and its Region', in M. Hicks (ed.), *Proceedings of the Fifteenth-Century Colloquium, Southampton 1999* (forthcoming).

Some Alternative Models

The almost infinite variety of potential influences on the course of economic and social development, combined with a chronic inability to measure with any pretence of accuracy the power which they may have exerted, has resulted in a plethora of alternative models and explanations, each of which makes its own claims for the truth. The eternal quest of historians for novelty and the plaudits that reward it will ensure that an equal or greater number of original ideas will be liberated in the future. The construction of a new explanatory model almost invariably begins with the selection of one or a limited number of historical elements or variables from among the profusion of potential claimants. These newly favoured variables, which have previously been ignored or assigned only subsidiary roles, are then raised to positions of prime significance, or combined together in ways which have not previously been attempted. Finally, in order to stress the novelty of the new approach, the roles of other potential dynamic factors, especially those which have commanded support in other models, are ruthlessly downgraded.

S. R. Epstein, for example, has recently added to the profusion of models by raising to pre-eminence a series of deleterious effects on production and trade which resulted from the quest by lords for income and from the exercise of power by cities. For him the expansion of trade and improvements in marketing across Europe in the twelfth and thirteenth centuries were ultimately brought to a halt by a range of institutional impediments stemming from the exercise of seigneurial rights, the monopolizing of trade, the raising of tolls, and the discrimination by one city against another, which combined to raise the costs of distribution, force up the prices of goods, and disrupt the flow of trade. The crisis of the early fourteenth century is therefore not a technologically or demographically determined agrarian crisis of production but an institutionally determined crisis of distribution, which Epstein terms an 'integration crisis'.[13]

The case for an increasingly unfavourable imbalance between population and resources is reduced by Epstein to just

three distinct claims: first, that the marginal productivity of land was in long run decline; second, that lower levels of food consumption, and particularly the greater incidence of harvest crisis from the 1280s onwards increased levels of background mortality and caused population to decline; and third, that medieval societies were incapable of applying preventative checks to nuptiality and natality that could mitigate the pressure on resources.

He then summarily refutes, in a few short paragraphs, each of his chosen claims. By believing that it was the behaviour of landlords which played the leading role in undermining the economy in the early fourteenth-century, Epstein might be thought to be in accord with Marxist historiography, but he is not. Whereas for Dobb and Brenner the crisis sprang from the excessive burdens placed by lords on their peasants, for Epstein it sprang from the stranglehold which landlords and other authorities exerted over trade.[14] Finally, he stresses that the later Middle Ages was an era of substantial commercial and industrial advance, as trade and industry benefited from the rise of the modern state and were liberated from the bonds of competing feudal lords. Epstein has thus not only sought to squeeze the experience of Europe over a number of centuries into a single explanatory scheme, he proffers views of the developments of the medieval era which contradict the main tenets of neo-Malthusian and Marxist modelling and confound all major versions of the commercialization thesis.

---

[13] Epstein, *Integration Crisis; idem, The Late Medieval Crisis* (forthcoming), ch. 3.

[14] This argument does not fit the English experience at all well. Unlike some parts of Europe, there were relatively few tolls on internal trade within England and English towns were incapable of exerting much legal or coercive influence outside their own walls.

The Role of Money

A number of more venerable alternative explanations of long-term economic change derive from emphazising the influence of monetary factors. As we have seen, models based upon the interplay of population and resources regard movements in the relative scarcity of land and labour as the major influences on long-term trends in commodity prices and economic fortunes, while Marxists generally accept that 'real' factors lay behind significant price movements, although in addition stress the influence of socio-economic laws specific to the feudal economy. However, the amount of money in circulation also affects prices and can, it is claimed, exert a powerful influence over the level of economic activity. Thus, the price of food will rise not only if demand outstrips supply, but if there is an increase in the amount of money circulating in the economy. When the amount of money in an economy rises but output does not, more money chases the same quantity of goods, with the result that money becomes more plentiful relative to goods thereby causing prices to rise. The ability of fluctuations in the money supply to move prices is therefore incontestable, but the extent to which the movements of medieval prices were dictated by monetary rather than real factors is a matter of considerable debate. Even more disputable is the contention that fluctuations in the stock of money were the major influence behind the output of the economy.

The relationship between money and prices may be represented by the expression $MV = PT$, called the Fisher equation, where M is the amount of money in circulation, V is the velocity at which it circulates, P is the mean price of commodities, and T is the sum of transactions which take place in the economy. If the equation is expressed in the form $P = MV \div T$, the relationship between prices and the amount of money is made even clearer. In fact, the Fisher equation is less an equation than an identity, since it is no more than a declaration of the obvious, which cannot be anything other than true. It simply states that the amount of money (M), multiplied by the number of times it is spent (V), must be the same thing as the total of goods that are bought (T) multiplied by the price that is paid for them (P).

However, even statements of the obvious can have considerable value when they help to focus analysis on key elements in economic relationships. But, unfortunately for medieval historians, P is the only variable in the Fisher identity which can be measured with any pretence of accuracy. Although there are excellent records of the output of English mints, the relationship between the numbers of new coins being minted and the total amount of money in circulation (M) is a matter of speculation. More advanced methods and thinking have of late been devoted to the tasks of estimating both the velocity at which money in England circulated, and the sum of transactions, or total national output, but these still remain highly speculative.[15] And when the best guesses for each of the variables in the identity are multiplied together the potential for extremely wide margins of error is considerable.

The stock of money in circulation in the Middle Ages owed relatively little to the direct influence of basic economic or social phenomena, and was instead decisively influenced by a range of random and exogenous factors, such as the chance discovery or exhaustion of silver deposits, improvements or insurmountable obstacles in mining technology, the onset or cessation of war and trade embargoes, and the capriciousness or probity of monarchs in the manner in which they managed the coinage of their realms. Because the overwhelming bulk of the money used in medieval economies was comprised of coins made of precious metals (silver and to a lesser extent gold) the output of European silver mines was of vital importance in determining how many coins could be minted. But the number of coins that could be produced from any given quantity of precious metal is dependent on their purity as well as their weight. The

---

[15] For example, Mayhew, 'Modelling Medieval Monetisation', in Britnell and Campbell (eds.), *Commercialising Economy*, 55–77; and *idem*, 'Population, Money Supply, and the Velocity of Circulation in England, 1300–1700', *EcHR*, 2nd ser., 48 (1995), 238–57.

mixing of base metals with silver and gold, called debasement, made it possible to mint many more coins and produced windfall profits for rulers. Finally, the balance of trade between countries and continents also helped to determine the numbers of coins in circulation, with deficits settled by the export of bullion and surpluses resulting in an influx of silver and gold which could then be turned into coins by the Crown.

It had been recognized as early as the sixteenth century that sharp increases in the amount of coin in circulation were likely to push up prices, and in the 1920s and 1930s the influential writings of Irving Fisher helped to stimulate renewed attempts to promote the role of monetary factors as a cause of medieval and early modern economic development. The massive influx of precious metals from the New World in the sixteenth and early seventeenth centuries and the scale of the simultaneous 'price revolution' ensured that monetary interpretations of this period soon gained greater favour. But their popularity among medieval historians was short-lived, and the growing influence of neo-Malthusian and Marxist interpretations of history soon saw explanations based on 'real' factors gaining ever greater dominance. In the last few decades, however, the tide has begun to turn once again, and the significance of the broad correlations which existed in the Middle Ages between mine production, bullion flows, and mint output, on the one hand, and the behaviour of prices and the economy, on the other, are being stressed by a new generation of monetary historians.[16]

In the twelfth and thirteenth centuries a protracted boom in the mining of silver ran parallel with massive and prolonged demographic and economic expansion and rising prices, and the swelling flow of silver from within Europe was supplemented by a substantial influx of gold from Hungary and Africa. By contrast, in the later Middle Ages, a time of price falls, plunging population, and economic contraction, the output of Europe's silver mines shrank, her trade

---

[16] For example, P. Spufford, *Money and its Use in Medieval Europe* (Cambridge, 1988); J. Day, *The Medieval Market Economy* (Oxford, 1987); J. H. Munro, *Bullion Flows and Monetary Policies in England and the Low Countries, 1350–1500* (Aldershot, 1992).

deficit with the Levant expanded, and the Sudanese gold trade was severely disrupted. As a result, it is claimed, Europe experienced a 'great bullion famine' of unprecedented proportions, when the output of mints collapsed and money became extremely scarce.

It is argued that these broad correlations demonstrate that the amount of money in circulation played a major role in determining price movements and a significant part in regulating the level of economic activity in both the early and the late Middle Ages. Some would go further and see monetary factors as the prime mover. But correlation must not be confused with causation. Although it is undeniable that neo-Malthusian and Marxist modelling has persistently denied sufficient weight to the influence of monetary factors, we must not now lurch to the opposite extreme and overinflate their role. The supply of money was a material element in the operation of the economy at all times, and there were some periods when sharp fluctuations in the money supply exerted considerable influence over prices,[17] but this is a far cry from demonstrating that the supply of money was consistently the pre-eminent variable in the promotion of medium- and long-term change.

Constructing a credible model which establishes the money supply as the chief engine of economic development, to stand in opposition to those based on population, class relations, or commercialization, is a task fraught with extreme difficulties which few have attempted. But there are some who do try to fashion arguments along these lines, and in a recent article it is claimed that 'the case for arguing that a lack of silver coin could by itself depress the medieval economy rests on . . . commonsense', and that monetary shortage also exerted a powerful influence over the ability of the population to recover in the mid-fifteenth century. The reasoning runs as follows: the lack of money depressed the economy, a depressed

---

[17] It seems probable, for example, that the stark contrast between the deflationary decades just prior to the Black Death, and the inflationary decades which followed, owed much to a large increase in the amount of money in circulation, and esp. per caput. See e.g. N. J. Mayhew, 'Numismatic Evidence and Falling Prices in the Fourteenth Century', *EcHR*, 2nd ser., 27 (1974), 1–15.

economy worsened the prospects for employment and thus for marriage and, since E. A. Wrigley has stated that 'marriage was the hinge on which the demographic system turned', not only in the early modern centuries but probably for 'far longer than its existence can be clearly demonstrated', it follows that delayed marriage and an increase in the proportions never marrying lowered the birth rate and depressed the level of population.[18]

The great economic slump of the mid-fifteenth century has attracted the particular attention of monetarists, and the proposition that a famine of bullion was its prime cause has been repeatedly stated with considerable conviction.[19] But it has little plausibility. The depression embraced not just falling imports and exports, and falling internal trade, commodity prices and rents, but falling industrial and agricultural profits, a crisis for commercial farming, the proliferation of vacant landholdings, and a severe shortage of people willing to farm the land at every level from smallholding peasants to yeomen. It owed its breadth and intensity to the conjuncture of a wide range of adverse forces. If a severe contraction of the supply of money had been the dominant problem experienced by the mid-fifteenth-century economy, then its first effect would have been to depress prices rather than economic activity, and its second effect would have been to make the remaining money work harder by circulating it more rapidly, as the Fisher identity demonstrates.[20] The third effect of a scarcity of coin in an economy which is otherwise

---

[18] P. Nightingale, 'England and the European Depression of the Mid-fifteenth Century', *Journal of European Economic History*, 26 (1997), 631–56 (citing E. A. Wrigley, *People, Cities and Wealth* (Oxford, 1987), 9, 239–40). For further arguments stressing the role of bullion and monetary factors in global history, see I. S. W. Blanchard, *The Middle Ages: A Concept Too Many?* (Newlees, 1996).

[19] Reviews of the issues and the historiography are contained in Day, 'The Great Bullion Famine of the Fifteenth Century' and 'The Question of Monetary Contraction in Late Medieval Europe', in Day, *Medieval Market Economy*, 1–71; Spufford, *Money and its Use*, 339–62. For a recent critique, see N. Sussman, 'The Late Medieval Bullion Famine Reconsidered', *Journal of Economic History*, 58 (1998), 126–54.

[20] From the Fisher identity, $MV = PT$, we can see that a decrease in the amount of money (M), will translate swiftly into a decrease in prices (P), unless it is compensated by an increase in the speed at which that money circulates (V). Any movement in T, total output, will of course take longer to come about.

thriving would be an increase in barter and credit in order to meet the needs of eager buyers and sellers short of ready cash. We know that credit contracted during the worst of the fifteenth-century recession, and therefore that did not compensate for any shortage of coin, but it is wrong to claim that it did so solely or primarily as a consequence of the contraction in the money supply.[21] A recession by definition means difficult trading conditions, and although the demand for credit from the increasing numbers of people experiencing financial problems will rise, lenders will become more reluctant to advance them credit as the chances of securing repayment worsen. Furthermore, as the businesses of solvent traders contract they will have less need of credit.

Although it is undeniable that a drastic shortage of coin would have created great inconvenience and made trade at all levels much more difficult to carry out, it is difficult to see how a 'famine' could have arisen suddenly in the mid-fifteenth century. Even a complete cessation of minting will take a considerable time to have a significant impact on the numbers of coins in circulation, since the production of new coins constituted but a small fraction of the total money stock. Furthermore, although the output of English mints did slump in the 1440s and 1450s, the numbers of coins minted in the 1420s and early 1430s had been high.

There are many extremely powerful reasons why money must be considered as one of a host of variables rather than the dominant variable, as may be briefly illustrated by examining the crucial relationship between prices and wages. Although there was a very rough synchronization over the span of the Middle Ages between rising food prices and rising money supply, and falling food prices and falling money supply, it is far from providing the whole story behind causation. For, if the measure of prices is broadened from foodstuffs to encompass the whole range of goods consumed by labouring and peasant households, then mean price levels are shown to be marginally *lower* when the series begins at the turn of the

---

[21] As Nightingale does in 'England and the European Depression', 639.

thirteenth and fourteenth centuries, than they were in the second half of the fifteenth century. But, in direct contrast, the price of labour was transformed over the same period: in 1500, despite the shrinkage in the stock of money, the wages paid to unskilled and semi-skilled labourers stood two or even three times higher than they had in 1300.[22] Whatever the role played by monetary factors in the movements of prices and wages in the thirteenth, fourteenth, and fifteenth centuries, it is impossible to deny immense power to the transformations which took place in the relative scarcities of the factors of production.

There was clearly far more to the operation of the medieval economy than the amount of money within it. Fortunately, there are welcome signs that it is increasingly being recognized that the priority should be to establish the rightful role of monetary factors alongside all the other influences rather than to assert their dominance over them.[23]

Institutional Change and Property Rights

The most ambitious and sophisticated new model of long-term economic and social change to emerge in recent decades is that devised by D. C. North, in association with R. Thomas. The North model stresses the central role of institutions and institutional arrangements, which are defined as sets of rules, compliance procedures, and moral and ethical behavioural norms designed to constrain conduct and allocate scarce resources.[24] Such rules, procedures and

---

[22] These data are necessarily drawn from the Phelps Brown and Hopkins index ('Seven centuries of the Prices of Consumables'), but many other collections of data also demonstrate the strong divergence of wages and prices in the later Middle Ages.

[23] For example, in the work of Mayhew cited in n. 15 above.

[24] See, in particular, D. C. North and R. Thomas, 'An Economic Theory of the Growth of the Western World', *EcHR* , 2nd ser., 23 (1970); D. C. North and R. Thomas, 'The Rise and Fall of the Manorial System: A Theoretical Model', *Journal of Economic History*, 31 (1971); D. C. North and R. Thomas, *The Rise of the Western World: A New Economic History* (Cambridge, 1973); D. C. North, *Structure and Change in Economic History* (1981).

norms, whose influence has previously been neglected by historians and economists, are seen by North to have performed a major dynamic role in determining the pace and direction of economic development and innovation, and to have undergone fundamental change over time.[25]

Economists have conventionally seen institutions and institutional arrangements as parameters rather than variables: that is, they have taken them as given and not assigned them an active role. Basic neoclassical economic analysis, for example, commonly works on the assumption that the world is 'frictionless', that knowledge and markets are perfect, that institutions, laws, customs, and rules do not exist, and that all actions by individuals or groups are determined simply by opportunities and choices made on the basis of a desire to maximize welfare, normally expressed through income and wealth. In North's model, by contrast, institutions and institutional arrangements are seen to have played a prime role in economic outcomes and in determining long-term economic and social change, either by restraining incentives or by channelling them into productivity-raising types of economic activity.[26]

In accordance with the premisses of this model, North and Thomas attempt to apply an economic theory of contracts to the manorial system in order to account for its rise and fall. They see the early stages of the feudal era as characterized by a sparse and scattered population and abundant supplies of good land, but since disorder was normally either present or threatened, trade was constrained and a considerable degree of self-sufficiency was practised. Such conditions led to contractual relationships whereby goods and services were directly exchanged between lords and peasants to their mutual benefit. The military elite offered land as well as protection and justice, and the peasantry offered in return payments in kind, notably labour. In an age of limited markets, direct exchanges of these kinds were the most efficient way of satisfying the respective

---

[25] 'Growth of the Western World', 5.   [26] See e.g. *Structure and Change*, 2–12.

needs of the parties, and involved the lowest transaction and bar-gaining costs. The contractual arrangement characteristic of the traditional manor was thus 'an appropriate response to the conditions of that day' and 'lasted as long as the conditions that made it efficient'.[27]

Institutional innovation does not occur spontaneously, and in this model the primary trigger in the Middle Ages was the forces generated by the interaction of population and resources. Growing population led to an expansion of towns and markets, and to the colonization of new lands with different regional factor endowments (i.e. different natural resources and climate), which in turn encouraged more specialization and thus promoted trade between regions. But, according to North and Thomas, eventually

[p]opulation pressure undermined the economic basis for the institutional organization of feudalism [i.e. the existing contractual relationships] by reversing the relationship of prices as a result of diminishing returns and by expanding the size of the markets. Increases in population relative to a fixed supply of good land led to agricultural prices rising relative to non-agricultural prices; this in turn increased the value of land and decreased real wages as the output per labourer fell.

Such dramatic changes 'destroyed the basic *raison d'être* of feudalism' and demanded the introduction of new institutional arrangements. Consequently lords sought to 'eliminate common-property use of land and to achieve private exclusive ownership' and to 'commute labour dues to payments in kind and in cash, and to lease the demesne lands in return for rent'.[28]

This model, when dealing with the Middle Ages, is notable for the manner in which it integrates central tenets from each of the three supermodels. Commercial development provides the backdrop, population is generally held to be the instigator of social and institutional change and to behave in a Malthusian fashion, and seigneurial

---

[27] 'Rise and Fall of the Manorial System', 792–4.
[28] 'Growth of the Western World', 10–11.

exploitation and conflict features in the relationships between classes. Ideally the fundamental premisses of the North–Thomas model would require contracts to be essentially consensual, freely negotiated between the respective parties and founded upon incentives, transaction costs, and rational economic behaviour, and with both lords and peasants deriving substantial benefits from them. And in the early stages of formulating their conspectus this is how North and Thomas did interpret the evolution of the manorial system in the late Anglo-Saxon era. But in response to sustained criticism North subsequently fled to the opposite extreme and claimed that 'a more accurate perspective . . . was that the warrior class was analogous to the Mafia in extracting income from the peasantry'.[29] Further strong redolences of Marxist thought are also in evidence when North and Thomas turn to the late medieval era of falling population, and they write that

[o]ur model, in these circumstances, would predict a period of rising social tension and of conflict between these groups, requiring an exploration of the structure and distribution of political power of the times to foresee its resolution. To the extent that the political power resided with the lord, he would be able to reimpose feudal obligations; to the extent that it was more widely diffused among diverse political interests, he might be less able to capture again the rents from labour.

In the event, the landlords lost out because of 'the flight of peasants, the competition between lords anxious to attract tenants and the stubborn refusal of villeins to obey orders'. The new arrangements resulted in lower rents, the relaxation of servile obligations, and the innovation of lengthy leases. Moreover, 'the decline in population . . . [reduced] the total size of the market and the difference between regions in Europe', and trade shrank, thus reinforcing developments on the manor.[30]

Much of this is familiar rather than iconoclastic. For the mainsprings of change in the early and central Middle Ages which force

[29] *Structure and Change*, 130.   [30] 'Growth of the Western World', 12.

the abandonment of old arrangements are deemed by North and Thomas to be the long-established ones of the pressure of people on resources (which leads to diminishing returns to land and labour) and the growth of the market, specialization, and the use of money (which leads to a reduction in transaction and search costs). Also familiar is their claim for the potential for the growth of trade and commerce to undermine the feudal system, which parallels the writings of Pirenne and Sweezy, and their depiction of a new balance of power and institutional arrangements between landlords and tenants being established in the later Middle Ages during a period of tension and struggle.

Since Douglas North and Robert Thomas are not medievalists their model was constructed at some distance from the historiography and sources of the Middle Ages, but the closer it gets to them the less it deviates from mainstream medieval scholarship and closer it approximates to description rather than projection or insight. North does not argue that during this period there were autonomous changes in institutions and property rights which determined the path which history took; on the contrary he insists that the changes in them were contingent upon preceding changes in the economy and in the relative disposition of class power. To argue that medieval societies tended to adopt the institutional arrangements which fitted prevailing economic and social realities and factor prices, and which reflected the interests of the most powerful of the parties embraced by them, and that substantial change in these realities was likely to lead to the evolution of new arrangements, is not to put forward propositions which the majority of medievalists would find either contentious or novel.

Likely to be much more upsetting for medievalists are the premisses upon which North and Thomas set forth on their task of building a new model, namely that the historiography of the Middle Ages 'is a chaotic output . . . in which bits and scraps of evidence are proffered for almost every specific explanation', and their confidence that with the 'application of the tools used by the new economic historian in analyzing the American experience . . . [o]ne can now do better—much better'.[31] In the event, however, the contribution this model makes to the advance of medieval history is distinctly limited, and lies more in its reaction against the application of the 'abstract, frictionless and static theoretical formulations' of neoclassical economics,[32] than in adding significantly to our understanding of the workings of the medieval economy.

The Social Dimension in Economic Development

One of the most telling criticisms that may be levelled against the three supermodels which dominate this book is that they all neglect social factors. Such an accusation is far from new, and ironically it has often been levelled by the proponents of these models against one another. In the 'Brenner Debate' of the late 1970s, for example, Robert Brenner accused members of what he termed the neo-Malthusian school of an excessively economistic approach. This charge drew a twofold response. First, that those who legitimately adopted the population and resources method of analysis did not seek to use it to explain all that occurred in the world, or even the abiding economic characteristics of the Middle Ages, but rather they used its framework merely to examine and explain the relationship between economic fluctuations and demographic changes over time. Second, that Marxist analysis, although superficially more concerned with social and political matters, in practice has an unacceptably narrow and rigidly defined agenda which focuses on the primacy of class relations, and by so doing neglects a host of relevant structures and influences, namely:

[f]amily structure, inheritance customs, attitudes to technological discovery and innovation, communal facilities and restraints, the prevailing

---

[31] 'Rise and Fall of the Manorial System', 717.
[32] J. L. Anderson, *Explaining Long-Term Economic Change* (1995), 49.

hierarchy of economic objectives and consumption needs, the special rank which the possession of land occupied in that hierarchy, the burdens and penalties of war, the vicissitudes of government and the rule of law.[33]

Negative as such exchanges might appear at first sight, this bout of mutual accusation does highlight some of the fundamental issues facing those who attempt to model the medieval economy. When Postan, the principal architect of the population and resources model, made the unequivocal statement that at best his model can only be used to explain a narrow range of economic relationships, he was unambiguously accepting that long-term economic change cannot adequately be explained without taking into account a wide range of social and political factors. In fact, the list of structures, elements, influences, and attitudes at work in the Middle Ages could be extended far beyond the compilation of his that has just been quoted, and all would have a claim to be represented in a model which fashioned a comprehensive explanation of every important element of long-term change. The dilemma for model-builders, as we have already stated many times, is that any attempt to incorporate even a small selection of such a wide range of variables into the structure of any economic model inevitably results in an unacceptable level of unpredictability and incoherence.

One method of dealing with the plethora of potentially significant social variables is, of course, to replicate the strategy adopted for the comparable range of economic variables, and apply theoretical concepts and methods which assist in the prioritizing of some of the variables over others and in predicting the nature and strength of outcomes. In other words, to use social theory and construct social models. This approach is pursued by S. H. Rigby in a recent study of late medieval English society, which applies closure theory, initiated by Max Weber and developed by a series of

---

[33] Brenner, 'Agrarian Class Structure and Economic Development', 10–12; Postan and Hatcher, 'Population and Class Relations', 64–6.

sociologists culminating in Frank Parkin.[34] Closure theory analyses society by focusing on 'the excluders and the excluded', using the notions of exclusionary closure and usurpationary closure. 'In the case of *exclusionary closure* one group attempts "to secure for itself a privileged position at the expense of some other group through the process of subordination", this downward exercise of power leads to the creation of "a group, class or stratum of legally defined inferiors"'. The complementary situation is *usurpationary closure*, in which the excluded and inferior group attempts to improve its position and win a greater share of privileges and resources at the expense of those above.[35]

In essence, therefore, closure theory is a simple and generalized notion which rests upon the innate desire of people to maximize their own interests and occupy a superior rather than an inferior position, and in which the success with which one group will be able to exclude others will be determined by the extent to which social distinctions and barriers are defined and enforced by laws and government. Moreover, expressed like this, the reader may be forgiven for seeing a close resemblance to the class relations and struggles central to Marxist historiography. But closure theory seeks to achieve an advance on Marxism by incorporating a far wider range of relations and conflicts than those between the owners of the means of production and the masses who are subservient to them. As well as birth, estate, and class, the defining characteristics on which exclusion can be based are extended to include race, gender, religion, and language. Thus, white protestant manual labourers may be exploited by their employers, but they may also adopt exclusionary strategies to protect their position against competition from women, blacks, catholics, and so on. This gives rise to a situation for which Parkin coins the term *dual closure*.

When Rigby applies closure theory to the specific circumstances of later medieval England he attempts to reduce its excessive

[34] Rigby, *English Society in the Later Middle Ages.*   [35] Ibid. 9–11.

generality by adding a dose of the social theory developed by W. G. Runciman. This branch of theory identifies the three types of power which could be used to sustain closure: economic, coercive, and ideological. Even so, despite Rigby's considerable efforts, we are left with the firm conclusion that closure theory is descriptive rather than explanatory, and he concludes his book by stating that 'closure theory offers us a set of intellectual tools, a unified vocabulary, and a package of concepts, which help to make particular social hierarchies intelligible to us, but it cannot provide universally valid explanations of why such hierarchies exist or how they came to change'.[36]

Closure theory thus reviews and defines social issues but does little to assist their integration into models of long-term economic and social change. It should also be noted that although closure theory is explicitly a social theory, one of its leading tenets is the concept of exploitation, which it shares with Marxism, and that tenet inevitably involves concentration on the struggle to maximize rewards and opportunities within which basic economic goals such as wealth and income loom large. Hence, we observe once again that the distinctions between social and economic modelling are blurred: social groups have economic goals, economic fluctuations have social effects, and social and political actions have economic effects.

A Case Study: Serfdom and Villeinage in England

The three leading models which are the focus of this book have repeatedly been used to explain change over prolonged eras of time across vast portions of the world. Somewhat paradoxically, they are normally at their most plausible when applied to the grandest of

---

[36] Rigby, *English Society in the Later Middle Ages*, 327.

historical vistas, primarily because their intellectual integrity, honed over many decades by generations of advocates, flourishes on the most abstract of generalizations. However, when brought to bear on specific situations they commonly thrive far less well. The trapping of supermodels within the confines of space, time, and subject is a sure way of exposing their weaknesses. In the writing of history, as in other areas of intellectual endeavour, it is best to proceed from the known to the unknown and not vice versa, so instead of proceeding from the models to the history as we have tended to do in the first four chapters, we shall now begin with the evidence relating to the history of one institution and use it to test the validity of the models.

Serfdom is an appropriate case study for our purposes. It played a principal role in the life of medieval England, and serfs and villeins probably encompassed the majority of the population and furnished a major portion of the income of the nobility, gentry, and Church. Accordingly, serfdom has featured prominently in all of the models which have been constructed.[37] The rise of money, towns, and trade helped to shape its evolution and ultimate demise; it was the focus of the struggle over rent between landlords and tenants; and it was directly affected by the rise and fall of population and by contingent movements in the prices of land and labour.

Yet even a cursory review of the evidence reveals that frequently the interrelationships between serfdom and commercialization, the class struggle, and the level of population did not take the forms which have been predicted by the builders of the various models, and that the range of influences upon serfdom were far from being restricted to those which are featured in those models. According to interpretations based on population and resources, the power of landlords over their tenants, as well as the rent which was charged for the land which they occupied, should have been determined primarily by the relative scarcities of land and labour. But over long

---

[37] For recent accounts of serfdom and villeinage, see Hatcher, 'English Serfdom and Villeinage'; Britnell, *Commercialisation of English Society*, 62–71, 140–6, 218–24; Rigby, *English Society in the Later Middle Ages*, 27–34, 41–5, 86–7.

periods of the Middle Ages this was not the case. In fact the power of lords over the persons and property of their peasants was arguably at its most oppressive during the centuries preceding and following the Conquest, when land was relatively abundant and labour relatively scarce. Furthermore, although in the course of the later twelfth and the thirteenth centuries the abundance of land was transformed into scarcity and the scarcity of labour into glut, the rate of increase in the rents and dues paid by the unfree fell far behind the rate of increase in the market price of land. Consequently, by the turn of the thirteenth and fourteenth centuries, a time of intense pressure on natural resources, lords generally received substantially less for the land which was held by those who were legally their chattels than they did from land which they leased to those over whom they had little or no seigneurial authority. It was perhaps only in the later fourteenth and the fifteenth centuries that serfdom at last behaved in a manner decreed by the laws of supply and demand, and withered away during a period of sustained population decline. But, lest even this final chapter in its history should be misinterpreted as support for a crude demographic determinism, we should remember that in parts of eastern Europe low population was to coincide with the directly contradictory phenomenon of the enserfment of a previously free population.[38]

Thus, the relations between landlords and their serfs and villeins patently did not follow a path dictated by the market forces which flowed from shifts in the relative scarcity of land and labour. Indeed they often proceeded in a direction quite contrary to them. The history of serfdom in medieval England thus attests the importance of non-economic factors, but does this mean that it lends support to models based upon the supremacy of class power and the resultant class struggle?

There is a prima facie case for arguing that effective class power must have been exercised by lords in the centuries before *c.*1100,

---

[38] The enserfment of Eastern European populations is discussed on pp. 223–8.

when at a time of abundant land and low population they imposed economic and social restrictions on people who would otherwise have enjoyed greater prosperity as well as personal freedom. Men and women at this time were a commodity made more valuable to their lords by their depressed legal status. In the eleventh and twelfth centuries they were bought and sold, and the children born to parents who were the serfs of different lords might be split between those lords. They had to be coerced into remaining on the land and rendering the rents and dues which their lords demanded, as the many instances of flight and pursuit testify. Yet, if this early era lends some support to a Dobb and Brenner type of 'class conflict' model, which portrays medieval lords as insatiable plunderers of peasant surpluses, the behaviour of lords in the succeeding era of rising agricultural prices and growing land scarcity directly contradicts it. For thirteenth-century lords were commonly restrained by the customs and traditions which had been established in more spacious times, which restricted the rate of surplus extraction which they imposed on the unfree. Whatever the origins of the conditions of unfree tenure may have been, in the longer term, as Marx had predicted, they tended to be transformed into a 'constant magnitude'.[39]

Nor is it plausible to interpret the development of the common law relating to villeinage in the later twelfth and thirteenth centuries, which defined and codified the extensive powers lords had over their unfree peasants, as a campaign in the class struggle, deliberately manipulated by the seigneurial class in their own interests.[40] On the contrary, the course taken by the common law has been seen by its most recent historian to be a 'by-product' of changes elsewhere in the legal system, and he 'refutes once and for all simple theories of common-law villeinage as a means of class oppression'.[41]

[39] See above, pp. 105–6.
[40] This opinion was put forward by Kosminsky (*Studies in the Agrarian History of England*, 328–31) and by Hilton ('Freedom and Villeinage'). See also the most recent discussion in Faith, *English Peasantry*, 245–65.
[41] P. R. Hyams, *King, Lords and Peasants in Medieval England: The Common Law of Villeinage in the Twelfth and Thirteenth Centuries* (Oxford, 1980), quote on 265.

In particular, there is no evidence to indicate that the rights of access to royal courts granted by Henry II to free tenants who were in dispute with their lords over matters relating to the tenure of land, deprived the unfree of any legal rights which they had previously enjoyed. The legal changes left many things as they were, one of which was that those who were not free remained subject in law to the will of their lords.

Whereas we may swiftly dismiss contentions that the fluctuating history of serfdom in England was solely determined by either the interplay of economic forces within the land and labour markets, on the one hand, or the depredations of a ruthless seigneurial class, on the other, the forces unleashed by the growing commercialization of the economy warrant a more detailed consideration. The postulation that self-sufficiency (represented by manorialism and serfdom) and exchange (represented by trade, industry, and towns) are incompatible is intellectually beguiling. What could be more plausible than to hypothesize that as commerce, urbanization, specialization, and the use of money advanced, so feudal institutions like serfdom were progressively undermined? They weakened because they were designed for a previous age which depended on production for use, rather than for the emerging world which was becoming more and more dependent on production for exchange.

But an acknowledgement of the historical fact that, in the broadest of terms, the rise of towns and trade coincided with the decline of serfdom is very far from proving a strong causal link between the two, and further still from proving that the rise of the money economy was consistently the prime reason for the changing character and ultimate demise of that system. As Postan wrote many years ago, the progress of the money economy for long periods reinforced rather than sapped manorial institutions, and the history of the exaction and commutation of labour services, considered by contemporaries and historians alike to be one of the hallmarks of unfreedom, was a series of ebbs and flows rather than a linear progression.[42] Although rents paid in agricultural commodities declined virtually continuously in the face of a growing preference for money, rents paid in labour grew in importance over much of the later twelfth and thirteenth centuries as landlords required more and more work to be performed on their expanding demesne farms. The commutation of labour services for money, which had been widespread on many manors before the later twelfth century, was reversed as landlords adopted the practice of running their demesnes as commercial farms, and then progressively expanded the scale of their operations.

Thus, an archetypal feature of a subsistence economy was adapted in a pragmatic fashion to serve the needs of the largest commercial enterprises during an era of massive commercial expansion. The pragmatic approach to the provision of labour extended yet further. For under conditions of increasing labour surplus in the late thirteenth century, lords were encouraged by the low wages of day labourers, and their higher productivity, to increase the use of hired casual workers on their demesnes while commuting into money payments the forced labour services of their villeins.[43]

Serfdom thus had a considerable degree of flexibility, and lords could and did choose to forgo their rights from time to time on a temporary basis. Yet the power of custom made the system very resistant to permanent change. Direct assaults by landlords on the customary defences of serfdom were surprisingly few in number and lacking in penetration, and it was the relative inflexibility of servile rents which led them to seek other ways of increasing their incomes in the long thirteenth century. Running what have been called 'federated grain and wool factories' on their demesne lands was one method, and commercializing the non-customary land market was another. As

---

[42] See, in particular, 'The Chronology of Labour Services' and 'The Rise of a Money Economy', in Postan, *Medieval Agriculture and General Problems*.

[43] Miller and Hatcher, *Rural Society and Economic Change*, 53, 233–4; 238–9; D. Stone, 'The Productivity of Hired and Customary Labour: Evidence from Wisbech Barton in the Fourteenth Century', *EcHR*, 2nd ser., 50 (1997), 640–56.

the thirteenth century neared its close, more and more lords took the opportunity to create leaseholds and competitive tenures rather new villein tenures when land came into their hands by virtue of assarting, the failure of heirs or the shedding of acres from the demesne.[44] The final and ultimately successful assault on the customs of serfdom, however, did not come until the late Middle Ages, when it was led by the villeins and serfs against the lords who were vainly seeking to maintain customary rents and rights in an age of plunging land values.

The opportunities which towns provided for the unfree to flee from oppression in the countryside has often loomed large in those models which see commercialization destroying feudalism.[45] But it is difficult to envisage the migration into towns by unfree peasants who abandoned their landholdings as making more than a subsidiary contribution to the operation of serfdom at any time in the Middle Ages. In the later twelfth and thirteenth centuries the pull of the towns was largely exercised over the landless and village craftsmen, the former because they had little to lose and the latter because their skills offered enhanced prospects. Scarcely any unfree tenants were tempted to give up viable landholdings in the countryside for the precarious life of an unskilled labourer in a town. Moreover, in this time of rising population even if large numbers of landed peasants had abandoned their holdings and fled to the towns it would have done little to weaken serfdom, for they would have been readily replaced from among the hoards of the landless and land-hungry who would have been pleased to accept land on servile terms.

Although the relative attractions of town life may have increased in the later Middle Ages, we must resist the temptation to exaggerate the contribution of migration from the countryside to the ultimate demise of serfdom. The numbers of people living in towns certainly did not grow in the later Middle Ages, and migration therefore could not have been more than a subsidiary cause of the

[44] Hatcher, 'English Serfdom and Villeinage', 19–21.
[45] For example, by Sweezy and Dobb (see above, pp. 76–7, 92–3).

severe slump which gripped the rural land market during much of the fifteenth century.

This brief review of some of the reasons behind episodes in the history of serfdom in England demonstrates once again that the influences shaping the medieval economy and society were so multitudinous and miscellaneous, and so variable in strength over time, that they cannot be encompassed satisfactorily within the parameters of any of the leading models. When these models are forced to confront historical reality the independence and exclusivity which they claim is shown to be an intellectual illusion, and their highly refined and abstracted prime movers are easily unmasked as conglomerations of arbitrary judgements and miscellaneous components. The class power of landlords in the struggle for rent with their unfree peasantry, for example, was a product of not only their military strength and the degree of solidarity which they displayed with their peers, but the efficiency of their officials, of the location of their estates and whether they were scattered or centralized, of the nature of their expenditure patterns, and of their political and personal priorities and so on. Moreover, many more influences, major and minor, played upon serfdom itself, among them such diverse and seemingly unconnected elements as the attitude of the Church to slavery and servility, the level of taxation on lords and peasants, the degree of efficiency in the market for labour and agricultural produce, and peasant kinship networks and family ties.

This chapter has focused once again on the generic weaknesses of the models which have been developed to describe and explain the history of the medieval economy, and in so doing it has inevitably raised serious doubts about the appropriateness of model-building for historians. Does this mean, therefore, that all explanatory frameworks are either too simple or too complex, and that in the writing of history the tasks of description and the collection of facts must be accorded far greater weight than those of analysis and explanation?

6

Beyond the Classic Supermodels

The central theme of this book has been an exploration of the intellectual strength, clarity, and historical accuracy of the three traditional supermodels of economic development in the Middle Ages and beyond. We have outlined the theoretical principles on which they are founded, and traced their intellectual origins; re-created each model on its own terms, marshalled the empirical evidence in support of the theory; and identified the strengths and weaknesses which each possesses. Our purpose has been twofold: first to provide a clear and accessible introduction to the conceptual frameworks which have dominated this subject for so many decades, and, secondly, to assess the extent to which these frameworks retain relevance and credibility. In doing so we have persistently commented that the great strength displayed by these models is also their profound weakness, because, when providing explanations of great historical events and processes, the price of lucidity and consistency is invariably simplicity and artificiality. Instinctively we know that historical outcomes are determined by a wide rather than a narrow range of forces and events, and that these forces and events are variable rather than fixed, and interdependent rather than independent. The more our historical knowledge is extended by research into unexplored archives and deepened by new interpretations or methodological approaches, the more complete becomes the failure of these grand models to accommodate and explain the complexity of historical experience.

The foundations on which each grand model is built, and the methods by which it proceeds, are essentially far too crude. At best they might be applicable to very simple systems, but modern research has confirmed that the medieval economy was relatively complex and that it operated within a sophisticated environment. It is not surprising, therefore, that the answers these models have provided lack validity or even real subtlety, and that their grading of causation is inevitably subjective. Whatever forces were exerted by the rise and fall of population, the progress and regress of commerce and technology, or the waxing and waning of the power of the various classes, they must have acted and reacted upon each other. But each model is founded on different and fixed convictions. And it is because they employ contrasting assumptions from the outset, and adopt distinctive interpretative priorities, that they inevitably produce radically contradictory answers.

Recent attempts at updating these models, or synthesizing the various elements within them, have not found a viable solution to this dilemma. New versions of a commercialization model have provided greater sophistication by exploring the importance of feedback mechanisms which involve a wider range of factors acting both negatively and positively in the dynamic process of change, but because they are still predicated on the consistently dominant role of commerce the argument even in its most powerful form of expression remains uncomfortably crude. Douglas North's recent institutional model has incorporated major elements from all three supermodels, but his promotion of the centrality of institutions and institutional arrangements seems to have more to offer as a corrective to unrealistic assumptions of the existence of 'frictionless' relationships and completely free markets in much economic theory, rather than as the new leading agent of historical development in the Middle Ages.

The perspective from which we have so far directed our criticism of the grand models has been largely a mixture of empirical evidence and commonsense, but the construction and application of explanatory models also involves a range of broad theoretical and philosophical considerations, and some of these will now be addressed briefly, including the nature of causality and explanation. In seeking to promote the central role of a 'prime mover' or leading instigator of change, the models are essentially establishing a hierarchy of causes within which one, or a small group from among a whole host of possibilities, is made pre-eminent while the vast majority are relegated to minor and supporting roles. Moreover, these models necessarily seek to make their chosen prime mover independent of other factors: in other words, rather than being subject to the influence of other forces it is the prime mover which does the influencing. These models also characteristically adopt what is termed a linear approach to explaining how the chosen system operates: that is they proceed on the assumption that a given cause has a single predictable effect or chain of effects. Thus, A leads to B, B leads to C, C leads to D, and so on; and it is not only the occurrence but the direction and scale of D that is directly attributable to A. This is commonly seen as an additive process, in which the outcome is the sum of the components. Thus, for example, the population–resources model in its crudest form assumes that movements in the land : labour ratio not only lead to changes in the price of land, food, and labour, and thence to a shift in the balance of power between landlords and peasants, but that movements in the ratio in a certain direction and of a certain scale will tend to promote predictable and proportionate changes in the economy and society at large. It is in this way that linear models serve the purpose of reliable maps, whose clearly marked paths guide historians through the density and complexity of a multitude of often conflicting details.

Although this approach represents a logical and plausible method, each of the fundamental assumptions of such lineally structured models is open to serious doubt. The selection of one factor as the prime mover must necessarily be based on a subjective ordering of other potential causal factors, and is therefore a choice which, by definition, is capable of being disputed. In the real world prime movers do not exist independently of all other forces and totally impervious to their influence, and the contention that historical change invariably followed a linear path, and contained no significant random elements, is similarly unrealistic. These potential weaknesses are implicitly acknowledged by most of the historians who have employed supermodels as explanatory tools, but their implications are rarely addressed explicitly. Indeed, they cannot adequately be addressed without questioning the basic premises on which the models are constructed. Linear models of economic development designed to answer difficult questions are seductive because they are relatively simple, and they are relatively simple because the vast majority of potential variables are either held more or less constant or excluded. Any attempt to incorporate neglected variables would —because of their almost infinite variety—quickly create unmanageable complexity in these models and deprive them of their predictive and transparent qualities, which are exactly those qualities from which they derive their virtues and strengths.

This is not to deny, of course, that it can be extremely illuminating to isolate a particular element or group of related elements, and model its behaviour while holding other elements constant. We have seen in the previous chapters how the assumptions behind the various models have encouraged the systematic gathering and analysis of evidence of the behaviour of key elements, which have resulted in major advances in our knowledge of such fields as demography, the processes of marketing and urbanization, the nature of serfdom and the relations between landlords and tenants. Methods of this kind have also been responsible for enormous advances in the natural sciences as well as the social sciences. Indeed, 'the bulk of current science is built on models that either use assumptions of linearity and/or independence or focus on them'.[1] This is not because non-linearity and interdependence are thought to be rare or exotic rather than 'utterly simple and common', but primarily because the linear approach makes difficult tasks infinitely more manageable, and because the analytical tools and concepts developed in fields as divers as physics and psychology—namely, linear algebra, linear regression, and linear correlation—have consistently kept the focus firmly on linear approaches. The almost universal application of these methods has led inexorably to a situation where, as in the physical sciences, '[A]ny integrable system may be represented as a set of units, each changing in isolation, quite independently of the others.'[2] Humans are even less predictable than elements in the natural world, but in order to make the outcomes of any given theoretical situation calculable it is essential to impose strict limits on their behaviour. Thus, in economic theory it has normally to be assumed that collective human behaviour is entirely predictable and governed by the maximization of satisfaction or profit, and that 'other things remain equal'; in other words, that all variables other than those under scrutiny will remain absolutely fixed.

However, a methodological revolution has been under way in recent years. It began in the natural sciences and is based on the recognition of 'the importance of interdependence in shaping the world from the molecular to the societal'.[3] As a result, '[A] simple view of how the world works is being replaced by an essentially complex and paradoxical one.'[4] Under the stimulus of extremely powerful computers

---

[1] S. J. Goerner, 'Chaos and Deep Ecology', in *Chaos Theory in Psychology*, ed. F. D. Abraham and A. R. Gilgen (Westport, Conn., 1995), 5–6.

[2] I. Prigorgine and E. Stengers, *Order Out of Chaos: Man's New Dialogue with Nature* (New York, 1984), 71.

[3] Goerner, 'Chaos and Deep Ecology', 3.

[4] D. Parker and R. Stacey, *Chaos, Management and Economics: The Implications of Non-linear Thinking*, Institute of Economic Affairs, Hobart paper, 125 (1994), 11.

which are capable of facilitating ever more complex modelling, emphasis is shifting from linearity and independence to non-linearity and interdependence. It is now possible to run programmes within which a host of variables can be integrated simultaneously, allowing a multitude of interdependent forces, and the processes which flow from them, to be analysed. Attention is thus shifting from the limitations of linear modelling to the potential of non-linear modelling. Such new modelling is still designed to establish patterns of change, predict behaviour, and forecast outcomes, but because the potential interactions and feedback systems are far more numerous and complex within non-linear models their calculations are far more elaborate and their predictions far less straightforward.

Such developments have facilitated the rise of Chaos Theory, which analyses the manner in which many and varied forces interact in complex ways to produce organized networks and structured systems. Chaos Theory is far more than the integration into models of more and more variables, and the endless chains of positive and negative feedback loops that flow between them. It lies beyond non-linear modelling because it demonstrates that the links between cause and effect are liable to be unpredictable as well as extremely complex. Chaos also recognizes that outcomes may be influenced massively by very small changes in the weighting of any of the variables, or in the feedbacks which are generated by their interrelation with any of the multitude of other variables. From this it follows that in any system any cause can have a multitude of possible effects, and any effect can have a multitude of possible causes. Moreover, the relationship between elements in a system is commonly not proportional, and the processes at work can produce flows of rapidly accelerating energy. While the patterns envisaged by Chaos are normally coherent, ordered, and stable for long periods, they can also provide a context in which a seemingly minor and random occurrence can trigger revolutionary change. Thus, expressed in the form of a poetical conceit, a medium so beloved of the practitioners of the hard sciences, we are told that a butterfly taking flight in Tokyo (or Peking) may trigger a hurricane in New York and, what is more, nobody will be able to trace the steps back from the hurricane to the butterfly.[5]

Consequently, the image we now have for the origins of life and the process of evolution is of an intricately interwoven ecological universe. Whereas the old view concentrated on life forms adapting to a relatively fixed environment, now life and environment are seen to co-evolve. Where traditionally competition led to the survival of the fittest, here cooperation and coordination are responsible for the greatest leaps in efficiency. Where once it was the evolution of species which was dominant, now it is the 'whole interwoven earth ecosystem'.[6]

Chaos Theory charts 'turbulence' as well as complexity, and it reveals that turbulence can occur in even the simplest of models, which otherwise might be thought to behave in a linear manner, resulting in unpredictable and disproportionate outcomes. For example, it is possible to demonstrate mathematically that under certain conditions linearity will give way to non-linearity and eventually to chaos in a classic Malthusian model based on only three ingredients—an equation relating the net birth rate to income, and functions describing the product of labour and the wages of labour.[7] However, Malthus would not have been surprised to learn of highly complex and non-linear processes resulting from the interaction of a very narrow range of variables, since he himself observed that 'A faithful history [of the dynamics of population and income] . . . would probably prove the existence of retrograde and progressive movements . . . though the times of their vibrations must necessarily be rendered irregular from the operation of many interrupting causes'.[8]

---

[5] A popular introduction to Chaos Theory is J. Gleick, *Chaos, Making a New Science* (1987).

[6] Goerner, 'Chaos and Deep Ecology', 14.

[7] R. H. Day, 'The Emergence of Chaos from Classical Economic Growth', *Quarterly Journal of Economics*, 98 (1983), 201–13.

[8] Malthus, *Essay on the Principles of Population*, ed. Winch, 27.

The lessons of Chaos Theory, therefore, are that in the real world most systems are capable of behaving in ways which bear little resemblance to the simple theoretical models that we have traditionally used to represent them. In fact, it teaches that the sort of systems economic historians conventionally study resemble a complex web spun from an almost infinite number of threads, and that their behaviour is an obscure blend of chance and inexorability. Chaotic dynamics provides the sternest warnings against placing much reliance upon forecasting outcomes from linear economic and econometric models, 'because of the essentially unknowable nature of chaotic futures'.[9] Indeed, since even the simplest of systems may behave in a non-linear or chaotic fashion, it has the gravest implications for any traditional attempt to model the behaviour of whole nations and their economies in history, and for our ability ever to comprehend fully why change took place when it did, and why it took the form that it did. Chaos forces us to acknowledge that there are a vast number of potential variables which have to be taken into account in any historical process, and that there is an infinitely greater number of interconnections between them. Further, it is not just a matter of the numbers of variables and the interconnections between them, it is the impossibility of measuring the strength of most of these variables and, *a fortiori*, the positive and negative forces which are generated when they interconnect with each other. Thus, the ineluctable conclusion is that causality even in relatively simple situations involves complexities and unknowns of such orders of magnitude that no satisfactory explanations of historical events are possible.

In the last few years there have been a number of developments in economics which relate to Chaos Theory, to history, and to what has been written in this book. In recognition of the unacceptable gulf which persists between much economic theory and the actual events and processes which it is intended to model, mainstream

9 Parker and Stacey, *Chaos*, 74–9.

economists have become increasingly interested in finding new ways of modelling which can incorporate and assign an adequate weight to non-predictable and non-economic influences. One major innovation has been the rise of 'path dependence analysis', which allows that 'important influences upon the eventual outcome can be exerted by temporarily remote events, including happenings dominated by chance elements rather than systematic forces'.[10] In such modelling it is conjectured that the influence of a small initial event, or sequence of small events, might through chance combination with other events, be progressively reinforced by positive feedbacks until it exerts considerable power over the path which a grand process of economic change eventually takes.

Path dependence analysis has been found to be especially useful in constructing explanations of why industries are born and thrive in certain regions and not in others, and why some of those regions experience exceptionally high levels of industrial agglomeration. Historical accident appears to have a major part to play in many cases. The reasons why a location was initially chosen as the site for establishing an industry can often depend on very particular circumstances which owe little to its purely economic advantages. Once an industry is established, however, its presence serves to attract other entrants through a process of what is termed 'agglomeration economies', although even in these subsequent stages of development historical accidents and non-economic factors will often continue to play a significant role in determining the rate of growth.[11]

In other words, economists are increasingly acknowledging the power of events, institutions, and accidents, and therefore realizing

[10] P. A. David, 'Clio and the Economics of QWERTY', *American Economic Review*, 75 (1985), 332–7. This article argues that the universal adoption of the QWERTY typewriter keyboard, despite the fact that it is demonstrably not the most efficient design, illustrates the importance of 'historical accidents' and the power of 'institutional constraints' on outcomes or 'end-states'.

[11] See e.g. P. A. Kattuman, 'The Role of History in the Transition to an Industrial District: The Case of the Indian Bicycle Industry', in P. Cadene and M. Holmstrom, *Decentralised Production in India: Industrial Districts, Flexible Specialization, and Employment* (Pondicherry, 1998).

that history matters. Models of this type frequently postulate the existence of a number of different paths which can lead to widely different outcomes, and they demonstrate that the choice of path is often a matter of 'historical accident' rather than the inexorable workings of independent economic laws. More than this, the thrust of the efforts of many economists in this field is to demonstrate the importance of small and frequently random events in shaping large-scale economic change. By so doing they are incorporating aspects of chaotic behaviour into their models, and reinforcing the notion that change is often a matter of chance rather than rational choice.

A further assault on the viability of our supermodels comes from traditional philosophical notions of the nature of causality, and it is a threat which has been reinforced in more recent years by the rampant scepticism that has been sown by postmodernism. The thrust of both these lines of reasoning is to prove that it is impossible to rank causes in order of importance, and that truth is unknowable. In 1843 John Stuart Mill expressed the cause of any phenomenon as 'the sum total of the conditions positive and negative taken together; the whole of the contingencies of every description, which, being realised, the consequent invariably follows'.[12] There is, therefore, an infinite chain of causes stretching backwards and outwards from any event, and the more general the nature of the event, the longer and wider the chains of those causes stretch. It follows that these 'causes' cannot be ranked according to importance, because they each played a role which was indispensable in determining the particular outcome. Even if we should believe that causes can be ranked, in practice it is invariably impossible to do so: first, because the influence or power of the vast majority cannot by their very nature be quantified and, second, because even if their influence is in theory quantifiable, the inadequacy of surviving records will rarely

---

[12] S. H. Rigby, 'Historical Causation: Is One Thing More Important than Another?', *History*, 80 (1995), 234–5.

permit this to be done with any pretence of accuracy. Thus, since any one cause cannot be held to be more important than any other, it follows that all causes must be of equal value.

Zealous postmodernists would go further by arguing that there can be no such thing as objectivity in the writing of history, and that historical truth can never be reconstructed.[13] It is commonly asserted in these intellectual circles that each surviving historical text is capable of a multitude of different readings—a standpoint with which few historians would disagree. Even if the author of a text or the compiler of a historical document was expertly and assiduously attempting to capture truth and reality, which most were not, they could only succeed in creating a construct. These constructs, which are the evidence historians have to rely on, are rendered all the more imperfect by the fact that information about the past is conveyed through language, and language and grammar are completely arbitrary signifiers of meaning and intention. Thus, when historians (none of whom are are capable of exercising true objectivity) seek to reconstruct the past from surviving texts in order to discover historical facts and truths, they are in fact engaging in the creation of a new construct based on a series of other constructs, which inevitably means that their histories will be far removed from representing the reality of the past.

Since all interpretations of history are essentially works of imagination, and no single interpretation can be proved to be the true one, all must be equally valid and invalid. More than this, since each document is capable of being read in an almost infinite variety of ways, none of which can be proved to be more correct than another, all 'texts' must be viewed as essentially the same, whether they be contemporary primary sources (such as a tax return, a court roll, or a customs account), works of fiction and creative writing

---

[13] A recent discussion of postmodernist theories of history and their impact on the writing of history is contained in R. J. Evans, *In Defence of History* (1997); see esp. 224–53. This book also contains a useful list of the main works in this field, embellished by the author's vigorous comments on their quality (291–301).

(such as Chaucer's *Knight's Tale* or Langland's *Piers Plowman*), or modern history books (such as G. M. Trevelyan's *England in the Age of Wycliffe* or R. H. Hilton's *Bond Men Made Free*). The result of the acceptance of such notions, as postmodernists rightly claim, is the shattering of history as a discipline because of the inherent inability either to 'demonstrate the superiority of one interpretation or story-type over another' or to establish that it is the evidence which provides the perspective rather than 'the historian's perspective [which] counts as evidence'. History is not the impartial seeker after truth but 'a mode of discourse . . . on the same footing as fiction and other modes of expression'. Historians must therefore be urged to 'abandon their false illusions about objectivity and their ability accurately to represent the past'.[14]

What then are the implications of these assaults from Chaos Theory, the philosophy of history, postmodernism, and path dependency, for our attempts to explain the rise and fall of the economies and societies of whole nations across the centuries? In this little book we have been remorselessly critical of the simplicity of the supermodels which have commonly been espoused in order to achieve this task, but have we missed the main point? Should the whole task of seeking explanations be abandoned because it can never be successful?

The response must be no. The great questions in history demand that answers to them continue to be sought, however misguided or partial these might eventually turn out to be. It is the function of others to point out the deficiencies of the answers which are provided, and also to suggest ways in which they might be improved. While few of the grander questions in history can be answered definitively, any more than can the grander questions of life and the natural world, there is a discipline to the writing of

[14] E. Somekawa and E. A. Smith, 'Theorizing the Writing of History, or "I can't think why it should be so dull, for a great deal of it must be invention"', *Journal of Social History*, 22 (1988), 150, 153, 159.

history, and it is enforced by the collective judgement of practitioners and readers. What becomes accepted, or worthy of serious consideration, is not simply the opinion or prejudice of a single historian, but the outcome of a process of collective assessment. The inadequacy of the answers so far provided to questions about the course that the economy and society of England and Europe took during the medieval and early modern centuries, is at least as much a reflection of the extreme complexity of the issues that are being confronted as of the ineffectiveness of the historians and social scientists who have attempted to resolve them.

Historians can use their training, their knowledge of the periods they are studying and their commonsense to progress beyond the nihilism of postmodernism. Whatever lessons may legitimately be drawn from the teachings of postmodernism, they do not include the bizarre contention that all explanations and are equally valid and equally invalid (including, of course, the opinions proferred by postmodernists themselves). This obvious point may be readily illustrated by the creation of a new historical model to explain the rise of the Western world, which shall be called the Pewter Theory. In this model the driving force of history is not the rise and fall of population, the struggles between the classes, or the advance of commerce and technology, it is the adoption, use, and ultimate abandonment of pewter tableware and domestic utensils—plates, bowls, cups, tankards, jugs, and suchlike.[15] Pewter is an alloy of tin and lead, sometimes with the addition of small amounts of antimony or copper. Excessive quantities of lead in the human body can cause lead-poisoning or plumbism, which in severe cases results in brain damage, including arteriosclerosis, and infertility. The Pewter Model, therefore, argues that the decline of the Roman Empire, which suffered from some disastrous leadership as well as a low birth rate among the aristocracy, owed much to the deleterious effects of

---

[15] The rise and fall of the use of pewter is surveyed in J. Hatcher and T. C. Barker, *A History of British Pewter* (1974).

lead-poisoning on the brainpower and fertility of the ruling classes, who not only ate and drank from utensils of pewter containing unhealthily high proportions of noxious lead, but also stored their wines and water in such vessels and smothered themselves in lead-based cosmetics and ointments. It further contends that the slow pace of economic and technical progress in the medieval and early modern world was causally related to the ubiquitousness of the use of pewter in these times. This proposition is strengthened by the counter-example of Italy where, unusually within Europe, pewter was scarcely used and where, of course, a prodigious renaissance of learning and culture took place. Finally, surely it was not mere coincidence that the great eighteenth- and nineteenth-century leap forward of technology, industrialization, and urbanization in Britain, as well as the accompanying population explosion, ran almost exactly parallel with the supplantation of pewter by newly available cheap hard-glazed pottery?

The Pewter Theory could be extended and developed, enshrined in full scholarly apparatus and supported by a forest of footnotes. And then perhaps there would be some postmodernists and like-minded theorists who would find it worthy of being placed alongside all the other hypothetical explanations of the rise of the Western world which, in the last resort, cannot be definitively proved true or untrue. However, the intermittent, superficial plausibility of such a schema would not have much appeal to practising historians, who would immediately appreciate its inherent absurdity, and how derisorily it performs when ranked against the firepower inherent in those models constructed on foundations laid down by the likes of Karl Marx, Adam Smith, and Thomas Malthus.

Nor are Mill's propositions on the nature of causality nearly as threatening to historians as they might appear at first sight. Even if causality were permitted to assume the shape of a chain rather than a web, that chain does not have to be allowed to stretch out into infinity with innumerable links all of equal weight. The issue of causality is self-evidently a complex and contentious subject, but people in everyday life routinely distinguish between major and minor causes and between conditions and causes. This may be illustrated by the much-discussed case of the glass bottle which broke when hit by a stone.[16] The answer to the question of why the bottle broke might appear obvious: because it was hit by a stone and because it was brittle. But the list of potential causal factors stretches far, far wider than this. Why did someone want to throw stones in the first place? How did it come about that they were able to hit the bottle, and with sufficient force to break it? Clearly, the size and weight of the stone is important, and also the thickness of the glass, but so too is the distance the thrower was from the bottle, to say nothing of the number of attempts that were made to hit it. The bottle might not have been hit at all if the thrower lacked reasonably good eyesight, or if he suffered from an injured arm, or if the light was poor. A complete answer to why the bottle was broken would also require knowledge of how the bottle came to be where it was, and the stone and the thrower where they were too, why no one stopped the stones being thrown, why the thrower was not run down by a car the day before, why the thrower was born, and so on and so on.

It is to be hoped that qualities such as commonsense, knowledge, experience, and good historical judgement will help to determine where the chain of causality in the explanation of historical events should be severed, and this will depend on which factors are thought appropriate for close scrutiny and which are considered to be minor or irrelevant and therefore to be ignored or left in the background. The precise point at which the chain of causality is severed will, of course, vary according to the nature of the event for which an explanation is being sought and the nature of the enquiry being conducted, but it may well also, and less justifiably, vary according to the preconceptions and prejudices of the historians involved. Indeed, as we have repeatedly noted, the chains of causality employed in the supermodels reviewed in this book are often extremely

---

[16] See also Rigby, 'Historical Causation', 234–5.

short. To continue with our analogy of the broken bottle, the debate about why it broke may be reduced not only to a thrown stone and a brittle bottle, but to an assertion that only one of these was the true cause, and the other was merely a condition. In other words, the explanation may be reduced to a choice between, on the one hand, the assumption that since people are always throwing stones at bottles it is the degree of brittleness of bottles, the thickness of their glass and so on, which determines whether they break or not, or, on the contrary, an assumption that since all bottles are brittle it is the stone and the manner in which it is thrown which determines whether a bottle is broken or not.

Historical debates often lack a precise focus, with the result that participants spend much time talking past each other, but the issue of causality, in both its philosophical and practical forms, is specifically addressed in the debate between Brenner and his critics over the relative significance of demographic and class factors in generating economic and social change in pre-industrial Europe. In his opening article Brenner pursued a comparative approach and cited two examples: first, that in the thirteenth century, an era of high population, peasant freedom grew in northern France but serfdom strengthened in England; and second, that in the fifteenth century, an era of low population, the peasantry were enserfed in many parts of Eastern Europe while serfs gained their freedom in England. Brenner then went on to assert that, since 'different outcomes proceeded from similar demographic trends at different times and in different parts of Europe', it could be questioned whether demographic change should 'be legitimately treated as a cause, let alone the key variable'.[17] His charge was answered with a question: 'Does Brenner mean that no causal factor can be proved true unless it can be shown to produce identical results in totally different

---

[17] 'Agrarian Class Structure and Economic Development', 21 (ignoring for this purpose the dating of the rise of serfdom in Eastern Europe, which most historians would see as occurring later than does Brenner).

circumstances?' To which Brenner in turn replied 'in kind' by asking 'Can Postan and Hatcher really wish to argue that a historical explanation can be counted adequate when the factor imputed to be cause (demographic increase/decline) can be shown to produce the opposite effects (in terms of income distribution) in very similar conditions?'[18]

This interchange is extremely revealing of the conflicting motives and beliefs of the participants. For it focuses not merely on the general issue of the nature of the causes of long-term economic and social change, but on the specific issue of whether there was a *single* cause and what that cause might be. Brenner might at first sight be thought to have made some telling points by indicating that different outcomes occurred under similar conditions of falling or rising population, but in fact he has scored only against those rare beasts who would see demographic factors as the sole driving force of economic and social change and who consider the outcomes of major fluctuations in the level of population to be entirely predictable. Moreover, when he goes on to deny influence to a factor, in this case population, simply on the grounds that it is not the sole determinant of an outcome, he is clearly in error. There are innumerable instances in history, and even more within the imagination, of powerful agents helping to promote change, but where the character of that change varies from place to place and from time to time according to the conditions and forces it reacts upon. But let us choose a single example from medieval agriculture. Excess rainfall at the wrong times of the year can be damaging to crops, but even in the almost constant deluges of the famine years of 1315–17, when harvests almost everywhere were unprecedentedly disastrous and in places the land barely returned the seed that had been sown, on a few manors, such as Fareham (Hants.), which were located on dry

---

[18] Postan and Hatcher, 'Population and Class Relations', 66; Brenner, 'Agrarian Roots of European Capitalism', 220.

chalky soils which normally suffered from a deficiency of moisture, yields actually *rose* above their average levels.[19] Can it be sensible to doubt that excessive rainfall 'can be legitimately treated as a cause' of both the increased and the decreased yields of these years?

Postan and Hatcher readily concurred with Brenner's non-contentious conclusion that population movements were not the sole significant determinant of economic and social change, and they went on to advocate a far more limited role for population, and to emphasize the significant influence played by a wide range of social, political, cultural, and ideological factors in shaping history.[20] But Brenner makes clear his contrary position: it is that the debate about the reasons for the development of medieval and early modern Europe should not be conducted as a battle between two armies of alternative explanations, each with hierarchies of causes and conditions, but as a gladiatorial contest between two rivals each claiming to be the supreme prime mover. Having demolished the case for demographic forces being the sole prime mover of long-term change, Brenner promptly seeks to put property and class relations in their stead. For Brenner property and class relations constitute a truly independent variable: 'as a rule, they are not shaped by, or alterable in terms of, changes in demographic or commercial trends', and it is they which determine what impact population movements will have, because the forces that are set in train by the rise or fall of population have to be mediated through them, and not vice versa.[21]

If we return to our glass bottles and stones, we may observe a similarity between the stones and falling population, and between the brittleness or otherwise of the bottles and property and class relations. If one takes it as given that stones will be thrown at bottles (i.e. that population will rise and fall), whether or not a bottle breaks when hit by a stone can be taken to depend solely upon the

---

[19] J. Z. Titow, *Winchester Yields: A Study in Medieval Agricultural Productivity* (Cambridge, 1972), 43–9, 53–9, 63–9.

[20] 'Population and Class Relations', 64–6; see also above, pp. 197–8.

[21] 'Agrarian Class Structure and Economic Development', 12.

thickness of its glass (i.e. the prevailing class structures). Therefore, if one takes as given the fact of falling population during the later Middle Ages or during the Thirty Years War in Germany, it follows that it is class power which determines what happens to the fortunes of landlords and the legal and economic status of the peasantry. By this reasoning, in England the ultimate demise of serfdom would be due to the strength of the peasantry and the relative weakness of their lords, while in Eastern Europe the outcome is reversed because so is the balance of power of the classes. Thus, for Brenner it is the relative strengths and weaknesses of lords and peasants which determine whether peasants will be enfranchised or enserfed, and whether lords prosper or not, and he proceeds to reduce not only the demographic factor but all other possible causal factors to the status of background conditions.

But by what objective criteria can it be proved to be valid to make property relations and the class struggle the cause and not a condition, and the demographic factor, and all other factors for that matter, conditions and not causes? Why should the pre-existing balances of class power in England and Eastern Europe not be taken as given, and the new element in the situation, demographic collapse, not be made the prime cause of both the decline and the rise of serfdom?[22] But this reversal of roles is equally invalid. To labour further this important though rather obvious point: if one (English) bottle breaks (the demise of serfdom) when hit by a stone (population decline), and another (East European) bottle falls over (imposition of serfdom) when hit by a similar stone (population decline), neither the stones nor the construction of the bottles can be isolated as the prime reason for the contrast in their subsequent condition. Even allowing for the possibility that identical stones were thrown with identical force, and that they hit two adjacent bottles in an

---

[22] For a discussion from the perspective of Eastern Europe, see A. Klíma , 'Agrarian Class Structure and Economic Development in Pre-industrial Bohemia', in Aston and Philpins (eds.), *Brenner Debate*, 192–212.

identical spot, the fact that one bottle was broken and the other knocked over was clearly due to both their differing composition and to the fact that they were hit by stones. Likewise, neither the decline of serfdom in England nor the enserfment of the peasantry in Eastern Europe would have occurred in the manner that they did and at the time when they did, if either the balances of class power or demographic conditions in these two regions had been materially different. Both were indispensable to the particular outcomes, and the selection of one or other and deeming it to be the prime cause, a contributory cause or a mere background condition can be justified by little more than the preferences of the person who is doing the choosing.

However, arguing that a complete explanation of such a crucial and complex process as the history of serfdom and freedom in Europe cannot be constructed from just one grand variable, does not take us very far towards providing that explanation. The changing level of population and the respective strength of lords and peasants were clearly of immense importance to the welfare of the peasantry in England and Germany, but the analysis of causality cannot stop here. For example, in order to explain the decline of serfdom in England we need to discover why English lords were relatively weak, why English peasants were relatively strong, and what was the precise timing and scale of the fall in population. Such an investigation would involve consideration of such matters as the scattered nature of baronial and ecclesiastical estates, the power of the king, the rule of law and the mentalities which conditioned the behaviour of great lords. A search for the reasons why population declined on the scale that it did would involve analysis of the manifold influences on fertility and mortality. If fertility was deemed to have contributed significantly to decline, then the potential causes of falling fertility would become relevant, and they may have included factors which tended to raise the age of marriage for women, such as an increase in the occupational opportunities open to women, as well as the possibility that people simply hesitated to bring children into the traumatic world of the later Middle Ages. On the other hand, if the basic cause of the decline of population was thought to be the onset and persistence of the second pandemic of plague, such a path would eventually lead to a study of possible changes in the structure of the bacillus which causes plague, and to changes in the behaviour of the fleas which carried the bacillus, or in that of the hosts which carried the fleas, in the lines of communication along which moved fleas or their infested hosts, in the climate and environment in which fleas and flea-carrying rodents lived, and so on and so on. Down this route, of course, lies non-linearity and ultimately Chaos. And the notion that it could have been the random mutation of a micro-organism carried in the gullets of fleas living on the backs of rodents inhabiting the remote high steppes of Asia, which was ulti-mately responsible for the collapse of the feudal system of the Western world, is a far more powerful illustration of the potential havoc that can be wrought by the unpredictable workings of a chaotic system than the oft-quoted example of a Tokyo butterfly causing a New York hurricane.

Once again, the task of providing complete and satisfactory explanations of the course of history can be revealed as impossibly massive. The more we learn from advances in Chaos Theory and related methodologies about the operation of complex systems, and even of simple systems, the more insubstantial the foundations of the grand, monocausal historical supermodels are shown to be, and the more absurd it becomes to try to construct explanations of what are immensely complex processes from the behaviour of a single or tiny group of independent variables isolated from a potentially infinite range. The linear models that are in current use to analyse the medieval economy might be thought suitable for modelling simple systems, but as we have seen, even in the simplest of Malthusian systems, dependent on the interaction of only three vari-ables, equilibrium can give way to turbulence and then to chaos.

The economies of nations are, by their very nature, not simple but immensely complex systems. The medieval economy was manifestly less complex than later heavily industrialized and urbanized economies, but the research of recent years has shown it to be a good deal less primitive than it was once thought to be. Moreover, the economy did not exist in a frictionless vacuum. It was run by people, buffeted by events, influenced by a vast battery of political, religious, and cultural institutions, shaped by custom and practice as well as by market forces, and subjected to shocks from external forces such as the weather, disease, and wars.

Chaos Theory and the mass of related and parallel developments currently taking place in mathematics and the natural and social sciences can help to provide a broad and highly generalized picture of the sort of system the medieval economy probably was, and it will stress webs and clusters rather than chains, interdependence rather than independence, an abundance of variables, and the positive and negative feedbacks of unpredictable strength and direction which their interaction generated. Mathematical programming and computer simulations now enable complex systems to be modelled in new and exciting ways. However, although methodological leaps in other disciplines will doubtless assist historians to discover far more about *how* the medieval economy operated, their contribution to discovering *why* it behaved as it did is likely to be far smaller.

The benefits and limitations of the new methods for medievalists may be conveniently illustrated by turning to A. G. Wilson's very recent mathematical progression of von Thünen's model of agricultural land use around an urban market.[23] Von Thünen's original framework was necessarily a simplistic representation of a far more complex reality, with concentric rings around a single market centre rather than overlapping spheres of influence emanating

[23] A. G. Wilson, *Complex Spatial Systems: The Modelling Foundations of Urban and Regional Analysis* (Harlow, 2000).

from multiple competing market centres, with a diverse and irregular pattern of geography, soil types, transport systems, and so on.[24] Now Wilson, using the latest mathematical techniques and computer simulations, has demonstrated how 'interactive modelling' can simulate the operation of complex systems which incorporate multiple markets and a wide range of other dynamic variables.

Such advances in modelling are likely to offer a far more realistic conceptual framework for those who work on the feeding and fuelling of medieval London, and the influence which the metropolis might have exerted over its agricultural hinterland. But for all their mathematical sophistication, the explanatory and predictive qualities of models can only be as strong as the assumptions that underlie them and the data that are fed into them. The modelling of complex spatial systems in the present day is based on masses of more or less reliable data, which can often be gathered to order. The scale and quantity of this data means that social scientists, urban geographers, and the formulators of planning and social policy have at their disposal most, if not all, of the information required to test and refine their models, to adjust the weightings of each variable and to vary the strength of the interactions between them. But for those working on the medieval 'Feeding the City' project hard data on vital questions are often impossible to obtain. The changing patterns of land use in southern and eastern counties in the late thirteenth and fourteenth centuries may be able to be mapped with a fair degree of accuracy, but there is scarcely any direct evidence of who purchased the produce of demesne farms, and virtually none at all about its ultimate destination. Likewise, Central Place Theory may be used to postulate a hierarchy of markets, with the smaller supplying those in the tier above and ultimately the metropolis at the top, but the extent to which the food supplies of large towns were derived from transactions made in small markets, and the proportions of production and trade which serviced the requirements

---

[24] Above pp. 131–3.

of local rather than distant consumers, must remain matters of conjecture rather than fact.

Furthermore, the considerable complexity of the systems which such spatial modelling attempts to re-create are revealed as extremely simple in comparison with those which are required to replicate the operation of the economy as a whole. At the last count the Treasury Model, used by the government to simulate the British economy and predict changes within it, contained more than 1,000 equations and identities. Yet it is important to stress the conceptual benefits that may be derived from advances in Chaos Theory and the modelling of complex systems, and not to overstate the negative impact which they have had on more traditional methods of analysis. Most traditional methods remain useful and, rather than being abandoned, they need to be used in a more discriminating manner. Thus, although the severe limitations of linear analysis and the errors which arise from its inappropriate use have been highlighted by recent advances, this form of analysis has not been rendered redundant. The laws of supply and demand, diminishing returns, comparative advantage, and so on are not invalidated by what we know of the complexity of the past, but it has become ever clearer that they can provide only partial answers to the large problems which history poses. If population rises or falls, then land will tend to become more or less scarce relative to labour, but whether and to what extent the price of land or labour rises or falls, or what happens to aggregate output or output per head or, even less predictably, what happens to the status of tenants or the incomes of landlords, will be the result of far more than the operation of theoretical economic laws.

The relationship between the general and the particular, and the construction of national trends from agglomerations of local evidence, is a vital component of the process of finding answers to big questions. But the more we learn about the complexity of the real world the more difficult this undertaking seems to become. Enormous resources have been devoted by the Cambridge Group for the History of Population and Social Structure to studying the demography of the sixteenth, seventeeth, and eighteenth centuries from entries in English parish registers.[25] But, while there can be no dispute that our knowledge of the processes of demographic change has been substantially enhanced as a result of the pioneering work of the Cambridge Group,[26] their histories inevitably fall short of being definitive. In particular, much remains to be done before there is a complete and satisfactory explanation of the relationship between economic change and demographic change and a clear picture of how and why England's population took the course that it did.

Wrigley and Schofield in their first book aggregated the listings of baptisms, marriages, and burials in the registers of 404 parishes with the intention of providing a definitive account of national trends. Using this huge database and employing a formidable armoury of mathematical and demographic modelling, they charted the course of England's population, weighed the respective impact of changes in fertility and mortality upon it, and, adopting a broadly Malthusian low-pressure framework, they offered an explanation of the changes in the 'national' demographic behaviour they observed which was primarily based on movements in the level of 'national' real wages, as measured by an amended version of the Phelps Brown and Hopkins index. The overall conclusion they drew was that fertility was of more significance than mortality in determining the population growth rate, and that shifts in fertility were largely accomplished by changes in the timing and incidence of marriage, which was in

---

[25] See, in particular, E. A. Wrigley and R. S. Schofield, *The Population History of England, 1541–1871* (1981) and E. A. Wrigley, R. S. Davies, J. E. Oeppen, and R. S. Schofield, *English Population History from Family Reconstitution, 1580–1837* (Cambridge, 1997).

[26] It is, however, a testament to the collective ability of historians that the new estimates of England's total population from the 16th to the 18th centuries, calculated by the Cambridge Group using the application of complex 'back-projection' techniques to vast quantities of new data (Wrigley and Schofield, *Population History*, 528–9) are uncannily close to previous estimates which had been hypothecated on the basis of a mixture of imperfect evidence and intuition. For example, the estimates of a selection of historians given by D. C. Coleman (*The Economy of England, 1450–1750* (Oxford, 1977), 12) are generally well within a 10% range of the results of back-projection.

turn strongly responsive to fluctuations in real wages. One of the main additional conclusions of Wrigley and Schofield's second volume, based on the reconstitutions of families from the registers of twenty-six parishes, is that English demographic experience was 'remarkably homogeneous'.

It is inevitable that such an ambitious exercise should provoke much debate on the accuracy with which the 404 aggregated parishes and the twenty-six reconstituted parishes represent the range of diversity present in England's villages and towns, but problems concerning the representativeness of these samples are eclipsed when the reasons for the behaviour of 'national' demographic processes are sought. This is because causality does not sum up in the same fashion as numbers, and looking for causal relationships between aggregated demographic indices and aggregated economic indices can lead to what is sometimes called 'the fallacy of composition'. The attempts of Wrigley and Schofield to explain movements in their 'national' data of births, deaths, and marriages, and rates of marital fertility, celibacy, infant mortality, illegitimacy, and so on, by reference to 'national' data on real wages, servanthood, migration, and suchlike are being called into question on the grounds that micro analyses at the community level have obvious advantages in getting closer to the truth than large-scale aggregate analyses. In fact, the averaging out of local variations and the seeking out of causal links between macro-level variables may fail to capture any particular reality.[27]

Work in progress is beginning to reveal the diversity of social, economic, and religious experiences across England which helped to comprise the context within which local demographic events occurred. By studying in detail all the available records of individual communities, and not just the parish registers, and by making 'more direct and immediate connections between the processes of

[27] J. Schlumbohm, 'Micro History and the Macro-models of the European Demographic System in Pre-industrial Times: Life Course Patterns in the Parish of Belm (Northwest Germany) Seventeenth to Nineteenth Centuries', *The History of the Family*, I (1996).

economic, social, cultural and demographic change, it is possible to uncover worlds of cause and effect very different from those which satisfy the aggregated variables and which dominate the large scale causal analyses'.[28] In fact, we are beginning to learn just how complex and divergent demographic experience was, with sharply contrasting and often contradictory behaviour exhibited by identifiable subgroups, cohorts, and families within the same parish. 'The power of human relationships, rooted in local vernaculars, to shape their own history' offers a potent challenge to explanations based on 'the primacy of generalised economic forces'.[29]

But the difficulties encountered by historians seeking to move from the particular to the general, from a single region or sector to the whole picture, are equally formidable. Even if surviving evidence is good enough to make it possible to trace a sequence in the life cycle of young women who migrated to post–Black Death York, which links the acute scarcity of labour to improved employment opportunities for such women, and thence to an increase in the age at which they married and to a consequent fall in their fertility, this does not by itself demonstrate that English fertility fell overall, still less that the reason for England's low and declining population in the later Middle Ages owed more to low fertility than to high mortality.[30] At any particular time, there are likely to have been a multiplicity of varying influences on the demographic behaviour of social and economic strata and groups, pushing with differing strengths in a variety of directions. In this case, we do not know what proportion of all English women delayed marriage or chose not to marry at all, we do not know what happened to the age of marriage in the countryside, or what was the impact of other forces on the number of children born to each marriage, nor indeed what

[28] P. Hudson and S. King, 'Two Textile Townships c.1660–1820: A Comparative Demographic Analysis', *EcHR*, 2nd ser., 53 (2000), 706.

[29] Ibid. 737.

[30] P. J. Goldberg, *Women, Work and Life Cycle in a Medieval Economy: Women in York and Yorkshire, c.1300–1520* (Oxford, 1992).

were the survival rates of the children who were born. To use the language of Chaos Theory, there are demonstrable sequences acting in accordance with known laws floating in any system, but how they link up with other elements, and the force which results from the linkages which they form, can be very unpredictable.

Yet a healthy scepticism about the ability of models to serve many of the purposes to which they are put, need not be accompanied by extreme pessimism about our capacity to reconstruct and explain the past. It remains possible to write good history which makes progress towards discovering the right answers. Specialization, the division of labour, and improvements in technology have brought their rewards in the writing of history, as well as in the operation of the medieval economy, and we now possess improved historical tools and a vast library of excellent studies on subjects as diverse as the workings of the land market, colonization and settlement, farming practices, estate management, freedom and villeinage, peasant discontent and rebellion, the lifestyles of the nobility and gentry, chivalry, monasticism, lay piety, internal and external trade, urban and industrial development. It is here that the supermodels can reveal their more positive qualities, by providing a framework within which the operation of chosen sectors or relationships can be located and analysed. Thus, historians with a special interest in such subjects as settlement patterns, the yield and price of grain, the manner in which the land was cultivated, have much to gain from an understanding of the theoretical underpinnings of population and resources modelling and the conceptual literature which surrounds it, just as historians of rural markets and manor courts have much to learn from the tradition of Smithian and Marxist analysis. The challenge remains, of course, to knit these diverse elements together to provide an overall account and explanation of the main developments in the medieval economy and society, but there can be no doubt that the concentration of research effort on particular subjects and sectors will ultimately render generalizations more accurate and more profound.

Further, many methodological issues, which from a philosophical perspective can be made to appear extremely destructive of all attempts to determine causes and reasons, often assume far less threatening proportions when particular historical events or interpretations are addressed in detail by those well grounded in the evidence and experienced in the methods. The difficulties of making substantial progress towards explaining, or simply describing, historical events are magnified when cases are argued in the abstract, without precise focus, boundaries or priorities. It can be no mere coincidence that the most negative accounts of the practice of history emanating from the pens of philosophers and postmodernists are written with scarcely a reference to a particular historical event or the evidence which survives for it.

There are many ways of writing history, and many types of history to be written. Historians embarking on research and writing choose from a variety of more or less limited tasks and proceed to ask a variety of more or less specific questions, all of which demand different approaches and are likely to result in different but equally legitimate answers. For a historian seeking to assemble a detailed reconstruction of the events which led to a particular bottle being broken by a stone, even the size and colour of the shoes worn by the stone-thrower might be deemed to be relevant information. But for the historian seeking to explain why bottles tend to break when hit by stones, or why people are inclined to throw stones at bottles, such information would be considered too trivial to be relevant. So too with our analysis of the Middle Ages. Why the population fell or why lords were powerful or weak are not the same questions as why history in the later Middle Ages took the path that it did. In any attempt to explain why serfdom declined in England it would obviously be important to assess the scale and timing of the population fall, but less important would be the mechanisms by which the fall was accomplished: the respective roles to be allotted to fertility and mortality, the prevalence of black rats and suchlike.

Rapid innovation in any academic discipline brings with it dangers of an over-enthusiasm for novelty, and in their quest to demonstrate the great power of the seemingly random and trivial many economists engaged in exercises in path-dependence analysis run the risk of exaggerating the potential significance of minor events at the expense of larger. In so doing they mirror those in the hard sciences who delight in constructing models whose purpose is to demonstrate the fortuitous and the bizarre. The notion that a Tokyo (or Peking) butterfly stirring its wings might cause a New York hurricane is intellectually intriguing, but the fact is that a Caribbean weather system has an almost infinitely greater chance of causing a New York hurricane than has the behaviour of an insect ten thousand miles away, and in any event hurricanes rarely happen in New York. Very small events need to generate extraordinarily powerful feedbacks to stand any chance of influencing great events, whereas very large events are able to do so with far less additional support.

One of the main reasons why the three leading explanatory models have remained so influential in medieval historiography is quite simply because they encapsulate vital and immensely powerful elements in the economy and society at the time. And it is precisely because each of these models espouses a leading, and in truth an indispensable element or collection of elements, that they are incapable of providing the whole answer by themselves. It has been a recurrent theme of this short book that many broad areas of agreement exist between the three supermodels, and in recent years some of the most promising work on explaining major developments in the medieval economy and society has involved the exploration of interconnections between the prime elements of the competing models. The later work of the Marxist historians Hilton and Bois, for example, allows considerable weight to demographic forces, and Britnell's work on commercialization is notable for its conscious eclecticism. Such approaches are not easily pigeon-holed into one model or another, but precisely because they consider the operation of feedback systems and the impact of interacting and mutually affecting forces, they have a better chance of reflecting more accurately the complexity of actual historical experience.

But such pluralism does not go unchallenged, for it muddies the waters and obscures traditional battle lines. For daring to acknowledge that the rise and fall of population had powerful ramifications for medieval economy and society, Bois was simultaneously chastised by Brenner for deviating from true Marxist principles, and ironically welcomed into the camp of neo-Malthusians by Ladurie.[31] In a similar fashion, Hatcher has been accused of plagiarizing sentiments which are supposedly the sole prerogative of Marxists, simply for arguing that social, legal, and political influences acted and reacted upon economic and demographic trends and fluctuations, and therefore played a vital part in determining outcomes.[32] A recent article by Bailey has been declared 'partisan', apparently because it argues that mortality was likely to have been more important than fertility in lowering the late medieval population and keeping it down.[33]

In the midst of the most complex and profound debates there are recurrent streaks of superficiality and foolishness. How can it be thought essential to minimize the role of demographic factors simply because one believes in the power of property relations? How can it be thought inconsistent to allow substantial weight to non-economic forces while also believing in the power of population? Such artificial divisions in approaches to historical issues are perpetuated by the eagerness with which medievalists sort the writings of their colleagues into ideological camps, which allegedly owe allegiance to the founders of particular approaches to the subject—such as Marx or Malthus—or to distinguished modern proponents of their views—such as R. H. Hilton or M. M. Postan. When at its most

[31] Brenner, 'Agrarian Roots of European Capitalism', 231–2, 242–6; Ladurie, review of Bois, *Crise du féodalisme* in *Le Monde*, 11 March 1977.

[32] Brenner, 'Agrarian Roots of European Capitalism', 222 n. 11.

[33] C. Dyer, *Standards of Living in the Later Middle Ages: Social Changes in England, c.1200–1520*, revised edn. (Cambridge, 1998), 326.

irrelevant, a newcomer to the subject might be forgiven for thinking that it matters more to some historians whether a particular article or book derives support from, or lends support to, the ideas of a (usually) long dead guru, than whether it presents an accurate picture of its chosen subject. A historian is not made a Malthusian, a 'stagnationist', or a partisan member of 'the Postan school' simply by accepting that the living standards of the mass of the peasantry were precariously low at the turn of the thirteenth and fourteenth centuries, and that the high level of the population at the time was a major part of the problem, any more than a historian who chooses to write at length about the struggles between landlords and peasants, kulaks and smallholders, elites and proletarians, and to trumpet the cause of the 'underdog', is necessarily a Marxist or a member of 'the Hilton school'.

With our continuing dependence on simplistic models and preoccupation with the traditional divisions and allegiances which spring from them, we are clearly in danger of passing the point where diminishing returns set in. To continue to make progress the models that are used to simulate the behaviour of the medieval and economy and society will have to become much less didactic, much more complex, and much more inclusive, laying stress on the interdependence of variables rather arguing for their independence. Towards achieving this end it will prove fruitful to integrate two venerable approaches to the writing of history which in this field have hitherto largely been kept separate. The search for better answers to the big questions of history has always demanded the adoption of an evolutionary or dialectical method in which, because the aim is to establish sequential processes, the agenda is dominated by change over time. But this approach ought not to be at the expense of the 'weaving of the whole cloth of an age'. The functionalist method places the institution or activity under study in a broad context by relating it to the other institutions and activities which existed in the same society and at the same time. In the Middle Ages, for example, the former method might concentrate on showing how and why the capitalistic farming system of the seventeenth century developed out of the villeinage of the Middle Ages, which in turn had developed out of the slavery of the Dark Ages and classical era; the latter approach would attempt to fit, say, thirteenth-century villeinage, the management of demesnes, or the operation of the common fields into the legal, political, religious, social, and literary environment of the time.

The amalgamation of these two approaches is self-evidently the best way to proceed. A detailed understanding of the broad context in which institutions or activities existed, and of the multiplicity of the relationships which they had with other institutions and activities, is essential if we are to weigh the significance of variables and identify the small but potentially powerful occurrences which Chaos Theory, complexity theory, and path dependency teaches us can influence large-scale and long-term outcomes. Ideally, any analysis of change over the centuries should be founded upon a dense series of cross-sectional studies of the totality of the relevant aspects of economy and society at successive points in time. But this remains a counsel of perfection, and the prodigious scale and difficulty of accomplishing such a task is one of the main reasons why our models were developed in the first place and why they have flourished ever since. Which takes us almost back to where we began.

Yet, as experience demonstrates, the writing of history is on the whole a progressive craft, and advances will continue to be made. One thing that does seem certain is that getting closer to a true explanation of the great changes which occurred in the course of the Middle Ages will require the abandonment of restricted agendas and the quest for simple answers.

◆ *Guide to Further Reading* ◆

I. Population and Resources in History

Theoretical Foundations

The works of the late eighteenth-century economists T. R. Malthus and D. Ricardo provide the inspiration for much of the modelling based on the relationship of population and resources and the relative scarcity of land, labour, and capital. Ricardo's main contributions to this field are contained in *The Principles of Political Economy*, first published in 1817, and those of Malthus are contained in *An Essay on the Principle of Population*, first published in 1798. The modern editions used in this book are T. R. Malthus, *An Essay on the Principle of Population*, ed. D. Winch (Cambridge, 1992) and *The Works and Correspondence of David Ricardo*, ed. P. Sraffa, 11 vols. (Cambridge, 1952–73). An accessible short introduction to the ideas of Malthus is D. Winch, *Malthus* (Oxford, 1987); informative commentaries on the work of Malthus and Ricardo are contained in D. P. O'Brien, *The Classical Economists* (Oxford, 1975); M. Blaug, *Ricardian Economics: An Historical Study* (New Haven, 1958); J. Dupaquier, A. Fauve-Chamoux, and E. Grebenik (eds.), *Malthus, Past and Present* (1983); and W. Peterson, *Malthus* (1979). E. A. Wrigley, *Population and History* (1969) and D. B. Grigg, *Population Growth and Agrarian Change: An Historical Perspective* (Cambridge, 1980), survey the application of Malthusian theory to historical situations. For more advanced reading, see the essays in M. S. Teitelbaum and J. M. Winter (eds.), *Population and Resources in Western Intellectual Traditions* (Cambridge, 1989); M. Turner (ed.), *Malthus and his Time* (New York, 1986); and D. Coleman and R. Schofield (eds.), *The State of Population Theory: Forward from Malthus* (Oxford, 1986).

Key Historical Works

M. M. Postan is the leading architect of neo-Malthusian and Ricardian explanations of medieval economic development. Many of his more important essays have been republished in *Essays on Medieval Agriculture and General Problems of the Medieval Economy* (Cambridge, 1973) and *Essays on Medieval Trade and Finance* (Cambridge, 1973). These volumes, together with his 'Medieval Agrarian Society in its Prime', in M. M. Postan (ed.), *The Cambridge Economic History of Europe*, i. *Agrarian Life in the Middle Ages*, 2nd edn. (Cambridge, 1966), 548–659, provide the best overview of his contribution. Postan's textbook, *The Medieval Economy and Society: An Economic History of Britain, 1100–1500* (1972), was written late in his life and lacks the sharpness of his earlier work. J. Z. Titow, *English Rural Society, 1200–1350* (1969), argues a powerful supporting case for the progressive impoverishment of large proportions of the English peasantry. The pre-eminent neo-Malthusian intepretations of European history have been made by W. Abel, *Agricultural Fluctuations in Europe from the Thirteenth to the Twentieth Centuries* (1980 edn., first published in 1935); and E. Le Roy Ladurie, *Les Paysans de Languedoc*, 2 vols. (Paris, 1966); 'En Haute-Normandie: Malthus ou Marx?', *Annales ESC* 33 (1978); and *Territoire de l'historien*, 2 vols. (Paris, 1973–8).

Related Reading

E. Miller, 'The Thirteenth Century: Implications of Recent Research', *P&P* 28 (1964); E. Miller and J. Hatcher, *Medieval England: Rural Society and Economic Change, 1086–1348* (1978); J. L. Bolton, *The Medieval English Economy, 1150–1500* (1980); B. M. S. Campbell (ed.), *Before the Black Death: Studies in the 'Crisis' of the Early Fourteenth Century* (Manchester, 1991); W. C. Jordan, *The Great Famine in Northern Europe in the Early Fourteenth Century* (Princeton, 1996); J. Hatcher, *Plague, Population and the English Economy, 1348–1530* (1977); *The Agrarian History of England and Wales*, ii. *1042–1350*, ed. H. E. Hallam (Cambridge, 1988); *The Agrarian History of England and Wales*, iii. *1348–1500*, ed. E. Miller (Cambridge, 1991).

The major conflicting interpretations of the Middle Ages are, of course, listed under the following sections, but additional direct criticisms of Postan's case for a Malthusian-style crisis in the early fourteenth century include: H. E. Hallam, *Rural England, 1066–1348* (1981 edn.), esp.10–16, 245–64; B. Harvey, 'Introduction: The "Crisis" of the early fourteenth century', in Campbell (ed.), *Before the Black Death: Studies in the 'Crisis' of the Early Fourteenth Century* (Manchester, 1991), 1–24; and M. Desai, 'The Agrarian Crisis in Medieval England: A Malthusian Tragedy or a Failure of Entitlements', *Bulletin of Economic Research*, 43 (1991). For criticisms of Postan's interpretation of the later Middle Ages, see A. R. Bridbury, *Economic Growth: England in the Later Middle Ages*, 2nd edn. (1975); P. Nightingale, 'England and the European Depression of the Mid-fifteenth Century', *Journal of European Economic History*, 26 (1997); N. J. Mayhew, 'Population, Money Supply, and the Velocity of Circulation in England, 1300–1700', *EcHR*, 2nd ser., 48 (1995). On a broader level, M. Levi-Bacci, *Population and Nutrition: An Essay on European Demographic History* (Cambridge, 1990), argues against the existence of a long-term interrelationship between subsistence or nutritional levels and mortality, and for the importance of epidemiological cycles.

II. Class Power and Property Relations in History

Theoretical Foundations

The central texts for Karl Marx's analysis of the feudal economy and the transition of capitalism are to be found in *Capital,* published in three volumes, 1867–94, and the *Grundrisse,* which was written in 1857–8 but not published until 1953. The modern editions used in this book are: Karl Marx, *Capital: A Critique of Political Economy,* ed. F. Engels, 3 vols. (London: Lawrence and Wishart, 1979 edn.), and H. J. Hobsbawm (ed.), *Karl Marx: Pre-capitalist Economic Formations* (1964). Among the plethora of commentaries on these works, B. Fine, *Marx's Capital,* 2nd edn. (1984) and A. Brewer, *A Guide to Marx's Capital* (Cambridge, 1984) are recommended for their brevity and accessibility. For informative discourses on Marxist theory and Marx's theory of history, see e.g. G. A. Cohen, *Karl Marx's Theory of History: A Defence* (Oxford, 1978); S. H. Rigby, *Marxism and History: A Critical Introduction* (Manchester, 1987); W. H. Shaw, *Marx's Theory of History* (1978); J. Elster, *Making Sense of Marx* (Cambridge, 1985). For a largely theoretical approach to history, written from a Marxist perspective, see B. Hindess and P. Q. Hirst, *Pre-capitalist Modes of Production* (1975).

Key Historical Works

The classic Marxist interpretations of England's medieval history are M. Dobb, *Studies in the Development of Capitalism* (1963 edn.); and E. A. Kosminsky, *Studies in the Agrarian History of England in the Thirteenth Century* (Oxford, 1956) and E. A. Kosminsky, 'The Evolution of Feudal Rent in England from the XIth to the XVth

Centuries', *P&P* 7 (1955). In more recent years R. Brenner has made a number of important contributions including 'Agrarian Class Structure and Economic Development in Pre-industrial Europe', *P&P* 70 (1976), and 'The Agrarian Roots of European Capitalism', *P&P* 97 (1982), which are both reprinted in T. H. Aston and C. H. E. Philpin (eds.), *The Brenner Debate: Agrarian Class Structure and Economic Development in Pre-industrial Europe* (Cambridge, 1985), and 'The Origins of Capitalist Development: A Critique of Neo-Smithian Marxism', *New Left Review*, 104 (1997). R. H. Hilton, is the leading Marxist historian of England, and from his voluminous publications the following are suggested as most central to the issues discussed in this book: 'Peasant Movements in England before 1381', *EcHR* 2 (1949), reprinted in E. M. Carus-Wilson (ed.), *Essays in Economic History*, i (1962); 'Freedom and Villeinage in England', *P&P* 31 (1965); *The Decline of Serfdom in Medieval England* (1969); *Bond Men Made Free: Medieval Peasant Movements and the English Rising of 1381* (1973); *The English Peasantry in the Later Middle Ages: The Ford Lectures and Related Studies* (Oxford, 1975) and *Class Conflict and the Crisis of Feudalism* (1985). Hilton's, 'A Crisis of Feudalism', *P&P* 80 (1978), is much influenced by the argument put forward in G. Bois, *The Crisis of Feudalism: Economy and Society in Eastern Normandy, c.1300–1550* (Cambridge, 1976), that thirteenth-century landlords experienced severe difficulties in increasing the burdens on their peasants.

There have been many debates among Marxists and between Marxists and non-Marxists, and particularly recommended are: R. Hilton (ed.), *The Transition from Feudalism to Capitalism* (1976), which contains a number of contributions to the important debate which arose from the publications of Dobb's *Development of Capitalism*; and Aston and Philpin (eds.), *The Brenner Debate*, a crucial collection of essays. Among the many overviews of Marxist interpretations of medieval history are R. J. Holton, *The Transition from Feudalism to Capitalism* (1985) and J. E. Martin, *Feudalism to*

Capitalism: Peasant and Landlord in English Agrarian Development (1983).

Related Reading

The oppressions of lordship and the resistance it provoked are stressed in R. H. Hilton and T. H. Aston (eds.), *The English Rising of 1381* (Cambridge, 1984), esp. the essays by C. Dyer, 'The Social and Economic Background to the Rural Revolt of 1381' and R. Faith, 'The "Great Rumour" of 1377'; C. C. Dyer, *Everyday Life in Medieval England* (1994), esp. 'Power and Conflict in the Medieval Village', 'The Rising of 1381 in Suffolk: Its Origins and Participants'; R. Faith, *The English Peasantry and the Growth of Lordship* (Leicester, 1997). E. B. Fryde, *Peasants and Landlords in Later Medieval England* (Stroud, 1996) and J. A. Raftis, *Peasant Economic Development within the English Manorial System* (Montreal, 1997) provide different perspectives. Apart from the key works listed in Section I, the most sustained challenge to the view that rural England was the battleground for a constant struggle between landlords and tenants, comes from the 'Toronto school' of historians. See e.g. J. A. Raftis, *Tenure and Mobility: Studies in the Social History of the Medieval English Village* (Toronto,1964); J. A. Raftis, *Warboys: Two Hundred Years in the Life of an English Medieval Village* (Toronto, 1974); E. B. Dewindt, *Land and People in Hollywell-cum-Needingworth* (Toronto, 1972); E. Britton, *The Community of the Vill: A Study in the History of Family and Village Life in Fourteenth-Century England* (Toronto, 1977). Z. Razi, 'The Toronto School's Reconstitution of Medieval Peasant Society: A Critical View', *P&P* 85 (1979), provides a critique of the methods used in these studies and an alternative interpretation of the evidence which they rely on.

III. Commercialization, Technology, and Markets in History

Theoretical Foundations:

Adam Smith's *An Inquiry into the Nature and Causes of the Wealth of Nations* was first published in 1776, and *The Theory of Moral Sentiments* in 1759. The modern edition of the *Wealth of Nations* quoted in this volume is that prepared by R. H. Campbell and A. S. Skinner (Oxford, 1976), and the same authors have written a valuable book on Smith's ideas: *Adam Smith* (1982). Also recommended is the essay on Smith in D. P. O'Brien, *The Classical Economists* (Oxford, 1975); A. S. Skinner and T. Wilson (eds.), *Essays on Adam Smith* (Oxford, 1973); E. G. West, *Adam Smith: The Man and his Work* (New York, 1969). Influential, and largely theoretical, expositions of the role of the market and improvements in efficiency and technology in economic development include P. Hall (ed.), *Von Thünen's Isolated State* (1966); E. Boserup, *Population and Technology* (Oxford, 1981); E. Boserup, *Population and Technological Change: A Study in Long-term Trends* (Chicago, 1981). J. Hicks, *A Theory of Economic History* (Oxford, 1969) has the evolution of the market at its core, and the importance of trade as a dynamic factor in history is also stressed in I. Wallerstein, *The Modern World System*, 2 vols. (New York, 1974–80). K. Polanyi, *The Great Transformation* (1944) and *The Livelihood of Man* (New York, 1977), provide some challenging interpretations of the role of exchange and markets over the centuries. K. G. Persson, *Pre-industrial Economic Growth: Social Organisation and Technical Progress in Europe* (Oxford, 1988), interprets medieval economic development from the perspective of commercialization and technical progress.

Key Historical Works

Although there are no modern studies of commercialization and technical progress in medieval England which provide tightly argued theoretical and empirical expositions comparable to those which have been written from the demographic and the Marxist perspectives, the following books and articles contain much that is indicative of recent research and interpretation in this area: B. M. S. Campbell, J. A. Galloway, D. Keene, and M. Murphy, *A Medieval Capital and its Grain Supply: Agrarian Production and Distribution in the London Region c.1300*, Historical Geography Research Series, 30 (1993); B. M. S. Campbell, 'Land and People in the Middle Ages: 1066– 1500', in R. A. Dodgshon and R. A. Butlin (eds.), *An Historical Geography of England and Wales* (1990); B. M. S. Campbell, 'Agricultural Progress in Medieval England: Some Evidence from Eastern Norfolk', *EcHR*, 2nd ser., 36 (1983), 26–4; R. H. Britnell and B. M. S. Campbell (eds.), *A Commercialising Economy: England 1086–c.1300* (Manchester, 1995); R. H. Britnell, *The Commercialisation of English Society, 1000–1500*, 2nd edn. (Manchester, 1996); J. Langdon, *Horses, Oxen and Technological Innovation: The Use of Draught Animals in English Farming from 1086 to 1500* (Cambridge, 1986); J. Masschaele, *Peasants, Merchants and Markets: Inland Trade in Medieval England, 1150–1350* (Basingstoke, 1997); G. W. Grantham, 'Espace privilégies: Productivité agraire et zones d'approvisionnement des villes dans l'Europe preindustrielle', *Annales ESC* (1997). L. White, Jr., *Medieval Technology and Social Change* (Oxford, 1962), is a forceful argument in favour of the revolutionary impact of technical progress.

Related Works

C. Dyer, *Standards of Living in the Later Middle Ages: Social Change in England c.1200–1520* (Cambridge, 1989); S. Reynolds,

An Introduction to the History of English Medieval Towns (Oxford, 1977); E. Miller and J. Hatcher, *Medieval England: Towns, Commerce and Crafts, 1086–1350* (1995); P. Spufford, *Money and its Use in Medieval Europe* (Cambridge, 1988); J. Day, *The Medieval Market Economy* (Oxford, 1987); M. Bailey, 'The Commercialisation of the English Economy, 1086–1500', *Journal of Medieval History*, 24 (1998).

IV. Historical Methods and New Interpretations

J. L. Anderson, *Explaining Long-Term Economic Change* (Basingstoke, 1991), provides a brief introduction to some of the leading models. S. H. Rigby, *English Society in the Later Middle Ages: Class, Status and Gender* (1995), uses social theory to illuminate the social history of the later Middle Ages, and also supplies intelligent critiques of various approaches to the writing of its economic history. N. Hybel, *Crisis or Change? The Concept of Crisis in the Light of Agrarian Structural Reorganisation in Late Medieval England* (Aarhus, 1989), provides a commentary on many of the major works on medieval English economic history.

For the writing of history using the methods and theory of the social sciences, see M. M. Postan, *Fact and Relevance: Essays on Historical Method* (Cambridge, 1971); D. C. Coleman, *History and the Economic Past: The Rise and Decline of Economic History* (Oxford, 1987); C. M. Cipolla, *Between Two Cultures: An Introduction to Economic History* (Oxford, 1991); W. N. Parker (ed.), *Economic History and the Modern Economist* (Oxford, 1986). K. Jenkins, *Rethinking History* (1991) and A. Munslow, *Deconstructing History* (1997) impart some of the flavour of recent excursions into the implications for history of postmodernism and structuralism; R. J. Evans, *In Defence of*

History (1997), mounts a spirited attempt to refute these fashionable modes of thought. A popular account of the development of Chaos Theory is J. Gleick, *Chaos, Making a New Science* (1987). S. J. Goerner, 'Chaos and Deep Ecology', in *Chaos Theory in Psychology*, ed. F. D. Abraham and A. R. Gilgen (Westport, Conn., 1995) and D. Parker and R. Stacey, *Chaos, Management and Economics: The Implications of Non-linear Thinking*, Institute of Economic Affairs, Hobart paper, 125 (1994), are useful essays on the implications of Chaos Theory for the social sciences.

The most significant of the plethora of alternative theories and models of economic and social development which have not received detailed attention in this book are: D. C. North and R. Thomas, *The Rise of the Western World: A New Economic History* (Cambridge, 1973) and D. C. North, *Structure and Change in Economic History* (1981); P. Anderson, *Passages from Antiquity to Feudalism* (1974) and *Lineages of the Absolutist State* (1974); I. Wallerstein, *The Modern World-System*, i. *Capitalist Agriculture and the Origins of the European World Economy in the Sixteenth Century* (Orlando, Fla., 1974).

ᵛᶳ *Index* ᶧᵛ